D1005636

Why Growth Matters

WHY
GROWTH
MATTERS

How Economic Growth in India
Reduced Poverty and the Lessons for
Other Developing Countries

JAGDISH BHAGWATI
ARVIND PANAGARIYA

A Council on Foreign Relations Book

PUBLICAFFAIRS
New York

Published in the United States by PublicAffairs™, a Member of the Perseus Books Group
All rights reserved.
Printed in the United States of America.
A Council on Foreign Relations Book.

The lyrics from "Taxman" were reprinted by permission from Sony/ATV Music Publishing LLC. ©1966 Sony/ATV Music Publishing LLC. All rights administered by Sony/ATV Music Publishing LLC, 8 Music Square West, Nashville, TN 37203. All rights reserved.

The Council on Foreign Relations (CFR) is an independent, nonpartisan membership organization, think tank, and publisher dedicated to being a resource for its members, government officials, business executives, journalists, educators and students, civic and religious leaders, and other interested citizens in order to help them better understand the world and the foreign policy choices facing the United States and other countries. Founded in 1921, CFR carries out its mission by maintaining a diverse membership, with special programs to promote interest and develop expertise in the next generation of foreign policy leaders; convening meetings at its headquarters in New York and in Washington, DC, and other cities where senior government officials, members of Congress, global leaders, and prominent thinkers come together with CFR members to discuss and debate major international issues; supporting a Studies Program that fosters independent research, enabling CFR scholars to produce articles, reports, and books and hold roundtables that analyze foreign policy issues and make concrete policy recommendations; publishing *Foreign Affairs*, the preeminent journal on international affairs and U.S. foreign policy; sponsoring Independent Task Forces that produce reports with both findings and policy prescriptions on the most important foreign policy topics; and providing up-to-date information and analysis about world events and American foreign policy on its website, www.cfr.org.

The Council on Foreign Relations takes no institutional positions on policy issues and has no affiliation with the U.S. government. All views expressed in its publications and on its website are the sole responsibility of the author or authors.

PublicAffairs books are available at special discounts for bulk purchases in the U.S. by corporations, institutions, and other organizations. For more information, please contact the Special Markets Department at the Perseus Books Group, 2300 Chestnut Street, Suite 200, Philadelphia, PA 19103, call (800) 810-4145, ext. 5000, or e-mail special.markets@perseusbooks.com.

Book Design by Jeff Williams

Library of Congress Cataloging-in-Publication Data
Bhagwati, Jagdish N., 1934–
    Why growth matters : how economic growth in India reduced poverty and the lessons for other developing countries / Jagdish Bhagwati, Arvind Panagariya.—First edition.
        pages cm
    Includes bibliographical references and index.
    ISBN 978-1-61039-271-6 (pbk. : alk. paper)—ISBN (978-1-61039-272-3 (e-book) 1. Poverty—India. 2. Poverty—Developing countries. 3. Economic development—India. 4. Economic development—Developing countries. 5. India—Economic policy. 6. Developing countries—Economic policy. I. Panagariya, Arvind. II. Title.

HC440.P6B45 2013
339.4'60954—dc23
                                                                                    2012042283
10 9 8 7 6 5 4 3 2 1

Contents

Preface

In the 1950s, as developmental economists began to consider which countries would break out of the pack and become role models for other developing nations for their developmental strategies, India and China were regarded as certain bets. These giants would awaken after a long slumber.

India enjoyed an advantage on some dimensions but a handicap on others: India had inherited a splendid civil service, a fiercely independent judiciary, a relatively free press, and above all, politicians who had fought for independence and put social good ahead of personal profit. These attributes, which are now called institutions and define the underlying elements of good governance, were rare among most of the countries that reached independence as the Second World War ended.

The agronomer Rene Dumont, in *A False Start in Africa,* famously denounced the lifestyle of the African rulers who took over from the departing French, comparing it with that of the French court of the Bourbons! Indeed, pretty soon India was the only major postcolonial developing nation left standing as a democracy, even what we call now a "liberal" democracy characterized by the institutions of free elections, a free press, and an independent judiciary. Few development economists would have discounted the favorable implications of India's political "exceptionalism."

By contrast, China had emerged from the Long March and a fiercely contested civil war, and the liquidation of the kulaks in the process. If the Soviet Union under Stalin was any guide, the prospects for growth were shrouded in political uncertainties. In fact, the Great Famine and the Cultural Revolution were upheavals that underlined the legitimacy of these doubts about China. Until the 1980s, the Chinese giant therefore did not awaken; it continued snoring.

Yet, developmental economists in the 1950s favored the prospects of China over those of India. Why? The reason lay in the fact that development economists typically deploy simple models to arrive at judgments about development outcomes. At the time, the favorite developmental model shared widely by the economists depicted growth as dependent on two parameters: how much you saved (and invested) and how much you got out of that investment. As it happened, it was customary to assume that the savings rate could vary, and was subject to policy manipulation—typically, the government could use taxes to raise the domestic savings rate—but that the productivity of that investment, which was reflected in the "capital-to-output" ratio, was not significantly variable and was treated as a "technological datum."

So, with the productivity factor neutralized, it was inferred that India would lose out to China simply because India, being a democracy, could not raise its savings rate through taxation as fast and as much as China, which was authoritarian and could extract savings—or what Marxists call a surplus—through draconian means from the population.[1] India, left on its own, would lose the developmental race to China.

But the fact that India was democratic meant that in the 1950s the West was rooting for its success against the communist behemoth, China.[2] Its inability to match China's savings effort thus had to be matched by the West's making up through foreign aid India's handicap in raising savings and hence investment.

So, India became a recipient of substantial foreign aid and should have grown rapidly, in consequence. Yet, it did not. The Indian giant also continued to slumber and snore.

Both India and China were unable to grow very much during nearly three decades: China because of ruinous politics with disastrous economic policies prompted by Marxist doctrines that required autarky and regimentation of the economy, and India because of a disastrous economic policy framework that undermined the productivity of its investment efforts.[3]

Productivity and Growth

India's growth rate turned out to be abysmal because the underlying assumption, that the productivity of the increased investment was a technical affair, turned out to be false. Domestic savings efforts were indeed being made,[4] but the resulting growth fell far below expectation. Investment rose predominantly in the public sector, where productivity was low and stagnant. A complex regulatory regime tied otherwise dynamic entrepreneurs of India into knots. The result was low and stagnant growth rates until reforms began first grudgingly in the 1980s and then in earnest in 1991 (as seen in Figure 1).

The Indian situation was reminiscent of the 1970s and 1980s Soviet Union, which exhibited high and increasing savings and investment rates but whose growth rate kept falling (see Figure 2): there was blood, sweat, and tears, but no results. The cause of this disconnect was that the Soviet system was not putting the investments to productive use. This

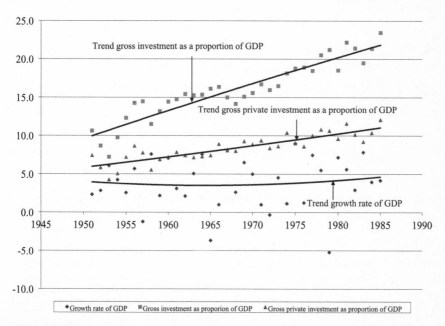

Figure 1. India: Low and stagnant growth rates despite rising investment-to-GDP ratio

Source: Author's construction based on data from the *Handbook of Statistics on India's Economy*, 2012, Reserve Bank of India, Mumbai

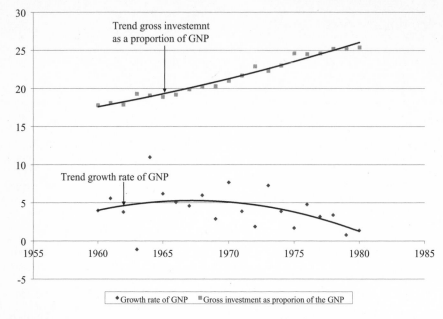

Figure 2. Soviet Union: Booming investment, collapsing growth

Source: Authors' construction based on data in Desai, Padma, 1987, *The Soviet Economic Slow-down: Problems and Prospects*, Oxford: Basil Blackwell

in turn had to do with the heavy hand of the central planning mechanism and the absence of incentives to produce and innovate that followed from the overwhelming dominance of public ownership of the "means of production."

By contrast, the East Asian economies registered extremely high investment rates but the investments were productive and thus the result was extraordinarily high growth rates, generally described as an "economic miracle" (see Figure 3). The investments were associated with extraordinary export performance, which resulted in imports of equipment embodying advanced technology.[5]

Economic Policies and Productivity

So what were the elements that reduced India's growth rate to almost 3.5 percent annually over nearly three decades spanning 1950 to 1980? Four factors played a critical role:[6]

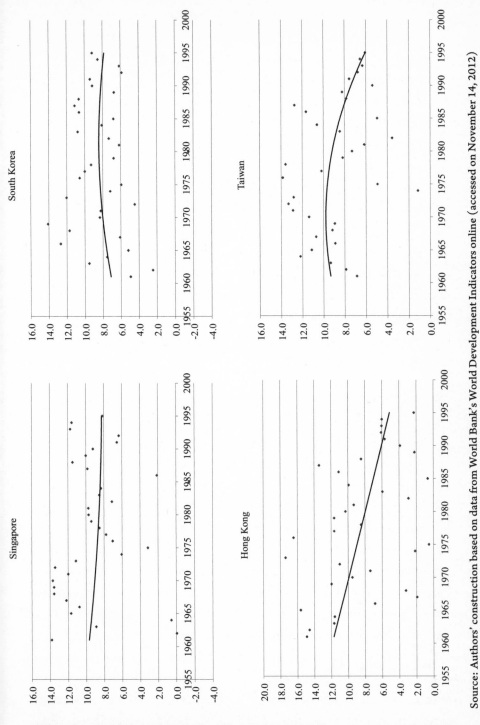

Source: Authors' construction based on data from World Bank's World Development Indicators online (accessed on November 14, 2012)

Figure 3. High growth rates in South Korea, Taiwan, Singapore, and Hong Kong in the 1960s and 1970s

1. There was an extensive system of controls over private investment and production. For example, industrial licensing regulated expansion of production, even its diversification;[7] import
   licensing regulated all imports; investment licensing regulated
   expansion of new capacity. The result was a Kafkaesque maze of
   regulations that stifled any innovation, production, and investment, while also encouraging inefficiency because effective competition from domestic entry of new firms and from imports was
   virtually eliminated.
2. The public sector was steadily expanded and even granted monopoly in many activities that went beyond the conventional
   areas, such as utilities. In turn, these public enterprises pre-
   dictably resulted in inefficient production and associated losses
   that also imposed a revenue burden on the state.[8]
3. Obsessive self-sufficiency defined trade policy. Domestic manufacture, once licensed, was automatically protected. The trade
   economist W. Max Corden has called this "made to measure"
   protection.
4. Similarly, India restrained direct foreign investment, which fell
   to dramatic lows during this period. When the reforms began in
   earnest in 1991, foreign investment flow amounted to barely
   $100 million, which is hard to believe for a country of India's
   size.

Two central follies stood behind the policy features that undermined
growth:

First, the heavy hand of the government in economic activity was so
pervasive that one of us had remarked that the problem with India (and
many other developing countries) prior to the reforms of the early 1990s
was that Adam Smith's Invisible Hand was nowhere to be seen.

Economist Joseph Stiglitz and financier George Soros talk of "market
fundamentalism" as having been practiced when liberal reforms were introduced. In truth, in India the reforms represented a move to the pragmatic center from a situation in which markets were sacrificed, with

grave consequences in efficiency and growth, to what can only be described as "anti-market fundamentalism."

Second, the counterproductive policy framework was also inward-looking on trade and hostile to direct foreign investment (DFI), which meant that India turned away from integration into the world economy, forgoing important gains from taking advantage of such integration.[9] The proponents of autarky in trade were of the view that, as the Chilean sociologist Oswaldo Sunkel put it, "integration into the international economy would lead to disintegration of the national economy." This "malign-impact" view of opening to trade turned out to be generally wrong.

While the favorable experience of East Asia was built partly, in Singapore and Taiwan, on a pro-DFI policy, with DFI leading to multiple benign effects such as diffusion of know-how to local entrepreneurs, the same was not true of South Korea, which followed instead the Japanese-style policy where technology was imported instead. India did neither effectively. No benefits were derived from a general skepticism about DFI and the absence of an active technology-importation policy.

Growth Follows Reforms

Reforms led to growth in India in exactly the same way as in Brazil after President Hernando Cardoso, who as an academic sociologist had opposed globalization as leading to dependency (this is the famous *dependencia* thesis), took Brazil toward globalization. The same happened in China, starting in the late 1970s and early 1980s.

Some economists, such as Dani Rodrik, have argued that economies have grown despite embracing anti-trade policies and disregarding markets, so it is wrong to attribute success on growth to these liberal and pro-trade reforms. But this claim is hollow because there is no compelling case where such policies led to significant growth over a sustained period. This was particularly true of the Soviet Union, where growth rates were high for nearly two decades but then declined steadily as the autarky and the absence of market-based incentives steadily undermined the economy.

The old saying insists that economists never agree, but the late Joan Robinson, a radical economist from Cambridge who admired pre-reform China, and Gus Ranis, the mainstream Yale University economist, were overheard astonishingly agreeing on how remarkable Korean development was. It turned out that she had North Korea in mind, whereas he was thinking of South Korea. Of course, down the road, she turned out to be wrong. The North Korean autarkic and heavily antimarket developmental strategy could deliver missiles and nuclear weapons, but not sustained overall development. South Korea, which instituted "liberal reforms," grew steadily.

The growth in China in the late 1970s and early 1980s was also led by the elimination of collective farming and the introduction of incentives to peasants. Subsequently, in response to sustained opening of trade and foreign investment, there followed the enormous expansion of exports from Guangdong province in the southeast, with large inflows of DFI and technology absorption resulting in an expansion of Chinese income and growth rate. A movement away from antimarket fundamentalism through the introduction of promarket policies and the removal of the disincentives against trade and DFI lay at the heart of the economics of Chinese gains in productivity and enhanced growth.

The East Asian miracle was also based on outward orientation in trade. The phenomenal growth in exports followed the deliberate integration into the world economy. Whereas India followed a policy of near-autarky in the pre-reform 1960s and 1970s, the East Asian economies looked ever more globally.[10] As a consequence the Indian industry was constrained by the internal domestic demand. This meant that the inducement to invest in industry was constrained by the domestic expansion of agricultural incomes. But since agriculture rarely grows at a sustained rate in excess of 4 percent in historical experience, the East Asian decision to exploit foreign markets meant that the inducement to invest was not so constrained. Investment expansion on a dramatic scale followed and the expansion of exports that was its flip side meant also that East Asian economies could import capital goods that embodied advanced technology.

This in itself would not have been enough, however, to generate extraordinarily high returns and associated growth. To get the most out of the new technology, the workforce had to be literate enough to work with the advanced machinery. If not, the embodied technical progressivity would have borne no fruits. Thus, for example, the older of us has a DVD player with the latest features, but he is able to play only Start and Stop on the remote control; the productivity of his DVD player is the same as if no technical progress had been embodied in his state-of-the-art machine.

East Asia fortunately enjoyed, partly as an unintended benefit of Japanese occupation and the example of Japanese tradition of educating the masses—see the splendid autobiography of Junichiro Tanizaki (1988), arguably Japan's greatest writer, which describes his school experiences—a primary and secondary education commitment that assured East Asian countries of astonishingly high levels of literacy. Besides, countries such as Singapore and Hong Kong freely imported skilled manpower at higher levels, making up for absent indigenous skills by importing foreigners with skills, and simultaneously sending masses of natives abroad to top universities to acquire the skills in the meantime and bringing them back at high remuneration. Benign attitudes toward trade and DFI combined with high and productive investment rates, importation of equipment with embodied know-how, and its successful exploitation by a highly literate population in a policy framework that additionally permitted incentives and rewards, created a virtuous circle that produced the East Asian miracle. But central to the phenomenon was the outward orientation in trade.

The experience of China, India, and East Asia—whose population amounts to not quite half of the global total population—demonstrates how growth is stimulated and sustained within the policy framework that exploits the opportunities provided by integration into the world economy, and also relies on a sophisticated use of market incentives in guiding production and investment.[11] Conversely, they also demonstrate that a shift away from such a policy framework undermines growth.

Three important caveats must be kept in mind. First, the liberal policy framework that has produced prosperity is not libertarian, nor is it one of "market fundamentalism." For instance, it allows environmental objectives, such as reducing domestic pollution, while proposing the use of price-based instruments, such as emission taxes instead of direct quantitative controls. If producers of a good can simply dump waste into a lake or a river in the country, that will lead to overproduction of the good since the private cost to the producers will be lower than the social cost, which should not ignore the damage to the environment. We therefore need a polluter-pay tax, which puts a cost on the discharge of pollutants. The correct way to diagnose this issue is to say that we have a "missing market" regarding pollution, and in effect the tax creates that market. You do not have to be an ideologue of markets to embrace it as part of the appropriate policy agenda.

Second, openness in trade is only an enabling mechanism. If other domestic policies create obstacles to taking advantage of the trading opportunity, the gains from trade will be minuscule. If domestic restrictions on production and trade prevent investment in new capacities to undertake exports, any opening to trade would have been frustrated: gains from trade could not be obtained in any significant way if resources could not be pulled toward the export industries, old and new. To use an apt analogy, if a door is opened but you do not have traction in your legs, you will not get through that door.

Finally, much is made of the so-called Washington Consensus as having driven the shift from the counterproductive policy framework. But this is nothing more than Washington Conceit. The shift in development strategy owed, not to any institutions in Washington, whether Bretton Woods or the US Treasury, but to the theoretical ideas and analysis of actual experience with autarkic policies and mindless interventionism that were the result of domestic experience. That they were then taken over and folded into coherent prescriptions for sound development strategy by Washington institutions, chiefly the World Bank, does not give ownership of these ideas to these institutions.

During the last quarter of the twentieth century, three extraordinarily important countries, India, the Soviet Union, and China, changed their counterproductive policies that had been based on antimarket funda-mentalism and autarkic inward-looking policies on globalization. The changes were self-motivated, as we discuss below, not imposed by Wash-ington. Public opinion and/or the politicians had realized that the "old" model, which some, including Stiglitz and Soros, would like to resurrect in their virtual embrace of what might be called "Jurassic Park Econom-ics," was not working and a drastic change was necessary.[12] "Washington Consensus" was also a popular phrase in the antireform circles because it would galvanize the antireform anti–US imperialism forces that were in retreat by suggesting that the United States, directly or indirectly, was behind the liberal reforms.

It has become fashionable among opponents of the liberal reforms to say that the Washington Consensus has now been replaced by the Bei-jing Consensus, an ambiguous phrase with little content, but aimed at suggesting that the liberal developmental strategy is now replaced by China's success with a very different state-dominated and state-driven developmental model.[13]

While China's export-led development appears to suggest that one element of the liberal development model—openness to trade—is part of China's developmental model, many features of China's econ-omy and political regime raise concerns instead of offering a role model. In particular, the huge reliance on the state-owned enterprises (SOEs) has not merely enabled the Chinese regime to have the Com-munist Party capture these enterprises—which many in the West, and increasingly in China itself, think of as SOBs instead of SOEs—to the advantage of the party functionaries. It has also meant that exten-sive corruption prevails in China as bureaucrats and party officials seek to put their children and spouses into every enterprise, siphoning a share of the profits themselves. This model is hardly sustainable as the common people begin to resent such corruption and their eco-nomic aspirations rise as the Chinese pie grows at an extraordinary pace. The authoritarian regime also denies political agitation for de-mocracy that inevitably is breaking out, as elsewhere. While therefore China has grown dramatically, it is unlikely that the growth perfor-mance is sustainable.[14] So the mix of political and economic features that characterizes China is hardly a role model for other nations to adopt for their development.

Growth and Poverty

If growth did follow liberal policies and reforms in the Indian economy, as we argue in this book, still some critics argue that the growth is not "inclusive," that it has failed to reduce poverty and has not spread to the marginalized groups in society. It is often argued that a policy of redistribution is preferable. This sounds plausible except that the Indian experience, and we might also add the East Asian experience, shows otherwise.[15]

In 1980, economist Gary Fields, who specializes in poverty, described India as a "miserably poor country." Yet the reforms that followed, especially beginning in 1991, transformed it from a basket case into a powerful engine of growth, with poverty declining at rates never before observed in the country. Because India experimented within the same democratic framework first with command-and-control and autarkic policies and then with a move away from those controls and toward a greater role for markets and globalization, its experience offers important lessons to other developing countries regarding their development strategies and for the many government aid budgets and NGOs that seek to end poverty in the developing world.

Common sense suggests that we should expect a rapidly growing economy to create more jobs and opportunities for the poor to escape poverty, whereas slow-growing economies would hardly do so. Poor and stagnant economies can no more offer hope to the poor than private-sector enterprises making losses can offer additional jobs. Pro-growth advocates are often confronted with the failure of "trickle-down" economics, which sounds like the Earl of Nottingham and his courtiers and vassals are eating venison and roast legs of lamb at the sumptuously endowed dining table and crumbs are falling to the serfs and dogs below. We don't care for the concept or analogy. Instead we use the now-popular phrase "pull-up" growth strategy, which much better describes what we have observed: a radical, activist set of policies to accelerate growth and to pull up more of the poor into gainful employment. In fact, with the shift to systemic reforms after the 1991 crisis, Indian growth did take off dramatically and poverty declined as well. And as we demonstrate, the benefits extended to the marginalized groups, with poll data also confirming that these groups actually consider themselves to be better off.[16]

What is the mechanism by which this happened? Bhagwati argued nearly a quarter century ago that growth would create more jobs (in the rural sector itself) and opportunities for gainful improvement in income (as, for example, through migration to growing urban areas), directly pulling more of the poor above the poverty line and additionally would allow the government to pull in more revenues, which would enable the government to spend more on health-care, education, and other programs to further help the poor.[17] Growth therefore would be a double-barreled assault on poverty.

The pre-reform policies produced little growth and therefore undermined any attempt at using growth to affect poverty directly. Slow growth failed to generate revenues, so the ability to finance health and education expenditures was stymied as well.

Why did the Indian government not find the moneys to finance these objectives by raising taxes or diverting, say, military expenditures? It is revealing that Mahbub ul Haq of Pakistan, who reminded us often how arithmetic showed that one less military tank would mean several additional primary schools, joined the cabinet of the military dictator Zia ul Haq, under whom military expenditures did not diminish, Islamism was encouraged, and education of the people was neglected. Arithmetic cannot solve the problem of lack of resources; only appropriate pro-growth policies will.

Besides, raising tax rates runs into the usual problem that this remains an unpopular course of action in democratic countries. This resentful attitude to taxes, unless they are to be paid by others and not oneself, is beautifully captured in the Beatles song "Taxman":

> *Let me tell you how it will be*
> *There's one for you, nineteen for me*
> *'Cause I am the taxman, yeah, I'm the taxman*

> *Should five per cent appear too small*
> *Be thankful I don't take it all*
> *'Cause I'm the taxman, yeah I'm the taxman*
> *If you drive a car, I'll tax the street,*
> *If you try to sit, I'll tax your seat.*
> *If you get too cold, I'll tax the heat,*
> *If you take a walk, I'll tax your feet.*

The closing stanza says it all:

> *Now my advice for those who die*
> *Declare the pennies on your eyes*
> *'Cause I'm the taxman, yeah, I'm the taxman*
> *And you're working for no one but me.*

Growth raises revenues without government's having to raise tax rates, as India experienced with the reforms since 1991. Only then, as our analysis shows, could the Indian government finally find the moneys to adequately fund the health-care, education, and other programs to help the poor.

Redistribution, as distinct from growth, cannot be the answer to removing poverty. In countries such as India, China, and Brazil, the large numbers of the poor mean that redistribution will do little and that, too, will not be sustainable. A peasant may get no more than another *chappati* or burrito a day: we quote the great communist economist Kalecki of Poland, who told one of us in 1962 that the problem for India is that "there are too many exploited and too few exploiters." The pie has to grow; growth is a necessity.[18]

We also discuss in this book that, while India has demonstrated that growth can be inclusive in its direct impact, the India policy framework, because of its bias against large-scale enterprises and rigid labor legislation that militates against hiring more labor, has not gotten as much "bang for its buck" as the Far Eastern economies. In short, both growth and its inclusiveness could have gone further if only these additional reforms had been undertaken.[19] The reforms are works in progress. The counterproductive policy framework was so extensive, and the difficulty of introducing reforms in a democratic framework is so arduous, that we have described it as "cleaning up after a tsunami."

Track I and Track II Reforms

We have called the reforms that produce growth and directly impact on poverty Track I reforms. Those that are aimed at providing health care and education, among other programs, such as guaranteed employment in rural areas, all made possible by increased revenues, we have called Track II reforms. Track II reforms can stand only on the shoulders of Track I reforms; without the latter, the former cannot be financed. Indian experience therefore shows how, starting with the post-1991 Track I reforms, revenues were generated that would finally enable the country to undertake the Track II reforms on a significant scale.

Interestingly, the sequence where Track I reforms led to revenues that made Track II reforms possible can also be observed in the case of Brazil. Track I reforms were undertaken by President Cardoso, whose successor, President Luiz Lula, stood on Cardoso's shoulders when he undertook Track II policies that additionally helped the poor.

Track II reforms involve social engineering, and some of the issues in health care and education are considered at length in Chapters 16 and 17; they are central today to delivering the poor from poverty and into well-being by judicious use of the new revenues (and for that matter, even inflows of foreign aid). We hope to demonstrate that the task of delivering the poor from poverty therefore has many dimensions, but they all center on using growth as the core strategy.

In fact, the *Economist* recently (September 8, 2012) ran the cover story "Countries Across the Continent [of Asia] Are Building Welfare States— With a Chance to Learn from the West's Mistakes." This story is really about Track II reforms. But it does not make frontally the connection with growth. In all cases covered in the story, the editors consider how, after long periods of sustained growth, resulting from Track I reforms, such countries as India, China, and (less dramatically) Indonesia have turned to Track II reforms, which, of course, have been made possible (as in Brazil, also as we discussed earlier) entirely because increased revenues have resulted from the growth produced by Track I reforms.

Interestingly, the country that has turned most prominently to Track II reforms, as distinct from frittering away the added revenues on expenditures other than for the poor, has been India. This shows, in turn, that India's liberal democracy has provided the political mechanism that channeled the revenues to Track II reforms. Countries such as South Korea grew fast for long periods of time, but Track II reforms have gained traction only after democracy progressively replaced an authoritarian regime. In the same vein, Track II reforms have lagged behind Track I reforms in China because of lack of democracy.

So, India offers a role model for reform today. Growth follows Track I reforms. Increased revenues, thanks to democracy, are spent on Track II reforms. In this way, growth works its twofold magic: through a happy and necessary marriage of economics and politics. Here is a model for other developing countries, indeed.

The Tryst:
The Vision and the Reality

W hen Jawaharlal Nehru, India's first prime minister, virtually handpicked by Mahatma Gandhi, addressed the newly independent nation at the "stroke of the midnight hour," as August 14 turned into August 15, 1947, he spoke in the tradition of the great orators over the ages: straight from the heart and in his own eloquent words, without the use of speechwriters[1] and the teleprompter that afflicts and mars the impact that even gifted politicians have today.[2]

He struck all the great themes that had marked the independence movement, defining the tasks before the leaders of independent India and the vision that framed them. In particular, he touched upon the two pillars on which he thought that India's destiny uniquely rested: the politics of democracy and the economics of poverty removal.

On democracy, it is clear that he defined it in the broadest sense in which we regard it, not simply equating the concept with elections but rather spelling out what today we would call the institutions of a liberal democracy. He reminded his audience that "our endeavor" should be "to build up a prosperous, democratic and progressive nation, and to create social, economic and political *institutions* which will ensure justice and fullness of life to every man and woman."[3]

On secularism, he reiterated his conviction, no doubt against the backdrop of communal violence that would soon engulf the subcontinent and claim the life of Mahatma Gandhi, that India ought to embrace multi-ethnicity and multi-religiosity, that "all of us, to whatever religion we may belong, are equally the children of India with equal rights, privileges and obligations. We cannot encourage communalism or narrow-mindedness, for no nation can be great whose people are narrow in thought or in action."

On the economics of poverty removal, he was even more impassioned. He may have been from a wealthy family—his father, Motilal Nehru, used to send his shirts to Paris to be laundered—but Jawaharlal had participated in India's independence struggle alongside Mahatma Gandhi, traveling the vast expanse of India's countryside and seeing poverty firsthand. So, his remarks on India's suffering masses and the immense task facing the nation in extending a generous hand to them and on Mahatma Gandhi's ambitions in meeting that challenge are particularly poignant:

> The service of India means, the service of the millions who suffer. It means the ending of poverty and ignorance and poverty and disease and inequality of opportunity.
>
> The ambition of the greatest man of our generation [Mahatma Gandhi] has been to wipe every tear from every eye. That may be beyond us, but as long as there are tears and suffering, so long our work will not be over.

But by the strangest irony, while India began its tryst with democracy with advantages that were unique among the newly liberated developing countries, its economic strategy began (except until the end of the 1950s) with an embrace of a policy framework that was so counterproductive that it produced an abysmal growth rate and therefore made little impact on poverty.

So, while India's democratic "surplus" was initially in abundance and it was only later that it yielded to the problems of governance that have defined the recent anguish, India's economics quickly collapsed into the disaster range, and it was only after the reforms began in earnest in 1991 that India's growth rate emerged from the doldrums and the accelerated growth rate began to make a serious dent on poverty and on the fortunes of the marginalized groups.

This "crossover" of the politics and the economics of India's post-independence history defines the backdrop against which we proceed to analyze India's performance on the tasks set before it by Prime Minister Jawaharlal Nehru on the fateful dawn of August 15, 1947.

But while we leave the problems of politics aside,[4] concentrating on the appropriateness of Indian economic reforms (since 1991) and the challenges that face us as we take these reforms forward, we should not forget that the sorry state of current politics in India and the crisis of governance that is the focus of much soul-searching, is not unrelated to the counterproductive economic policy framework that India had embraced prior to 1991.

Institutions are not exogenous to policies, as many seem to believe; they change as a result of incentives that the policies provide. As we will often observe later, the license-and-permit raj that undermined India's economy was also the major cause of the degeneration of Indian politics. Thus, politicians discovered that they could make money by diverting remunerative licenses to applicants offering cash, while senior bureaucrats enjoyed the power and patronage that licensing gave to them. The economic policies clearly undermined the efficacy of India's political institutions that defined a "liberal" democracy, taking them from an exceptional high to a commonplace low.

Therefore, the conjunction of the politics of democracy and the economics of poverty reduction in Jawaharlal's famous "Tryst with Destiny" speech is apt. It also provides us with the opening theme of our economic analysis: the role of Nehru's socialism in defining the politics and the economics of India after independence in 1947. It additionally provides us with a way to challenge and rebut several myths that have developed around both Nehru's ideas and policies, and around related critiques of India's earliest approaches (or alleged lack thereof) to reducing poverty and improving health care and education of the poor and the underprivileged.

In the chapters that follow, we debunk these myths and clear the debris of ex cathedra critiques of India's reforms. This helps us lay the groundwork for our subsequent analysis of the ways in which the reforms can now be broadened and deepened.

We cannot emphasize enough that our analysis, while it is addressed to India's development experience and underlines the centrality of growth in reducing poverty, has clear lessons for aid and development agencies, as well as NGOs that continually work to affect poverty.

The Indian experience also shows clearly that antimarket fundamentalism and autarkic policies are surefire ways to undermine growth and hence turn off the most powerful means of accelerating poverty alleviation.

Part I

Debunking the Myths

Chapter 1

Indian Socialism and the Myths of Growth and Poverty

If we squander our resources in merely acquiring for the state existing industries (that we have acquired them may be for the nation's good), for the moment we may have no other resources left, and we would have spoiled the field for private enterprise too. So, it is far better for the State to concentrate on certain specific, vital, new industries than go about nationalizing many of the old ones though, as I said, in the case of some specific vital industry of national importance that might be done.

—Jawaharlal Nehru in a speech to the
Constituent Assembly (Legislative), New Delhi, February 17, 1948

I am saddened though not surprised, to find that several critics of the NIP [New Industrial Policy] have denounced this as anti-Nehruvian, which only shows how little they knew of the dynamic mind of Pandit Nehru, which faced with the havoc in the economy, would have been the first among the first to salute the NIP.

—J. R. D. Tata in "Berlin Walls Should Fall," *Times of India*, August 1, 1991

Socialism, which was part of the rhetoric under Prime Minister Jawaharlal Nehru (who had been schooled in Fabian socialism), did not fully dominate and constrain the policy framework that was adopted under his leadership.[1] Indeed, Bhagwati, who had been educated at Cambridge University and was influenced by Joan Robinson, his tutor, on his return to India in 1961 went so far as to condemn the policy framework for being deficient on socialism. Working on poverty at the Indian Planning Commission at the time, he went on to characterize the "socialistic pattern of society," which in December 1954 the parliament had adopted as the guiding principle of social and economic policy, as mere "socialist patter."[2]

Socialism came to occupy a far more prominent place in the Indian policy framework only under Prime Minister Indira Gandhi, Jawaharlal Nehru's daughter.[3] Whereas, for instance, Jawaharlal Nehru had not embraced nationalization of existing private-sector enterprises (including foreign multinationals) and instead had adopted a "gradualist" policy of increasing the relative size of the public sector by planning a steady increase in the share of investment in it presumably with each five-year plan, Indira Gandhi chose the more radical and rapid path of nationalization on the one hand and ever-tightening regulation of the private sector on the other.

Beginning with the dramatic decision to nationalize the fourteen largest banks in 1969, Indira Gandhi went on to nationalize general insurance, oil companies, and coal mines in the following four years. At the same time, she went after the large private firms, both domestic and foreign, to combat the concentration of wealth and economic power. Among the measures she took were forcing the dilution of foreign equity in virtually all firms to 40 percent or less; confining investments by large domestic and foreign firms to nineteen narrowly defined highly capital-intensive industries; reserving a large number of labor-intensive products for exclusive production by small-scale enterprises; strictly limiting the size of urban land holdings; and restricting the layoff of workers in large firms. To further enhance government control, she additionally extended government monopoly over the imports and exports of several new products. She also attempted a government takeover of wholesale trade in food grains but had to retreat midway once it became clear that this was beyond the government's capacity.

This comprehensive turn to socialism was unsustainable. The economy took a nosedive with per capita incomes rising just 0.3 percent annually between 1965 and 1975, and private final consumption rising even more slowly. By the mid-1970s, evidence was visible that the rapidly expanding government controls had closed nearly all avenues to growth, and at least some within the government began to recognize the need for unwinding the system. A process of ad hoc and piecemeal liberalization strictly within the existing policy framework therefore soon got under way.

This process continued haltingly in the 1980s with some acceleration under Prime Minister Rajiv Gandhi, especially in 1985–1986 and 1986–1987. The liberalization, complemented by large fiscal deficits, led to some acceleration in growth in the 1980s. But since the deficits had been financed through substantial external borrowing and the export earnings necessary to finance the resulting debt service payments were small due to inward-looking policies, the economy wound up facing a balance-of-payments crisis in 1991. That crisis provided the occasion for turning the ad hoc reforms into a more systematic and systemic process.

This happened to the chagrin of the intellectuals on the Left. Indeed, during the first half of the 1970s when Indira Gandhi was implementing her socialist agenda, these intellectuals had sought to justify her policy changes by propagating many critiques, indeed myths, about the development strategy that India had adopted at independence. Principally, they had argued that India had pursued growth for its own sake, and that growth had failed to alleviate poverty. They had also insisted that redistribution offered the only effective avenue to alleviating poverty. These and related critiques would now be revived as weapons to undermine the reforms that were clearly a massive shift away from socialism.

The critics had little option but to retreat from reality into fantasy if they were to carry any conviction. By 1980 the wave, in fact a tsunami, of socialist measures had virtually drowned out the prospects for rapid growth of the Indian economy. The long-standing commitment by Indian leaders to the objective of eradicating poverty had also been frustrated by the stagnant economy. It was abundantly clear to those who did not wear ideological blinders that the socialist path Indira Gandhi had chosen had failed to deliver on the promise forcefully conveyed in her memorable slogan, "Garibi Hatao"—end poverty.

The shift to the "liberal" (or "neoliberal," which sounds more sinister) reforms meant that the myths that had fed the turn to socialism by Indira Gandhi were revived to shift the focus from socialism's failures. The psychological need to decry the liberal reforms, gathering steam since

1991, was all the greater precisely because they were so successful, not merely in accelerating India's growth rate, but also in finally reducing poverty.

These myths in fact are manifold and define a rich tapestry, relating to growth, poverty, and social goals. Among the litany of complaints, one can find passionate assertions that the reforms address growth but not poverty or social goals, that the growth they may generate is in any event not "inclusive," that the reforms have increased inequality, that they have increased corruption, that they even hurt the socially disadvantaged Scheduled Caste (SC) and Scheduled Tribe (ST) groups, and indeed much else that makes one wonder if the critics have let their ideology and political preferences entirely cloud their judgment.

These myths, endlessly repeated in different forms and contexts in virtually all developing countries that seek to combat poverty by embracing outward-oriented and pro-market policies, and in international forums by self-proclaimed development experts and nongovernmental organizations (NGOs), muddy the discourse on economic reforms. Indeed, the myths are used as effective weapons to wound and maim the reforms in the public eye. Therefore, it is important to sort them out and to refute them systematically with logic and facts.

Chapter 2

Myths About the
Early Development Strategy

P rime Minister Indira Gandhi came to power in 1966 with no real socialist convictions. At the time, a right-of-center coterie of Congress Party leaders known as the Syndicate controlled the organizational wing of the party, and it handpicked her for the country's top post following the sudden death of Prime Minister Lal Bahadur Shastri, the immediate successor to Nehru. The Syndicate's choice had been based on two considerations: it saw Indira Gandhi's connection to Nehru as a major asset in the elections that were due in 1967, and she had no political base of her own, which offered the Syndicate the prospect of ruling the country by proxy.

But Indira Gandhi proved herself to be a determined, ambitious, and skillful politician. She made common cause with the only substantial force within the Congress willing to openly challenge the Syndicate: the party's left wing, loosely organized under the Congress Forum for Socialist Action that included several firebrand young socialists known as the "Young Turks." Within three years of becoming prime minister, she successfully unseated the Syndicate, split the Congress Party, and firmly established control over its faction that stayed with her. But while doing so, she also made the agenda of her socialist allies her own.

Known as the Ten-Point Program, this agenda included the social control of banks, nationalization of insurance, nationalization of foreign trade, limits on urban incomes and property, tightening of controls on large firms, and an end to the privileges and privy purses of the former rulers of princely states. As Indira Gandhi proceeded to implement the agenda, many intellectuals on the Left sought justification for it through the propagation of a number of myths about the wisdom of the development strategy India had pursued during the preceding two decades.

Myth 2.1: Indian planners pursued growth as an end in itself, ignoring poverty reduction and other "social" objectives.

As Indira Gandhi embarked upon her socialist agenda, many analysts came to argue that the development programs initiated immediately after independence—the First Five-Year Plan spanned 1951–1952 to 1955–1956—had pursued growth for its own sake and ignored poverty alleviation. This assertion would be revived later in the wake of the assault on socialism by the post-1991 reforms.

The myth eventually found its way into the first Human Development Report published by the United Nations Development Program (UNDP 1990). In its technical note (p. 104), the report noted, "While the pioneers of measurement of national output and income stressed the importance of social concerns, economic growth became the main focus after the Second World War. . . . The growth rate of per capita GDP became the sole measure of development." It added, "As GNP became the goal of development in the 1950s and 1960s, the question of promoting individual well-being receded."

This narrative is wide off the mark, surely in the Indian context and very likely for other countries as well. The notion that GNP became during the 1950s and 1960s the "sole measure of development" to the neglect of poverty and related "social" objectives can be made only by ignorant critics. Not merely was growth seen from the earliest times, even before independence and not just when India began its Five-Year Plans, essentially as a strategy to achieve "social" objectives, especially poverty reduction. But there is also simply no evidence for the assertion that the Indian planners shifted away from these objectives during the 1950s and 1960s. In fact, there is plenty of evidence to the contrary from numerous evaluation reports on these objectives, and from extended attention to these objectives in the texts of the First, Second, and Third Five-Year Plans.

The immediate postindependence leadership in India had thought of, and indeed written about, growth as the *instrument* and poverty alleviation as the *objective*. Well before independence in 1947, as early as 1938, the Indian National Congress had taken the initiative to appoint a fifteen-member National Planning Committee under the chairmanship of Jawaharlal Nehru to evolve the development strategy that would be implemented once independence was achieved. The members of the committee were picked from diverse disciplines and were important thinkers in their respective areas. They included three economists as well.[1]

In his monumental work, *The Discovery of India,* Nehru (1946) offers the following fascinating account of the thinking behind the committee's decision in favor of a growth-centered strategy: "Obviously we could not consider any problem, much less plan, without some definite aim and social objective. That aim was to be to ensure an adequate standard of living for the masses, in other words, to get rid of the appalling poverty of the people. . . . To . . . ensure an irreducible minimum standard for everybody the national income had to be greatly increased. . . . We calculated that a really progressive standard of living would necessitate the increase of the national wealth by 500 or 600 per cent. That was, however, too big a jump for us, and we aimed at a 200 to 300 per cent increase within ten years."

The Planning Committee's ideas eventually influenced the design of India's development plans. While poverty alleviation and equitable distribution figured as true goals, growth remained the central element in the strategy, with redistribution serving as only a subsidiary instrument.[2] For example, the First Five-Year Plan stated at the outset, "The urge to economic and social change under present conditions comes from the fact of poverty and of inequalities in income, wealth and opportunity. The elimination of poverty cannot, obviously, be achieved merely by redistributing existing wealth. Nor can a program aiming only at raising production remove existing inequalities. The two have to be considered together; only a simultaneous advance along both these lines can create the conditions in which the community can put forth its best efforts for promoting development."

The evidence therefore lends no support to the claims that India pursued growth for its own sake, ignoring poverty reduction, in the immediate postindependence era. Nor did the objective shift from poverty alleviation to "growth for its own sake" alongside the launch of the liberalizing reforms. For starters, we could look for the corroborating evidence in the 2004 Bharatiya Janata Party (BJP) election manifesto since the BJP is the party that has been blamed most vociferously for pursuing the "India Shining" agenda, to the neglect of the poor. A quick search through the *Vision Document* the BJP issued in 2004 shows, however, that not only was the party not guilty of this error but, like the early Five-Year Plans, it drew an explicit connection between growth as the instrument and poverty alleviation as the objective.[3] The same message echoes in the speeches of Prime Minister Atal Bihari Vajpayee, who stated in his Independence Day address on August 15, 2000, "We have to accelerate and broaden our development process, so that no child of Mother India remains hungry, homeless, unemployed or without access to medical care. We have to reduce regional and social disparities. We have to make our brethren belonging to Scheduled Castes, Scheduled Tribes, Other Backward Classes and other minorities equal partners in our development process. To realize this goal, we have decided to achieve the target of doubling India's per-capita income in the next ten years." Programs such as the universal elementary education, Prime Minister's Rural Road Program and major rural electrification program were all part of the policies of the Vajpayee government.

Myth 2.2: Health and education are belated add-ons to development objectives.

The recent drives to recognize education and health as fundamental rights, culminating in the passage of the 2009 Right to Education Act and proposals for a similar act on health, have been accompanied by assertions that even if the early leaders saw poverty eradication as a key goal of policy, they failed to recognize the importance of education, health, and other similar determinants of human welfare.

Of course, eradicating poverty may have been regarded implicitly as leading to a richer existence of which education and health are integral parts. However, this is not the case. Instead, these objectives were given star billing by the Indian planners. The assertion of neglect of health and education as developmental objectives is so insidious that we must provide fuller documentation of its falsehood.

The 1938 Planning Committee, mentioned above, explicitly considered virtually every economic aspect of human existence that determines welfare. The relevant part of the account Nehru (1946) provides of these deliberations is once again worthy of reproduction in this context. After explaining why a significant rise in the national income was essential to combating poverty, he goes on to state,

> We fixed a ten-year period for the plan, with control figures for different periods and different sectors of economic life.
> Certain objective tests were also suggested:
>
> (1) The improvement of nutrition—a balanced diet having calorific value of 2,400 to 2,800 units for an adult worker.
> (2) Improvement in clothing from the then consumption of about fifteen yards to at least thirty yards *per capita* per annum.
> (3) Housing standards to reach at least 100 square feet *per capita*.
> Further, certain indices of progress had to be kept in mind:
>   (i) Increase in agricultural production. (ii) Increase in industrial production. (iii) Diminution of unemployment. (iv) Increase in *per capita* income. (v) Liquidation of illiteracy. (vi) Increase in public utility services. (vii) Provision of medical aid on the basis of one unit for 1,000 population. (viii) Increase in the average expectation of life.

Clearly the committee's concerns went well beyond the abstract eradication of poverty by some monetary metric and explicitly included education, health, shelter, and clothing. These concerns were subsequently incorporated into the Five-Year Plans. A detailed consideration of the contents of the First Five-Year Plan in health and education demonstrates the depth and breadth of the planners' concerns.[4]

After emphasizing the need for both growth and redistribution to eradicate poverty, Chapter 1 of the First Five-Year Plan states that the policy's objective is to remodel the socioeconomic framework to accommodate the impulses that express themselves "in the demands for the right to work, the right to adequate income, the right to education and to a measure of insurance against old age, sickness and other disabilities." Chapter 2 reiterates the importance of social objectives, stating, "We have not only to build up a big productive machine—though this is no doubt a necessary condition of development—we have at the same time to improve health, sanitation and education and create social conditions for vigorous cultural advance."

The plan goes on to devote entire separate chapters to each of health and education. These chapters are remarkable for the thoroughness of their coverage of relevant policy issues and documentation of the conditions in these sectors. The chapter on health begins by recognizing that "health is fundamental to national progress" and that "for the efficiency of industry and of agriculture, the health of the worker is an essential consideration." It adds, "Health is a positive state of well being in which the harmonious development of physical and mental capacities of the individual lead to the enjoyment of a rich and full life."

In the plan, the chapter explicitly discusses life expectancy, infant mortality, child mortality, maternal mortality, and cause-specific mortality. It then addresses in careful detail the issues of medical personnel and physical facilities and identifies as policy priorities the provision of water supply and sanitation, control of malaria, preventive health care of the rural population through health services for mothers and children, health education, self-sufficiency in drugs and equipment, and family planning and population control.

The chapter sets specific targets for hospitals, rural and urban dispensaries and medical personnel, and the number of beds in each of them by the end of the plan period. It also contains a long section on nutrition, identifying the need for cereals, pulses, fruits, vegetables, milk, sugar, eggs, and meat for 300 million adult Indians. Finally, it discusses a number of specific diseases, including malaria, tuberculosis, venereal diseases, leprosy and even cancer, a disease barely known at the time.

The education chapter exhibits similar depth and breadth. It begins by noting that the existing enrollments at 40 percent for children ages six to eleven, 10 percent for ages eleven to seventeen, and 0.9 percent for ages seventeen to twenty-three are highly inadequate. It goes on to note that the directive principles of the Constitution require that "free and compulsory education should be provided for all children up to the age of 14 within ten years of the commencement of the Constitution." Thus, the concern for universal free education up to age fourteen, embodied in the Right to Education Act of 2009, has a very long history.

Next the chapter discusses the structure of the educational system at various levels and its internal consistency, pointing out that the provision at the university level is larger than what the secondary and primary levels can profitably support. It finds the allocation of 34.2 percent of the total educational expenditures to primary education in 1949–1950 to be exceptionally low. It recommends shifting in favor of primary and secondary education and away from higher education. After a careful analysis, the plan sets explicit goals for expanding primary and secondary enrollments to 60 percent and 15 percent, respectively, by 1955–1956.

A number of committees recommended key changes on the health front. For example, the recommendations of the Health Survey and Planning Committee (Mudaliar Committee 1961) led to the establishment and expansion of primary health care centers and subcenters in the rural areas beginning in the early 1960s. Likewise, the Kartar Singh Committee Report on Multipurpose Workers (1973) and the Srivastava Committee Report on Medical Education and Support Manpower (1975) provided recommendations on distributing health cadres at the primary level. The buildup of rural health infrastructure got particular impetus during the Fifth Five-Year Plan (1974–1975 to 1978–1979) under its Minimum Needed Program.[5]

· The goal of universal free education for children between six and fourteen years of age by 1960 was missed by a wide margin. Indeed, two national policy statements in 1968 and 1986 (revised in 1992) and the passage of four more decades still left India some distance away from the goal. In 2001, the country launched the *Sarva Shiksha Abhiyan,* or National Movement for Universal (Elementary) Education. The country even passed the eighty-sixth constitutional amendment in 2002, elevating the right to education from a directive principle of state policy to a fundamental right. However, the implementing legislation, the Right to Education Act, was not passed until 2009.

This brief review of very broad developments shows that a lack of awareness of the importance of health and education or the absence of good intentions was not behind the slow progress in these areas. Instead, as we will argue more fully below, progress was inhibited by slow growth. With limited national income, the government could muster only limited revenues.[6]

In the area of education, although the government had amended the Constitution to make elementary education a fundamental right in 2002 and had prepared a first draft of implementing legislation as early as 2003, the Finance Committee and the Planning Commission rejected it, citing lack of funds. It took four more years of negotiations among various constituencies to modify the bill to a point where it could be financed.[7]

Similarly, following the recommendations of the report "Health for All: An Alternative Strategy," jointly sponsored by the Indian Council of Medical Research and Indian Council of Social Science Research, the 1983 National Health Policy adopted the provision of universal, comprehensive primary health services as its goal. But it quickly became clear that financial resources for it were lacking.[8] The subsequent National Health Policy 2002 and the National Rural Health Mission 2005 stayed away from the goal of providing universal health care. The issue has forcefully returned recently. Right-to-health legislation is being actively discussed but financial resources, even with more revenues now available, remain a significant hurdle.[9]

Myth 2.3: Growth is not *necessary* for poverty alleviation; redistribution can do the job.

This proposition may have some salience in industrial countries, which have had the benefit of growth for more than a century. In principle, the high levels of income made possible by prior growth may generate enough revenues to sustain large-scale antipoverty programs even during long-term stagnation. In practice, the situation is not so simple. As we have witnessed during the recent crisis and the associated Great Recession, the need to reduce the huge debt overhang has created a crying need for growth even in the developed countries so as to avoid having to cut spending on social programs.

The situation is many times worse in poor countries, such as India, which at independence already had an overwhelming proportion of its population in abject poverty. Other developing countries, such as Brazil, China, Indonesia, South Korea, Taiwan, Malaysia, and Thailand, mirror India in this respect. The option to eradicate (rather than making only a minuscule impact on) poverty through redistribution, even if politically feasible, was not available.

There were too few from whom the government could take and too many to whom it needed to give. Furthermore, the government needed to attack poverty on a sustained basis rather than approach it as a one-shot affair. With the country's rising population and stagnant growth, any favorable effects of redistribution on poverty would have quickly eroded.

When the founding fathers opted for a growth-centered strategy, they did so in full knowledge that India's poverty problem was too immense to be solved by redistribution alone—hence Jawaharlal Nehru's insistence that "to remove this lack and ensure an irreducible minimum standard for everybody the national income had to be greatly increased" (Nehru 1946, p. 438).

Whether poverty could be overcome without growth figured in the First Five-Year Plan and then again in the Second Five-Year Plan, with the planners opting in each case to endorse the critical role of growth in the assault on poverty.[10] In the early 1960s, when poverty and income distribution became the subject of heated debates in the parliament and Prime Minister Nehru became concerned with the question of where the growing incomes were going, the Perspective Planning Division of the Planning Commission took another careful look at the policy options. Among other things, the fifteen-year plan it produced offered a coherent and clearheaded analysis of why growth was necessary.

The plan (Pant 1962) began by noting that the income and consumption distribution data showed that approximately 50 percent of the population lived in abject poverty on 20 rupees or less per month at 1960–1961 prices. It then proceeded to argue the need for growth:

> The minimum which can be guaranteed is limited by the size of the total product and the extent of redistribution which is feasible. If at the current level of output, incomes could be redistributed equally among all the people, the condition of the poorest segments would no doubt improve materially but the average standard would still be pitifully low. Redistribution on this scale, however, is operationally meaningless unless revolutionary changes in property rights and scale and structure of wages and compensations are contemplated. Moreover, when even the top 30% of the households have an average per capita expenditure of only Rs. 62 per month, it is inconceivable that any large redistribution of income from the higher income groups to the other can be effected. To raise the standard of living of the vast masses of the people, output therefore would have to be increased very considerably. (pp. 13–14)

Moreover, Pitambar Pant's document had a novel argument about the need to grow the pie rather than share it more generously. Based on Bhagwati's work in Pant's division, the document went on to examine the income distribution data available at the time for several countries and argued that the distribution of incomes in countries at very different levels of income followed a remarkably similar pattern.[11] In particular, the proportion of incomes earned by the lowest 30 or 40 percent of the population appeared stable across countries. Therefore, it followed that a strategy of redistribution, or changed political orientation, did not offer a panacea and that "growing the pie" seemed to be the only effective way to bring the groups at the bottom of the distribution up to "minimum" standards of living.

Since there were groups such as tribes that were outside the mainstream economy, the document recommended a strategy of poverty reduction that relied on growth for the population that was or potentially could be integrated into the economic mainstream, and on redistribution for those outside the mainstream. Using a formal model, it calculated that in fifteen years a 7 percent growth combined with redistribution to those outside the mainstream could potentially eliminate abject poverty measured by 20 rupees per capita income at 1960–1961 prices.

On the other hand, the argument that poverty could be overcome without growth acquired some salience among Indian intellectuals following its advocacy by Mahbub ul Haq, a Pakistani economist. In his 1972 article "Let Us Stand Economic Theory on Its Head: Joining the GNP Rat Race Won't Wipe Out Poverty," Haq argued that whereas China, with only modest rates of growth, had eradicated through redistribution the worst forms of poverty, illiteracy, and malnutrition with only modest rates of growth, other countries including India, which had focused on growth, had missed the boat.[12]

We now know that the premise on which Haq based his argument was false. On the one hand, China had struggled to achieve speedy growth by extracting surplus from agriculture for investment in urban industry and in the process allowed millions of people to lose their lives. On the other hand, China was quite far from eradicating the worst forms of poverty, illiteracy, and malnutrition as late as 1971.[13]

In India itself, despite the justified skepticism about redistribution as the solution to sustainably assault poverty, modest redistribution did take place through expenditures on health and education. For instance, as the fifteen-year plan by Pitambar Pant noted, the 40 percent increase in income between 1950–1951 and 1960–1961 had allowed improvements in the social sphere, such as an 85 percent increase in school enrollment and a 65 percent increase in the number of hospital beds. But this was hardly a drop in the ocean of poverty.

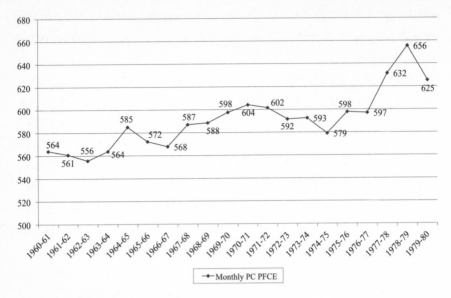

Figure 2.1: Monthly per capita private consumption expenditure, 1960–1980

The situation did not much improve until almost the late 1970s. This is demonstrated by Figure 2.1, which shows countrywide per capita private final consumption expenditure per month from 1960–1961 to 1979–1980 at 1999–2000 prices.[14] We can see that the private final consumption expenditure rose from 564 rupees per capita per month in 1960–1961 to just 597 rupees in 1976–1977—a mere 2 percent increase in sixteen years! The scope for redistribution had scarcely risen beyond what was feasible in 1960–1961.

Myth 2.4: Growth is not *sufficient* to reduce poverty; redistribution is necessary.[15]

Remember that the Pakistani economist Mahbub ul Haq was the most prominent writer in the early 1970s to condemn the growth-centered strategy and to celebrate the alternative policy of redistribution instead.[16] With India turning to socialism under Indira Gandhi, Haq found a constituency of left-wing journalists, academics, and policy makers in the country eager to embrace him. A cottage industry under the self-congratulatory rubric of "New Economics," whose basic premise was that growth by itself was not going to lead to any reduction in poverty, soon grew.[17]

Even Prime Minister Indira Gandhi seemed to give the premise a nod when she stated in her famous March 25, 1972, speech to the Federation of Indian Chambers of Commerce and Industry, "Growthmanship which results in undivided attention to the maximization of GNP can be dangerous, for the results are almost always social and political unrest. Therefore, increase in the GNP must be considered only as one component of a multi-dimensional transformation of society."[18] That this multiplicity of instruments (and a broad range of social objectives around the main theme of poverty reduction) was indeed what the Indian planners had long embraced was lost in a flourish of false assertions by her speechwriter of the novelty of her claims and the erroneous condemnation of what was the true situation earlier.

True enough, as we have stressed, state-financed programs to aid the poor can (when efficiently planned and run) help speed up poverty reduction in a growing economy that progressively enlarges the scope for such spending through increased revenues. Thus, remember that growth helps by drawing the poor into gainful employment, and it *additionally* helps by generating revenues that can be used to aid the poor through programs targeted at the health and education of the poor.[19]

But we cannot emphasize enough that the view expressed by Indira Gandhi—that even without this revenue effect, if India had only growth by itself, it would have done nothing for the poor (and would in fact have been "dangerous")—finds little support in either conceptual analysis or empirical reality.

Conceptually, in an economy with widespread poverty, labor is cheap. Therefore, it has a comparative advantage in producing labor-intensive goods. Under pro-growth policies that include openness to trade (usually in tandem with other pro-growth policies), a growing economy will specialize in producing and exporting these goods and should create employment opportunities and (as growing demand for labor begins to cut into "surplus" or "underemployed" labor) higher wages for the masses, with a concomitant decline in poverty.

Countries such as South Korea and Taiwan offer ample empirical evidence precisely in support of this argument. These countries managed to put in place the right mix of policies from the second half of the 1950s onward and were able to achieve high rates of growth. In turn, they were able to pull workers from agriculture in the hinterland into labor-intensive manufacturing in ever-larger volumes, resulting in steadily rising wages. The end result was a massive reduction of poverty. Rapid growth had "pulled up" the poor into productive employment and out of poverty.[20]

We will discuss in later chapters that growth has had a direct impact on poverty in India as well. However, continuing regulations that have prevented this process from fully working have handicapped the linkage. In particular, as we document in Part II, until at least 2000, the small-scale industries reservation, which required virtually all labor-intensive products to be produced exclusively in very small enterprises, kept India uncompetitive in these products in the world markets. But even though this regulation was considerably weakened by 2000, labor-intensive goods, such as apparel, footwear, and light manufactures, failed to show rapid growth on account of continuing labor-market inflexibilities.

The protection to labor in larger firms is extremely high in India and translates into excessively high effective labor costs. As an example, Chapter VB of the Industrial Disputes Act of 1947 makes it nearly impossible for manufacturing firms with one hundred or more workers to lay them off under any circumstances. Such high protection makes large firms in labor-intensive sectors in which labor accounts for 80 percent or more of the costs uncompetitive in the world markets. Small firms, on the other hand, are unable to export in large volumes.

Because of this limitation, growth in India has been driven instead by the capital- and skilled labor–intensive sectors, such as automobiles, two- and three-wheelers, engineering goods, petroleum refining, and the software and telecommunications industries. Despite this limitation, growth has helped alleviate poverty through an indirect mechanism.[21] Rising incomes in the fast-growing sectors have led to expenditures that led to gainful employment in the non-trade-services sectors. Thus, for example, the proliferation of automobiles generates the demand for drivers and mechanics. As cell phones proliferate, retail outlets for their sales must expand. Rising demand for housing gives rise to employment opportunities in construction. Generally rising expenditures also increase the demand for passenger travel; telecommunications, fax, and courier services; tourism; restaurant food; beauty parlors; education; medical, nursing, and veterinary services; and garbage collection. Employment in these non-trade services thus offers an alternative avenue to poverty reduction as growth accelerates.

Evidence linking poverty reduction to growth can also be gleaned by comparing per capita incomes and poverty rates across states in India. There is a strong negative correlation between per capita incomes of states and the poverty ratios.[22] Making the plausible assumption that redistribution policies across states do not vary much or that they are biased in favor of states with larger concentrations of poverty, this correlation would imply a positive relationship between per capita income and poverty reduction.[23]

Indeed, the evidence that the old policy framework had undermined growth and that growth would reduce poverty and be inclusive was so strong that only die-hard proponents of the old policy framework, many on the Left who professed to be pro-poor, were in the skeptical, or hostile, camp in the battle for reforms. Since nearly everyone had started on the same bus that they had boarded when being educated in England, perhaps the apt analogy was that, while many such as Bhagwati and Manmohan Singh had gotten off that bus as they observed the devastation around them, these opponents were still on the bus. They fancied themselves as Rosa Parks; in truth they were just intellectually lazy and unwilling to learn from the ruin they had visited on India and its poor. So, when the reforms started in earnest, they would oppose them, developing a new set of myths about the downside of the new reforms and the upside of the old policy framework that was being discarded.

Chapter 3

Reforms and Their Impact on Growth and Poverty

The economy is in crisis.... We are determined to address the problems of the economy in a decisive manner.... This government is committed to removing the cobwebs that come in the way of rapid industrialization. We will work towards making India internationally competitive, taking full advantage of modern science and technology and opportunities offered by the evolving global economy....

We also welcome foreign direct investment so as to accelerate the tempo of development, upgrade our technologies and to promote our exports. Obstacles that come in the way of allocating foreign investment on a sizable scale will be removed. A time-bound program will be worked out to streamline our industrial policies and program to achieve the goal of a vibrant economy that rewards creativity, enterprise and innovativeness....

Our vision is to create employment, eradicate poverty and reduce inequality. We want social harmony and communal amity. We want a more humane society. As the twentieth century draws to a close, we cannot live with poverty and destitution among large sections of our population. [Mahatma] Gandhi said that it was his ambition to wipe every tear from every eye. That is the vision which will inspire the work of my government. *Jai Hind.*

   —**Prime Minister P. V. Narasimha Rao in an address to the nation upon taking the office, June 22, 1991**

By the second half of the 1970s, the sorry plight of the economy, accentuated dramatically with the turn to socialist policies under Indira Gandhi, had become evident to those who did not wear ideological blinkers.

But the grip of socialist rhetoric on the national psyche was so overpowering that few dared to challenge the policy framework itself. Therefore, the response was a very gradual, almost imperceptible process of unwinding the controls without disturbing the underlying framework.[1]

This process accelerated somewhat under Prime Minister Rajiv Gandhi, who took the reins of the government at the end of 1984 following the assassination of his mother, Indira Gandhi.

Through the 1980s, doubts concerning the controlled regime grew steadily even if only gradually. But as the decade ended, the doubts were greatly heightened and confidence in the model India had followed was at a low point. It was further shaken by two external events: the success China had achieved after it turned outward—this was "learning by others' doing"—and the demise of the Soviet Union—which was "learning by others' undoing"—that had served as the model for Indian planners from the 1950s until at least the end of the 1970s. Therefore, when a balance-of-payments crisis in 1991 offered the opportunity to make more dramatic changes, newly elected Prime Minister P. V. Narasimha Rao, who came to the helm due to the assassination of Rajiv Gandhi during the election campaign and who had experienced the tyranny of central controls as the chief minister of Andhra Pradesh in the early 1970s, did not hesitate.[2] He launched a process of systemic reforms that firmly put India on a dramatically different course from the one Indira Gandhi had set for the nation.

These reforms posed the greatest challenge to the long-standing proponents of socialism, who now faced an existential threat. Unsurprisingly, their response was to take an offensive strategy designed specifically to undermine the credibility of the reforms. This required the creation of several new defensive myths. In this chapter, we address these myths, which relate to the alleged malign impact of the reforms on growth, poverty, and socially disadvantaged groups. Additional myths relating to the presumed deleterious impact of the reforms on inequality, education, health, and related issues are discussed in Part II.

Myth 3.1: Reforms do not explain the faster growth in India since 1991.

The most surprising myth, surviving among a few economists, is that although growth did occur after reforms, it was not a result of the post-1991 reforms and that instead it can be traced back to the 1980s.

We have seen that the command-and-control regime had peaked by the mid-1970s and a quiet process of loosening some of the controls began soon after, accelerating somewhat in the 1980s, especially under Prime Minister Rajiv Gandhi. It was this halting, partial process of reforms, introduced as it were "by stealth," that was replaced in 1991 by the reforms package that brought the liberalizing process into the open, made reforms more comprehensive across important issue areas, such as industrial licensing, and represented a fundamental shift in the policy framework.[3]

So, we must ask: How can serious economists maintain that the reforms had no effect on the post-1991 acceleration of growth? Their argument takes one of two forms. They claim that first, the growth acceleration really started in the 1980s, and second, even that was a result not of the piecemeal reforms of the 1980s, but of "attitudinal changes," which trumped the effects of any specific, concrete reform measures.

The economic historian Bradford DeLong (2003) was the first to argue that the post-1991 reforms followed rather than preceded the growth acceleration. But his claim that growth acceleration started in the 1980s did not automatically imply that reforms as such had nothing to do with the shift in the growth rate. Indeed, DeLong acknowledged that the reforms in the 1980s may have led to the acceleration in growth in that decade, and so one could not conclude that reforms and growth were not related. Going a step further, he also speculated that the 1980s growth acceleration might have proven to be just "a short-lived flash in the pan" in the absence of more comprehensive reforms of the post-1991 variety (as is indeed true).

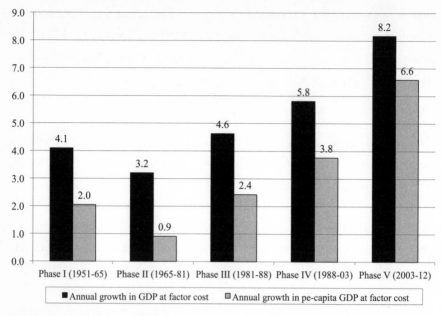

Figure 3.1. Annual growth rates of the GDP and per capita GDP during various phases, 1951–1952 to 2011–2012

Source: Authors' construction based on data from the *Handbook of Statistics on India's Economy*, 2012, Reserve Bank of India, Mumbai

The real problem lay with the separate assertion by Dani Rodrik (2003), in his editorial introduction to the volume carrying DeLong's paper, that the 1980s growth had little to do with reforms in any case. He argued that "the *change in official attitudes* in the 1980s, towards encouraging rather than discouraging entrepreneurial activities and integration into the world economy, and a belief that the rules of the economic game had changed for good, may have had a bigger impact on growth than any specific policy reforms" (emphasis added).[4]

However, both DeLong's statistical assertion about allegedly robust pre-1991 growth and Rodrik's explanation for it are wrong.[5]

First, the claim that growth in the 1990s was no higher than in the 1980s carries what might be called a fallacy of aggregation. The acceleration in the early 1980s was in fact quite modest (see Figure 3.1), with the bulk of the growth back-loaded in the last three years of the decade. Once we exclude the years 1988–1991, growth in the remaining years—1980–1981 to 1987–1988—turns out to be just 4.6 percent, which is closer to the 4.1 percent growth that had already been achieved between 1951–1952 and 1964–1965 and perceptibly lower than the 5.8 percent during 1988–2003 or 6.3 percent between 1992–1993 and 1999–2000.[6]

Chetan Ghate and Stephen Wright (2008) have recently applied state-of-the-art techniques to detailed state- and industry-level data to identify the turning point of the economy. The authors' careful and comprehensive work places this turning point at fiscal year 1987–1988, just as Panagariya's (2004b) did.[7]

Second, the "super-high" annual growth of 7.2 percent during 1988–1991 was preceded by significant, though partial reforms, especially in 1985–1986 and 1986–1987. It was also helped by significant depreciation of the rupee in the second half of the 1980s.[8] But more important, this growth was also driven by fiscal expansion and external borrowing that were not sustainable. Unsurprisingly, the surge ended in a balance-of-payments crisis in June 1991.

Even if we ignore the differences in growth rates in the 1980s and 1990s, the 1980s growth could not have been sustained without the post-1991 reforms.

Third, the shift to 8.2 percent growth during the nine years between 2003–2004 and 2011–2012 represents a significant jump in the growth rate following the post-1991 systematic reforms. Surely attributing this latest acceleration to some vague "attitudinal" change in the 1980s strains credulity.

In fact, many of the structural changes since 1991 have a direct link to the liberalizing reforms. Could the trade-to-GDP ratio have risen from 17 percent in 1990–1991 to more than 50 percent by the later 2000s without steady trade liberalization?[9] Could foreign investment have risen from $100 million in 1990–1991 to more than $60 billion in 2007–2008 without the liberalization of the foreign investment regime? Could the number of phones have risen from 5 million total at the end of 1990–1991 to new additions of over 15 million every month without the liberalization of telecommunications? Could automobile production have risen from 180,000 in 1990–1991 to 2 million in 2009–2010 without delicensing of investment and opening up to foreign investment? The list goes on.[10] Policies matter; "changes in bureaucratic attitudes" in the absence of policy changes are ephemeral.

Myth 3.2: There has been no reduction in poverty after the reforms.

Critics also complain that the reforms have done precious little for the poor. The complaint has taken different forms depending on the time and context. Initially the claim was simply that reforms had not helped bring down poverty. But as the reforms and growth progressed through the 1990s and 2000s and evidence on poverty reduction accumulated, these claims shifted first to asserting that reforms had not led to acceleration in poverty reduction from that in the pre-reform period and then to arguing that they had failed to reduce the absolute number of poor. We address each of these claims below.

Empirical evidence showing that poverty failed to decline during the heyday of socialism and that it has seen a steady decline in the post-reform era is now incontrovertible. Figure 3.2 shows the evolution of

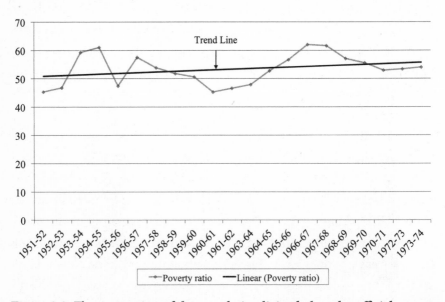

Figure 3.2. The proportion of the population living below the official poverty line, 1951–1952 to 1973–1974

Source: Authors' construction based on estimates in Dah, Guarov, 1998. "Poverty in India and Indian States: An Update," Discussion Paper No. 47, International Food Policy Research Institue (July)

the proportion of those below the official poverty line, called the poverty ratio, at the national level from 1951–1952 to 1973–1974. The figure also includes the trend line for the poverty ratio during this period. It is evident from the figure that poverty fluctuated between 50 percent and 60 percent during this period with a slight *upward* trend. Because India had begun at a very low per capita income and grew at a very slow pace during the first twenty-five years of the development program, the country could make no dent in poverty whatsoever.

Figure 3.3, which shows the poverty ratio in rural and urban India and the country as a whole at various points between 1977–1978 and 2009–2010 presents a sharp contrast to Figure 3.2.[11] Once the stranglehold of controls was loosened and reforms took root, growth accelerated and poverty fell in both rural and urban India and nationally. One can argue about the *level* of poverty since it depends on where precisely we draw the poverty line, but one cannot argue about the declining *trend* in it. Indeed, official estimates for 1993–1994, 2004–2005, and 2009–2010 are at a higher poverty line and these also show a declining trend in both rural and urban India.

Recognizing the compelling nature of the evidence on the decline in poverty under reforms and accelerated growth, critics have shifted

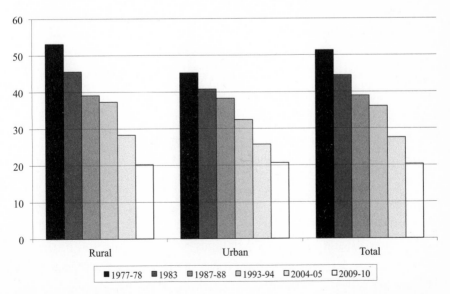

Figure 3.3. Poverty ratio in rural and urban India, 1977–1978 to 2009–2010
Source: Authors' construction based on estimates in Mukim and Panagariya (2013)

ground. They now argue that the decline during the post-reform era has not accelerated and even slowed down relative to the pre-reform era. For this, they compare the annual percentage-point decline between 1983 and 1993–1994 and that between 1993–1994 and 2004–2005. But this argument has two serious problems.

First, true comparison of pre- and post-reform performance is not the one that critics draw but rather the one between the first three decades, spanning 1950–1980, and the past three decades, 1980–2010. Even though liberalizing reforms in India became more systematic in 1991, they were already under way during the 1980s.

Second, and a tough nut for the critics to crack, is the poverty estimate based on the latest expenditure survey, conducted in 2009–2010, which captures the effect of the 8.7 percent growth during 2005–2006 to 2009–2010. This estimate shows that poverty during these five years fell at a rate far exceeding that in any other period. Indeed, the acceleration during this period is so large that when we combine it with the earlier period and compute the average percentage-point decline per year during 1993–1994 to 2009–2010, this number turns out to be larger than during 1983 to 1993–1994, the period critics favor the most.[12]

But some critics reject the evidence of declining poverty by arguing that there has not been a major dent in the *absolute* number of people living below the poverty line and that this fact undermines the claim that poverty fell after the reforms. According to the official estimates provided by the Planning Commission, at the traditional poverty line, the India-wide absolute number of poor was 323 million in 1983, 320 million in 1993–1994, and 302 million in 2004–2005. Presumably, therefore, the number of poor has at best declined marginally.[13]

However, the practice, once popularized by the World Bank, of citing the absolute number of poor makes for a flawed method of measuring poverty in the face of a rising population.[14] This approach to measuring poverty will in fact downplay the decline in poverty because it does not distinguish between changes in the absolute and in the relative or proportionate number of poor.

The use of absolute number of poor biases the poverty measure upward. (One might cynically speculate that the biased measure was popular at the World Bank and diffused to the client nations, so as to increase the alarm over poverty and bolster the critiques of a reforms-oriented development strategy.)[15]

Shifting, however, to the "proportionate" measure of poverty, we get a more meaningful idea of what happened in India. According to official poverty estimates, provided by the Planning Commission, the proportion of the population below the poverty line in India fell from 44.5 percent in 1983 to 27.5 percent in 2004–2005. During the same period, population rose by approximately 374 million. Unless you make the ludicrous assumption that the entire net addition of 374 million to the population was non-poor, a reasonable expectation would be that in the absence of an effective poverty-alleviation strategy, the poor would have been 44.5 percent of the additional 374 million people, or a further 166.5 million poor people.[16] Adding this number to the original 323 million poor in 1983, this would have meant a total of 489.5 million poor people in 2004–2005. But since the actual number of poor people in 2004–2005 was only 302 million, this suggests the exit of 187.5 million people from poverty.

This substantial decline is properly captured by what economists call the "poverty ratio," which fell to 27.5 percent in 2004–2005 from 44.5 percent in 1983. This clearly demonstrates the absurdity of the contention that the unchanged absolute number of poor people is equivalent to no change in poverty.

A final form in which some critics make the argument that the reforms have not helped the poor is by citing continuing or even increased poverty among certain individuals or groups of individuals. But this will not work either since we discuss below that poverty has gone down among all broad-based groups, such as the Scheduled Castes and Scheduled Tribes, and across all states.

There is no doubt that there are many who were poor prior to the reforms and who remain so today. Nor can we rule out the possibility that reforms have impoverished some individuals, for example, when they are displaced from land to make way for alternative activities without proper compensation.[17] However, this approach to the criticism of reforms is ill conceived since we can measure the efficacy of a set of policies only at some aggregate level, even when we disaggregate the effects by groups such as the Scheduled Castes and Scheduled Tribes (the impact on whom we examine in Myth 3.3 below). We know of no policy that makes everyone within each disaggregated group better off and hurts literally no one.

The reality for the critics of the reforms is stark: in regard to poverty reduction, the regime of socialist policies did far less good for (and indeed even inflicted harm on) the poor and the underprivileged groups than turned out to be the case under the regime of reformed policies. India ultimately moved away from the old policies precisely because those policies, with their deleterious effect on economic performance, had failed to deliver on poverty reduction and other social goals.

Myth 3.3: Reforms have bypassed, even hurt, the socially disadvantaged groups.

Some NGOs and journalists as well as international organizations argue that the reform-led growth may have reduced poverty overall but it has not helped bring down poverty among the socially disadvantaged groups, principally the Scheduled Castes and Scheduled Tribes but possibly also Other Backward Castes (OBC).

For example, a submission by the National Campaign on Dalit Human Rights to the House of Commons of the UK Parliament, published on January 14, 2011, states, "In spite of high economic growth rate the poverty rate among excluded communities in India has increased, coupled with the insecurity of livelihoods."[18]

In a similar vein, writing in the *Financial Chronicle* (December 29, 2010), journalist Praful Bidwai argues, "Rising inequalities highlight what is wrong with India's growth trajectory, driven as it is by elite consumption and sectoral imbalances, *which exclude disadvantaged groups from the benefit of rising GDP*, while aggravating income disparities" (emphasis added).[19]

Most strikingly, even the World Bank has joined the chorus alleging that growth in India has done precious little for the tribal population of the country. A recent country brief by the bank puts the matter in these stark terms: "India is widely considered a success story in terms of growth and poverty reduction. In just over two decades, national poverty rates have fallen by more than 20 percentage points, from 45.6 percent in 1983 to 27.5 percent in 2004–05. However it is widely acknowledged that growth has not touched everyone equitably and that many groups are left behind amid improving living standards. Among them are tribal groups identified by the Constitution as Scheduled Tribes."[20]

Once again, there is now irrefutable evidence that sustained growth alongside liberalizing reforms has reduced poverty not just among the better-off castes but across all broadly defined groups. It is true that the poverty ratios were and still remain significantly higher among the disadvantaged groups, reflecting historical injustices, but it is not true that these groups have not benefited from the recent growth. Indeed, evidence along all dimensions shows the Scheduled Castes and Scheduled Tribes gaining alongside the OBC and "forward" castes.

Mukim and Panagariya (2013) strikingly show that poverty fell for the Scheduled Castes and the Scheduled Tribes between every pair of successive surveys in rural and urban areas (see Figure 3.4). For the Scheduled Castes, the nationwide poverty ratio fell from 58.5 percent in 1983 to 48.9 percent in 1993–1994, 38 percent in 2004–2005, and 28.6 percent in 2009–2010. For the Scheduled Tribes, the ratio fell from 64.4 percent in 1983 to 51.2 percent in 1993–1994, to 46.3 percent in 2004–2005, and to 30.7 percent in 2009–2010. The authors also calculate the poverty ratios by states and find that they fell in all major states between 1983 and 2009–2010.

An extremely important recent development is the significantly larger decline in poverty among the Scheduled Castes and Scheduled Tribes relative to non-scheduled castes during the latest high-growth phase. Poverty for the Scheduled Castes fell by 9.4 percentage points and that for the Scheduled Tribes by a gigantic 15.3 percentage points relative to 6 percentage points for non-scheduled castes between 2004–2005 and 2009–2010. The disadvantaged groups by definition have had much higher poverty rates than other groups, but the gap has finally begun to be bridged decisively.[21]

There is an impression among some scholars that growth acceleration has not helped the Scheduled Tribes. This impression has derived partially

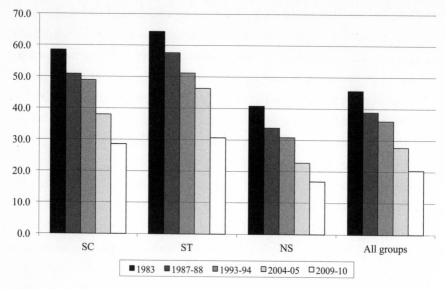

Figure 3.4. Evolution of the poverty ratio for various social groups
Source: See Figure 3.3

from the existence of the Maoist insurgency in certain regions where the tribes are concentrated and partially from a sense that when displacement happens from projects involving mineral extraction, tribes are not adequately compensated. While the adverse impact of these factors on the tribes can scarcely be denied, the evidence of the decline in poverty among the Scheduled Tribes is unequivocal. In this regard, two factors must be kept in mind. First, while the beginning of the poverty decline can be traced to the early 1980s, as demonstrated by Figure 3.3, the Maoist insurgency and even the acceleration in mineral extraction activity are of more recent origin. And second, the states with the largest populations of Scheduled Tribes, which include Madhya Pradesh, Maharashtra, Rajasthan, and Gujarat, have not been hotbeds of the Maoist insurgency.

Finally, we may also briefly mention the trends in poverty by religious groups. Here as well, estimates by Mukim and Panagariya (2013) show declining levels across all groups. In particular, they show poverty among Muslims declining from 52.2 percent in 1983 to 25.8 percent in 2009–2010, with the largest decline—9.7 percentage points—coming between 2004–2005 and 2009–2010.

Dehejia and Panagariya (2012a) take a different route to analyzing the impact of liberalization on different social groups. They consider the status of entrepreneurship among the Scheduled Caste and Scheduled Tribe groups in the service sectors, using the survey data gathered by the National Sample Survey Organization in 2001–2002 and 2006–2007.[22] They find for entrepreneurship a pattern very similar to the one found by Mukim and Panagariya (2013) for poverty. The share of each of the Scheduled Caste and Scheduled Tribe groups according to the value added and the number of workers employed in the enterprises was and remains well below its corresponding share in the population, reflecting the historical injustices. But each social group experiences healthy growth in the value added and in the number of workers employed in the enterprises owned by its members.[23]

The Scheduled Caste and Scheduled Tribe entrepreneurs have experienced significant growth in their enterprises. Some anecdotal evidence is beginning to appear even on the rise of Dalits (untouchable castes that are included among the Scheduled Castes by the Indian Constitution) to large fortunes. In particular, newspapers have widely reported on thirty Dalit *crorepatis* (a *crore* equals 10 million and a *crorepati* refers to someone having an accumulated wealth of 10 million rupees or more), almost all of them first-generation entrepreneurs, who were invited to a Planning Commission meeting specially organized for them in January 2011. The groups included Milind Kamble, who serves as chair of the Dalit Indian Chamber of Commerce and Industry, formed in 2005. According to him, "Including mine, most of the big Dalit-owned businesses are 15 years old. With the emergence of globalization and the disappearance of the License-Permit Raj, many opportunities appeared and many of us jumped on them."[24] Referring to the meeting at the Planning Commission, he reportedly said, "The Planning Commission was stunned when they asked how many of us used government schemes to build their businesses. Only one entrepreneur from Mumbai raised his hand and described how he'd applied for $20,000, spent three years visiting government offices to chase his money and finally got $15,000."

Thus, contrary to the general impression and especially the a priori fears of some critics, reforms and growth, and not governmental assistance, seem to have opened opportunities for the Scheduled Caste and Scheduled Tribe entrepreneurs to seize, in enterprises large and small.

Myth 3.4: The Planning Commission plays politics with poverty lines.

The suggestion that the Planning Commission plays fast and loose with the poverty lines couldn't be farther from the truth.[25] In setting the poverty lines, India has adhered to the highest standards of professionalism throughout its history.

The official poverty lines used until they were revised in 2011 were based entirely on the recommendations of the Lakdawala Committee of 1993.[26] These poverty lines had been set such that anyone above them would be able to afford 2,400 and 2,100 calories' worth of consumption in rural and urban areas, respectively, in addition to a subsistence level of clothing and shelter. A committee headed by Professor Suresh Tendulkar was likewise behind the revisions to the Lakdawala poverty lines, adopted in 2011 and reported to the Supreme Court by the Planning Commission. The integrity and qualifications of Tendulkar are beyond reproach.

In the second half of 2011, the media created the distinct impression that the Planning Commission, in its affidavit to the Supreme Court, had deliberately lowered the poverty lines to exclude many genuinely poor from the benefits reserved for the poor. The same impression was conveyed yet again when the Planning Commission released a report in March 2012 showing acceleration in poverty reduction between 2004–2005 and 2009–2010 over that between 1993–1994 and 2004–2005. These allegations are false.

In the first case, the Planning Commission had actually raised the poverty line, while in the second case it had made no change. In 2011, the Planning Commission reported to the Supreme Court poverty lines based on the Tendulkar Committee recommendations of raising the rural poverty line from the original level while keeping the urban poverty line at its previous level. The Planning Commission had simply complied with the Tendulkar Committee recommendations.

The claims of reductions in the poverty lines prominently surfaced yet again when the Planning Commission reported in March 2012 that poverty reduction had accelerated between 2004–2005 and 2009–2010 over 1993–1994 and 2004–2005. For instance, a headline on the NDTV website declared, "Planning Commission further lowers the [urban] poverty line to Rs 28 [from 32 rupees in the Supreme Court filing]." But once again, the Planning Commission had done no such thing. The 32-rupee line, reported to the Supreme Court, related to the year 2010–2011 and 28 rupees to 2009–2010, with the difference fully accounted for by the higher price level in 2010–2011.

One final accusation is that the Planning Commission has set the poverty lines at ultra-low levels so that it may exclude a large part of the population from benefiting from the government's redistribution programs. While reasonable people may differ on whether it is desirable to further raise the poverty line, the subject is far more complex than is commonly appreciated. The guiding objective behind the poverty line in India and indeed worldwide has been to monitor progress in combating destitution. Therefore, poverty-line expenditures have traditionally been set at levels just sufficient to allow above-subsistence existence.

The dilemma in raising the poverty lines is best brought out by considering the implications of poverty lines that are significantly higher than those currently in use and are advocated by many of the current critics of the Planning Commission. Thus, for example, suppose we were to raise the rural poverty line to 80 rupees and the urban one to 100 rupees at 2009–2010 prices.

What would these lines imply? First, based on the expenditure survey of 2009–2010, they would designate as poor 95 percent of the rural population and 85 percent of the urban population. But few analysts would suggest that all but 5 percent of the rural and 15 percent of the urban population live in destitution today. Even if we were to argue that poverty goes beyond the destitute, measuring progress at the 95th percentile in rural and the 85th percentile in urban areas is unlikely to tell us very much about success in combating poverty.

Second, turning to the implications for redistribution, how much good to the bottom 30 percent or 40 percent who represent the truly destitute will we do if the tax revenues raised from the top 15 percent urban population were spread evenly over 95 percent of the rural and 85 percent of the urban population? With the tax revenues still relatively modest, significant redistribution in favor of the destitute requires limiting such redistributions to the bottom 40 percent or so of the population. Spreading them thinly over a vast population would give too little to the destitute to make a major dent in poverty.

To dramatize this argument, suppose we redistributed all expenditures, as reported in the 2009–2010 expenditure survey, equally across the population. Astonishingly, such redistribution would leave each individual with just 45 rupees per day in expenditure. This level is well below even the lowest poverty line any critic of the Planning Commission has advocated during the recent debates on poverty lines.

Myth 3.5: Trade openness has exacerbated poverty.

The final myth we consider in this chapter folds into the criticism that globalization is bad for the poor. It also links a specific policy reform—increased openness to trade—to an increase in poverty. It got a boost from a study by the International Monetary Fund economist Petia Topalova (2007), who argued that enhanced openness adversely impacted poverty in India.[27]

However, several economists have successfully challenged her findings, showing that increased openness has reduced poverty instead. Given the importance of this issue, and the Topalova Myth, below we summarize these studies (which can be skipped by readers not interested in the necessary technical arguments).

Topalova asked whether rural and urban districts, which are subject to different degrees of competition from imports depending on which goods they produce and in what quantities, experienced increased or reduced poverty as a result of trade liberalization in India. She measured the openness by tariffs correcting for the levels of employment in high- versus low-tariff sectors. Working at the district level, she found that increased openness had been associated with, and presumably had led to, increased incidence of poverty in the rural districts but had no statistically significant effect in the urban districts. She found no evidence in either rural or urban India that openness was associated with alleviating poverty. These were startling results because, as we argued earlier, trade openness in a labor-abundant economy stimulates growth in general and the expansion of labor-intensive industries in particular so that it can be expected to lower rather than raise poverty.

Hasan, Mitra, and Beyza Ural (2006–2007) have therefore revisited this question. They note that the analysis of poverty and trade openness at the district level poses several problems. For example, the data from the 1993–1994 expenditure survey by the National Sample Survey Organization do not readily allow the identification of urban districts. District boundaries also shift over time. There are also questions of randomness of the sample at the district level. Finally, sometimes the number of observations in a district is insufficient to yield a reliable estimate of poverty.

Therefore, these authors study the question at the level of the state and (National Sample Survey Organization identified) regions within states. There being one or more regions within a state, regions are greater in number than states and therefore allow greater degrees of freedom. As such, their research offers an improvement over the Topalova approach: the focus on regions allows a tighter estimation of poverty than the district-focused approach and also allows for a tighter estimation of regression equations than a pure state-focused approach.

These authors also note that assigning zero tariffs to non-traded sectors in measuring openness, as done by Topalova, is erroneous. Many goods and services may be non-traded precisely because the barriers to trade are prohibitive. So they define openness as an employment-weighted sum of tariffs such that only exportable products are assigned zero tariffs, with non-traded sectors excluded from the calculation. These authors also take into account non-tariff barriers, which Topalova ignored.

In sharp contrast to Topalova's claim that trade openness was not associated with reduced poverty, these authors' superior methodology failed to encounter even a single case in which reductions in trade protection worsened poverty at the state or regional level. Instead, they found that states more exposed to foreign competition had lower rural, urban, and overall poverty ratios, with this beneficial effect being more pronounced in states that had more flexible labor-market institutions. The authors also found that trade liberalization led to greater poverty reduction in states more fully exposed to foreign competition. The results held for overall, urban, and rural poverty with varying strengths and statistical significance.

Moreover, Jewel Cain, Hasan, and Mitra (2012) have also revisited the issue and reinforced the findings of Hasan, Mitra, and Ural, using data from the more recent round of the sample survey conducted in 2004–2005. They find that every percentage-point reduction in the weighted tariff rate led to 0.57 percent reduction in the poverty ratio on average. This implies that of the overall reduction in poverty during 1987–2004, on average, 38 percent can be attributed to change in the exposure to foreign trade. Since the authors control for time-fixed effects, and poverty has declined over time, they can infer that the greater exposure of the labor force to foreign competition speeded up poverty reduction. The magnitude of impact and its statistical significance naturally vary across rural, urban, and the two sectors considered together, as well as across the different tariff and non-tariff measures used. However, in no case do these authors find increased openness to result in increased poverty.

Finally, Mukim and Panagariya (2012) split the data by social group and analyze the impact of trade openness on poverty within each of the social groups in rural and urban areas. They find no evidence whatsoever in favor of the hypothesis that rising incomes or openness have adversely impacted poverty among any one of the groups. They also find that one or more measures of openness have had a statistically significant and favorable impact on poverty levels in the Scheduled Castes and non-Scheduled castes in rural and urban regions and in both regions taken together. As for the Scheduled Tribes, they find a statistically significant effect of openness on poverty in urban areas only.

Chapter 4

Reforms and Inequality

T he surge of the growth rate during the eight years beginning in 2003–2004 to 8.5 percent from less than 4 percent until 1980 has meant the creation of substantial wealth. While there were no billionaires in dollar terms in India as recently as 2000, the 2007 list by *Forbes* reported as many as fifty-five of them.

This new wealth has in turn led to claims that reforms have generated massive income inequalities and that India has entered a state similar to the American Gilded Age in the late nineteenth century. But while such claims may appear superficially plausible, they crumble in the face of close scrutiny.

Myth 4.1: Reforms have led to increased inequality.

At the outset, we need to emphasize that what is an appropriate measure of inequality is not simply a technical issue—for example, whether the index of inequality should be the economists' measure of what is called the Gini coefficient (explained below and more fully in Appendix 2), which is widely used by economists studying inequality in India and elsewhere. An appropriate measure of inequality must also reflect broader questions of relevance to the popular concerns.

Thus, for a measure to be relevant to the public-policy discussion, it must have political and social salience. For example, if incomes increase in Mumbai but not in the Ratnagiri district of Maharashtra, evidently inequality of income has increased between Mumbai and Ratnagiri. But if those living in Ratnagiri are not comparing themselves to what is happening in Mumbai, why is this inequality measure of any relevance? So, measures of urban-rural inequality may have little relevance as well.

On the other hand, when *within*-Mumbai inequality becomes more acute, the poor there are more likely to notice as they compare themselves with the rich in their own neighborhoods. Similarly, within our own university (Columbia University in New York), the inequality between the top salaries—the president enjoys the highest salary—and the lowest salaries is a salient issue, but (at least as of now) not the discrepancy between our salaries and those on Wall Street.[1] In short, an increase in inequality within one's own village or institution is likely to raise hackles but not inequality between groups that have little relationship or contact with one another.

Then again, the political and social implications of any increase in appropriately measured inequality would depend on the social context in which it occurs. Thus, if inequality increases and the rich spend money on conspicuous consumption, that could become socially explosive. But if mobility is high, the poor may react by celebrating the conspicuous inequality rather than resenting it, because they think that they too may someday "make it big" in that way.

Keeping these caveats in mind, consider some general economic arguments that bear on income distribution between the rich and the poor in an economy such as India's. First, some forms of inequality can be expected to rise in a rapidly growing economy. Growth involves wealth creation. Insofar as a small number of entrepreneurs lead this wealth creation, and those creating wealth are unlikely to redistribute all of it in an act of altruism, disparity among the richest and the rest of the population in both income and expenditure is likely to rise.

Likewise, rapid growth is often led by the formation of a small number of agglomerations (i.e., concentrations of economic activity in limited geographical areas), which generally form in urban centers, leading to urban–rural as well as regional inequality. On the other hand, in a labor-abundant economy, pro-growth policies are also expected to lead to specialization in the labor-intensive goods, which raises employment and wages of the poor. The poor can move from lower-paid jobs in the countryside to higher-paid jobs in rapidly growing urban agglomerations, thereby producing less inequality.

Against this background, what has been the Indian experience? As it happens, the evidence we discuss below shows that contrary to widespread impressions, inequality measures do not point to an unambiguously rising trend in inequality.

Thus, Krishna and Sethupathy (2012) have recently measured inequality in India, using the household expenditure survey data from the NSS rounds conducted in 1987–1988, 1993–1994, 1999–2000, and 2004–2005.[2] They show that inequality between states and between urban and rural areas is dwarfed by inequality among households within each of these aggregates. For example, inequality within states accounts for more than 90 percent of the total inequality over the country (see Figure 4.1). Inequality between states accounts for less than 10 percent of the total inequality across the country. Likewise, inequality within rural and urban areas accounts for 90 percent or more of the total inequality across the nation.

Importantly, the overall inequality exhibits only modest variation over the period, rising slightly between 1988 and 1994 and again between 1994 and 2000, but by 2005 dropping to a level slightly above that in 1988 (see Figure 4.1). Inequality trends within states mirror the national experience: it rose between 1994 and 2000 and then fell between 2000 and 2005 in most states. Indeed, between 2000 and 2005, only four states—Mizoram, Maharashtra, Orissa, and Haryana—experienced significant increases in inequality. The picture is almost exactly the same for rural and urban areas within states; the vast majority experienced rising inequality between 1994 and 2000 but falling inequality between 2000 and 2005.

The results of other researchers, comprehensively surveyed by Weisskopf (2011), echo the basic message of Krishna and Sethupathy that, rather than exhibit secular trend, inequality has gone up and down during the growth process with at most a modest net rise since the 1980s. These researchers rely on the Gini coefficient, which usually varies by two or three percentage points, changing only rarely by five percentage points. What is interesting, however, is that some researchers have gone

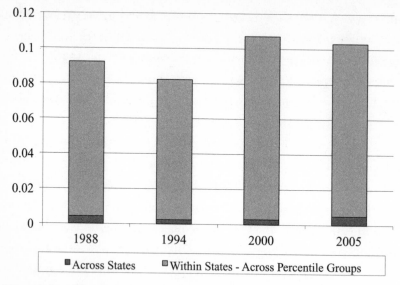

Figure 4.1. Changes in inequality over time and within households versus across states

Source: Krishna and Sethupathy (2012, Figure 6.9)

on to interpret these changes as representing "significant" or "pervasive" increase in inequality.

Thus, Deaton and Drèze (2002) report estimates that exhibit no clear trend in rural inequality and a small increase in urban inequality. But in the text of their paper, they surprisingly conclude, "To sum up, except for the absence of clear evidence of rising intra-rural inequality within states, we find strong indications of a pervasive increase in economic inequality in the nineties. This is a new development in the Indian economy: until 1993–94, the all-India Gini coefficients of per capita consumer expenditure in rural and urban areas were fairly stable" (p. 3740). Evidently their stark conclusion is not consistent with their statistical findings.

In almost an identical spirit, Weisskopf (2011) quotes Patia Topalova approvingly as stating that "all measures point to significant increase in overall inequality in the 1990s" (p. 46). Yet, the Gini coefficient calculated by Topalova and reported by Weisskopf changes from 31.9 in 1983–1984 to just 30.3 in 1993–1994 and 32.5 in 2004–2005. One would think that the difference between 31.9 and 32.5, which may not even be statistically significant, would hardly warrant the inference that there has been a *significant* increase in inequality.[3]

An extra dividend from Krishna and Sethupathy's analysis is the finding that there is no correlation between the change in inequality across households within states and the change in state-level measures of tariff and non-tariff protection. Trade openness is not linked to increased inequality.

The critics of the reforms have also raised a different concern: that growth has been uneven across states and that this has resulted in increased inequality among them. This is correct since richer states have grown faster than the poorer states *on average.* This phenomenon may have political salience if it leads to resentment by the states lagging behind, which are poor to begin with. But four qualifying facts must be kept in view.

First, as Panagariya (2010a) and Chakraborty et al. (2011) show, the years 2003–2004 to 2010–2011 have seen nearly all states growing significantly faster than they did in any prior period. Therefore, the rise in interstate inequality does not reflect the poorer states' remaining poor or being further impoverished. Instead, it represents the richer states growing faster than the poorer states in an environment in which all states are growing faster.

Second, two of the poorer states—Bihar and Orissa—are among the fastest-growing states today. Their success shows that when the national policies are conducive to growth (as they have been after the significant reforms began) and some of the states grow rapidly, the door to poorer states' achieving similar success is also opened wider. As Bhagwati and Panagariya (2004) and Panagariya (2009a) have argued and Gupta and Panagariya (2012) have analyzed in detail, there will likely be a diffusion effect: when the rest of the economy is growing rapidly, the electorate in the poorer states will demand more from its leaders, prompting policy changes that increase prosperity. Both Bihar and Orissa have elected and reelected chief ministers who have performed well.

Third, faster growth in some states opens the scope for larger-scale redistribution programs in favor of poorer states. A program such as the

National Rural Employment Guarantee Scheme, which benefits the poorer states proportionately more, would not be feasible without certain states' having large enough incomes to make the necessary revenues available.

Finally, labor is not immobile across states. It is well known that labor from Bihar has traditionally moved to Mumbai and Kolkata for jobs, as have people from the Punjab and from the hills. That means that faster growth will attract migrants from the slower-growth states and regions, so that the prosperity (as distinct from growth) will diffuse to the slower-growth areas through the usual channels, such as remittances.

A further dimension of inequality relates to the socially disadvantaged groups. Once again, critics often assert that the income differences between the Scheduled Caste and Scheduled Tribe on the one hand and non-scheduled castes on the other have gone up during the years of rapid growth. But in a comprehensive analysis, Hnatkovska, Lahiri, and Paul (2012) show that such claims are not supported by empirical evidence.

Using Employment-Unemployment Survey data from the NSS rounds conducted in 1983, 1987–1988, 1993–1994, 1999–2000, and 2004–2005, they show that the wages of the Scheduled Castes and Scheduled Tribes have been converging to those of non-scheduled castes since 1983. They demonstrate also that differential education levels of the two groups drive most of this convergence. Likewise, the occupation structure of the Scheduled Castes and Scheduled Tribes has also been converging toward that of non-scheduled castes. The Scheduled Castes and Scheduled Tribes have been able to take advantage of the rapid growth and structural changes in India during the post-reform period and have rapidly narrowed their huge historical economic disparities with non-scheduled castes and tribes.

Myth 4.2: Thanks to the reforms, India is now in the Gilded Age that prevailed in the late nineteenth-century United States.

The emergence of billionaires and the exposure of a few mega-corruption cases have led some, especially Sinha and Varshney (2011), to argue that

India has now entered a Gilded Age much like the United States in the late nineteenth century.[4]

During this period in the United States, four main strands of criticism were rampant. The first was that American business elites had succumbed to "gross materialism," which was manifest in conspicuous consumption and crass displays of wealth. Second, this was made possible by the accumulation of great wealth by the likes of John D. Rockefeller and Andrew Carnegie, and indeed many others, while the vast masses toiled for minuscule wages. Third, these tycoons were not "captains of industry" to be admired but were rather "robber barons" who had built their fortunes on abusive business practices and high-handed suppression of attempts at unionizing labor. Fourth, (in modern terminology) there was a business-political complex, such that these robber barons and corrupt politicians had greased one another's palms and defrauded the nation.

Mark Twain's 1873 novel with Charles Dudley Warner was titled *The Gilded Age,* a phrase that gained wide circulation.[5] The book was a reaction to the excesses that accompanied the remarkable growth of the American economy as the production of iron and steel took off with rail transport expanding rapidly to bring primary resources from the expanding western frontier to the east. Oil and banking expanded at an unprecedented pace as well, leading to massive fortunes for tycoons. The vignettes from this Gilded Age amply illustrate the criticisms that attended the extraordinary growth.

Lavish parties were a way of life for the nouveaux riches. An account of the time says: "Sherry's Restaurant hosted formal horseback dinners for the New York Riding Club. Mrs. Stuyvesant Fish once threw a dinner party to honor her dog who arrived sporting a $15,000 diamond collar."[6]

There was also a populist resentment of the extreme wealth contrasted with the tragic reality of slums and subsistence wages in the overcrowded tenements in the growing urban towns and cities. The general perception, reflecting that contrast, was that while the rich wore pearls, the poor were in rags. There was growing talk of retribution through emerging violence: fears grew of "carnivals of revenge."

Against this backdrop, labor began to organize against long hours and low wages, and the robber barons occasionally reacted by breaking the strikes brutally. Thus, even Andrew Carnegie, who professed sympathy for the poor, reacted to the Homestead Strike of 1892 by supporting his manager, Henry Frick, who locked out workers and hired Pinkerton musclemen to threaten the strikers. This was no isolated incident.

The offending titans also operated in a governance vacuum regarding business practices they used to gain monopoly control. Notorious for such business practices was John D. Rockefeller of Standard Oil Company, who in 1870 turned his company into one of the nation's first notorious monopolistic trusts. Antitrust legislation came later: the Sherman Anti-Trust Act of 1890 and the later, tougher, and more effective Clayton Anti-Trust Act of 1914.

The era was also marked by corruption at the highest levels of government, including the president, but more typically at the levels of local governance where, as today, businesses and governments shared the spoils from local grants of cash subsidies and land gifts, presumably for a "social purpose" (such as constructing a railroad) but in fact for the sole purpose of defrauding the commonwealth.

Is India today in such a Gilded Age? There are superficial similarities, for sure. True, in the same way that fast growth in the nineteenth-century United States created the Vanderbilts, Carnegies, Rockefellers, and Morgans, it has created a large number of billionaires in India. Again, like the robber barons of the American Gilded Age, Indian billionaires have tilted the playing field to their advantage through securing mining and land resources, seeking regulations favorable to them, and blocking foreign entry. But the similarity ends there.[7]

The conditions characterizing the American Gilded Age and current-day India are vastly different. At the beginning of the Gilded Age, the dominant economic philosophy in the United States was laissez-faire. There was virtually no effective regulatory, labor, or social legislation at the federal level. Two key pieces of regulatory legislation—the Interstate Commerce Act of 1887, which aimed to limit the monopoly power of the railways, and the Sherman Act of 1890, which provided for antitrust action against businesses—were enacted during this period. Key laws providing protection to industrial labor, the poor, and the elderly came much later. With rare exceptions, only white males enjoyed voting rights.

In contrast, post-reform India and its growth explosion have been preceded by several decades of a command-and-control system complemented by stringent legislation in favor of industrial workers so that it is impossible to have business tycoons breaking strikes the way the American robber barons did. India, it may be recalled, has had a long-standing national commitment to eradicating poverty and achieving universal adult suffrage since independence. The country has all elements of a liberal democracy with the poor and the underprivileged having access to effective politics at the ballot box.

The economic reforms have allowed freer play to private entrepreneurs but can hardly be characterized as laissez-faire. Railways remain a public-sector monopoly and the government remains a major player in such key sectors as steel, coal, petroleum, and engineering goods. Despite private-sector entry in airlines, telecom, insurance, and electricity, the public-sector players have remained active. In banking, the role of domestic and foreign private players has been expanded but the public sector again remains dominant. And several sectoral regulatory agencies, topped by an all-encompassing Competition Commission, oversee business practices.

Whereas during America's Gilded Age major sectors such as steel, oil, sugar, meatpacking, and the manufacture of agriculture machinery came to be dominated by "trusts," the opposite is true in India today. There are multiple domestic firms within many sectors, competing against one another as well as with imports and foreign investors. Increased competitive pressures have led to reduced prices and improved quality of products and services in such diverse sectors as airlines, telecommunications, automobiles, two-wheelers, refrigerators, and air conditioners.

The treatment of industrial workers in India today stands in sharp contrast to that in late nineteenth-century America. During the Gilded Age, factory workers toiled sixty-hour weeks without pensions, compensation for job-related injuries, or insurance against layoffs. In contrast to the strikebreaking actions of the robber barons at the Homestead Steel Mill in 1892 and George Pullman's railroad in 1894, labor laws in India provide a high degree of protection to industrial workers.

Finally, whereas the state provided no protection to those at the bottom of the income distribution, including farmers in the United States during its Gilded Age, the government in present-day India is sensitive to the fate of the poor. Indeed, growth and the social programs it has made feasible have helped bring down poverty significantly. The changes have also benefited the underprivileged groups, as we have already documented, and as we noted, there are now a handful of Dalit *crorepatis*.

But what about the corruption? How does today's India compare to America's Gilded Age? Critics contend that the post-reform era has been driven by crony capitalism. This implies that Indian entrepreneurs have accumulated wealth mostly by redistributing it in their favor through outright fraud in collaboration with politicians, rather than by creating it.[8] But the allegation is not persuasive. Unlike Mexico, for instance, where the billionaire Carlos Slim Helú has used every conceivable means to generate monopoly profits for himself, most Indian entrepreneurs have become rich by creating wealth while operating in a highly competitive market. Recent empirical work by Alfaro and Chari (2012) also points to the existence of a highly competitive market in India with substantial entry of new firms on the margin. To be sure, one can find examples such as those of the Reddy brothers, who, according to their recent indictment, have accumulated wealth from illegal mining; but that is not the case with the vast majority of Indian entrepreneurs from the information technology, telecommunications, pharmaceuticals, or engineering goods industries.

So, while the American Gilded Age produced Rockefeller and Vanderbilt, India today has given rise to Narayana Murthy of INFOSYS, Azim Premji of WIPRO, and Uday Kotak of Kotak Mahindra Bank. There is not a hint of corruption or shady practices among these successful tycoons. All of them are associated with extensive engagement with society, and have embraced corporate social responsibility and private social responsibility. Whereas Carnegie and Rockefeller gave away their fortunes on their death, the Indian tycoons have given away massive sums of money even as they have earned them. Besides, their lifestyles are simple, not extravagant.

While the tycoon Mukesh Ambani has built a much-condemned high-rise in Mumbai, the display of personal wealth and gross materialism is far less rampant in India than in nineteenth-century America or in the New York of the 1970s prior to the current crisis and even after the financial sector's recovery. Perhaps the worst displays take the form of flamboyant and unseemly weddings costing millions, but that is a long-standing cultural tradition.

While, therefore, India is not a throwback to the American Gilded Age, one might ask: What about China? Here the parallel is closer. Union rights are nonexistent; ostentatious displays of wealth are common; and there is little attempt at corporate and personal social responsibility. So here again India scores against China and handsomely at that.

Chapter 5

Reforms and Their Impact on Health and Education

T here is one final area of criticism that has been leveled at the re-form programs that have liberalized the economy and promoted growth: that they have failed to promote education and health. Critics have suggested that India lags behind much poorer countries in these areas; that states such as Kerala, which chose an alternative path, have performed much better; and that states such as Gujarat that have relied on growth have fallen short of satisfactory progress. But these assertions are little more than myths that fail to stand up to careful analysis and examination of data.

Myth 5.1: Poverty may have come down but India scores poorly on health even when compared with much poorer countries.

Recent focus of the media on child nutrition indicators, which place India below virtually all sub-Saharan African countries, has created the widely shared impression that India has performed poorly not just in nutrition but in health *in general* relative to these countries.

On the one hand, India is compared by the critics with much richer China and to significantly poorer Bangladesh to drive home the message that whether one takes rich or poor countries for comparison, India is a serious laggard in health achievements despite growth and successful poverty alleviation.[1] But these inferences are plain wrong. India is by no stretch of the imagination an exceptional underachiever in health generally. In fact, India is hardly out of line with other countries with similar per capita income levels. Moreover, when countries with similar or lower per capita incomes outperform India along a specific indicator, such as life expectancy, it is often because they started well ahead in the race. Superior past achievements may continue to ensure high current *levels* of indicators despite poor achievements in more recent decades. Progress over a given period must be judged by the *gains* made during that period.

At the outset, we should dispel any lingering doubts about India's having done poorly relative to the countries in sub-Saharan Africa in terms of vital statistics in the context of its per capita income. In Figure 5.1 we show the position of India relative to that of all sub-Saharan African countries along four indicators of health plotted against per capita income in 2009: life expectancy, infant mortality, maternal mortality, and deaths due to malaria. As is readily seen, India scores very well relative to the countries with the same per capita income or less and, indeed, in many cases relative to countries with higher per capita income as well.

But how does India compare with the critics' favorite countries, Bangladesh and China? Table 5.1 provides vital statistics for these countries and India, as reported in the 2011 World Health Organization (WHO) publication.

Take Bangladesh first. Without discounting its achievements, we must deflate them relative to those of India, refuting the unwarranted encomiums for Bangladesh and the exaggerated criticisms directed at India.

The performance of Bangladesh relative to that of India in terms of health indicators is significantly more equivocal than has been reported by the critics. Indians and Bangladeshis enjoy the same life expectancy at birth. Bangladesh has a lower infant mortality rate than India (41 per 1,000 live births against the latter's 50) but its rate of stillbirth more than offsets the difference (36 per 1,000 births against India's 22): an inconvenient fact that almost all observers emphasizing the lower infant mortality in Bangladesh ignore.[2] The maternal mortality rate in Bangladesh is, in fact, much higher than in India. Mortality due to malaria is similar while Bangladesh edges out India only marginally on nutrition indicators.

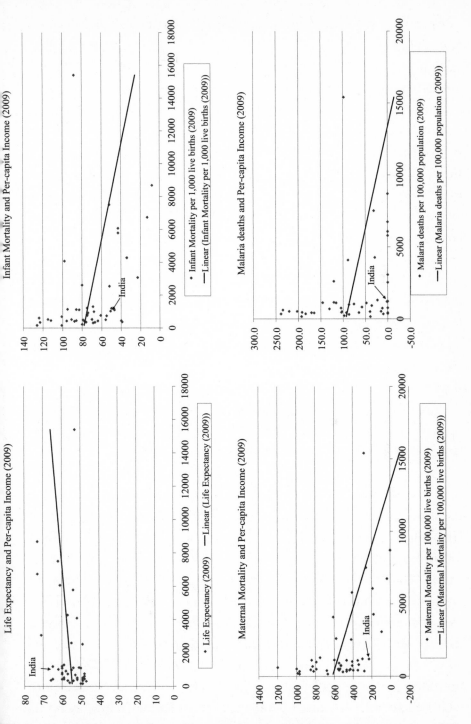

Figure 5.1. Comparing India to the countries in sub-Saharan Africa in terms of life expectancy, infant mortality, maternal mortality, and deaths due to malaria

Source: World Development Indicators for per capita incomes and WHO (2011) for other indicators

Table 5.1. Selected indicators: Bangladesh, China, and India, 2009

Health Indicator	India	China	Bangladesh
Per capita income, 2009 (current dollars)	1192	3744	551
Life expectancy at birth in 2009 (years)	65	74	65
Stillbirth rate (per 1,000 total births)	22	10	36
Infant mortality, 2009 (per 1,000 live births)	50	17	41
Maternal mortality, 2008 (per 100,000 live births)	230	38	340
Death from malaria, 2008 (per 100,000 population)	1.9	0	1.8
Percent children stunted, 2000–2009	47.9	11.7	43.2
Percent children underweight, 2000–2009	43.5	4.5	41.3

Source: World Development Indicators of the World Bank for per capita GDP and World Health Organization (2011) for the remaining indicators

In comparing Bangladesh and India, we must also take into account history. According to the United Nations (World Population Prospects, the 2010 revision), life expectancy in Bangladesh during 1950–1955 was forty-five years compared to just thirty-eight years in India. The 1971 war led to a major dip in most health indicators of Bangladesh but they recovered in the following decades. At least some of the accelerated progress Bangladesh has achieved during the 1980s and beyond is therefore to be attributed to its return to the initial conditions.

This point is reinforced when we compare Bangladesh to West Bengal, with which it has a shared history and geography. Not only are the two entities located in the same region, but they also were once part of the same larger state in preindependence India. It turns out that West Bengal outperforms Bangladesh in terms of health indicators. Already during 2002–2006, it enjoyed a life expectancy at birth of sixty-five years. And its infant mortality rate of 33 per 1,000 live births in 2009 and maternal mortality of 141 during 2004–2006 were considerably lower than the corresponding rates reported for Bangladesh in Table 5.1.[3]

Turn next to the India–China comparison. Some critics of Indian performance on health argue that despite acceleration in growth since the 1980s, India has done poorly relative to China in improving its health indicators. Such assertions are misleading for at least two reasons.

First, growth in the 1980s, 1990s, and early 2000s has been much faster in China than in India.[4] And second, like Bangladesh, China has enjoyed a historical advantage over India. For example, China had already gained much of its lead over India in life expectancy by the early 1970s (see Figure 5.2).

Indeed, the gap in life expectancy between China and India has steadily declined in recent decades, falling from 13.2 years at its peak in 1971 to 9.3 years in 2009. It is ironic that Amartya Sen, who has been criticizing India for its poor achievements in health vis-à-vis China, himself made this point in 2005: "The gap between India and China has gone from 14 years to seven [since 1979] because of [China] moving from a Canada-like system to a U.S.-like system."[5]

There is little doubt that India has some ways to go in the area of health. But this requires a realistic assessment of both achievements and failures. If income increases have indeed helped in improving health outcomes, this needs to be recognized. Otherwise we would erroneously conclude that income increases are not crucial to improving human welfare after all.

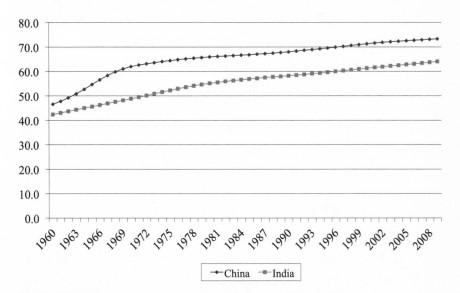

Figure 5.2. Life expectancy in India and China, 1960–2009

Source: Based on the data from World Development Indicators of the World Bank

Myth 5.2: India suffers from the worst malnutrition anywhere in the world.

There is constant repetition by Indian as well as foreign-based civil society groups, journalists, international institutions, bloggers, and even academics that India suffers from the worst malnutrition anywhere in the world. Some also contend that the country is making no progress in bringing down malnutrition. This is the latest illusion to which the critics of Indian reforms are clinging.

As a representative example, a blog post by Meg Towle on the website of Columbia University's Earth Institute asks, "India is booming—so why are nearly half of its children malnourished?" Towle opens the article thus: "India has more hungry people—and the highest burden of child malnutrition—than any country in the world. The 2010 Global Hunger Index designates national levels of hunger as *alarming,* and India scores lower than many Sub-Saharan African countries despite having a considerably higher GDP." She adds, "The percentage of children under age three who are underweight has virtually not changed between 1998–1999 and 2005–2006, hovering under 50%."[6]

Nutrition among children as well as adults is indeed an important and urgent problem in India. This being said, addressing it effectively also requires proper analysis. To date, however, rhetoric and journalistic assertions such as Towle's, which unfortunately are carried on websites of institutions that claim to be scientific but fall short in practice, and resort to dubious indices, have filled the public policy space, misleading many. Our critique below shows why.

Child nutrition. There are very serious measurement issues with translating the heights and weights of children into stunting (low height for age) and underweight (low weight for age).[7] Before we discuss them, however, it is useful to consider the evidence, such as there is, being utilized to reach judgments on the issue.

Recall that health as an objective received ample attention from the beginning of development planning in India. Nutrition, within health, was no exception: the First Five-Year Plan (1951–1956) devoted a substantial separate section to it. More important, India is perhaps the only developing country where systematic and comparable surveys at regular intervals aimed at measuring nutrition among children as well as adults have been conducted since the 1970s.

As early as 1972, the Indian Council of Medical Research, Hyderabad, had established the National Nutritional Monitoring Bureau (NNMB), which has conducted regular nutrition surveys of rural populations in nine states. The NNMB surveys provide comparable nutrition indicators for 1975–1979, 1988–1990, 1996–1997, and 2003–2006.

Figure 5.3 depicts the evolution of the proportions of the underweight and stunted children between ages one and five years according to these surveys. The estimates are based on pooled observations from all nine NNMB states. We cannot overemphasize the fact that both measures show a *steady improvement* in child nutrition status, contrary to Meg Towle's claim (though that improvement is consistent with India's still showing exceptionally high levels of malnutrition, a separate issue where Towle chides India and which we address below).

Evidence from a more recent comprehensive source, the National Family Health Survey (International Institute for Population Sciences and Macro International 2007), corroborates the trend indicated by the NNMB estimates. This newer source covers virtually all states and rural as well as urban areas, and has conducted three rounds of surveys, in 1992–1993, 1998–1999, and 2005–2006. Comparable child nutrition estimates are available for children under three years of age for 1998–1999 and 2005–2006. It turns out that the proportion of stunted children fell from 51 percent to 45 percent and that of underweight children from 43 percent to 40 percent between these two periods.

The decline in malnutrition notwithstanding, it is the high absolute level of malnutrition that has grabbed media headlines. Not a day goes by without some TV channel or newspaper running the headline that the world's fastest-growing economy suffers worse malnutrition than sub-Saharan Africa. Journalists, NGOs, politicians, and international institutions within and outside India have all accepted these levels entirely uncritically.

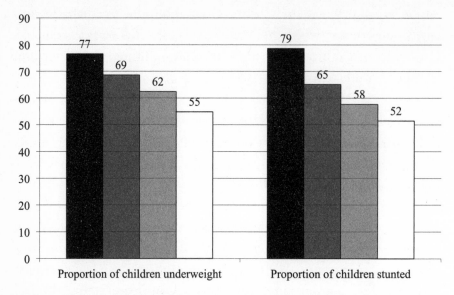

Figure 5.3. Malnourishment among children above one and below five years of age in rural areas of nine states

Source: Authors' construction based on NNMB (1999), Report of Second Repeat Survey—Rural, Indian Council of Medical Research, Hyderabad, Table 19, and NNMB Fact Sheet 2003–06 at www.nnmbindia.org/downloads.html (accessed June 27, 2011)

But first consider India in relation to sub-Saharan Africa (SSA). In terms of vital statistics, such as life expectancy at birth, infant mortality, and maternal mortality, India fares better than all except one or two SSA countries with comparable or lower per capita incomes. So it is puzzling that according to WHO statistics, the country suffers from a higher proportion of underweight children than every one of the forty-eight SSA countries and a higher rate of stunting than all but seven of them. Such countries as Central African Republic, Chad, and Lesotho, which have life expectancy at birth of just forty-eight years compared with India's sixty-five, have lower rates of stunting and underweight!

To further underline the obvious absurdity of the malnutrition numbers for India, compare Kerala and Senegal. Kerala exhibits vital statistics edging toward those in the developed countries: life expectancy of 74 years, infant mortality rate of 12 per 1,000 live births, under-five mortality of 16 per 1,000 live births, and maternal mortality rate of 95 per 100,000 live births. The corresponding figures for Senegal are far worse at 62, 51, 93, and 410, respectively. But nutrition statistics say that Kerala has 25 percent stunted children compared to 20 percent of Senegal, and 23 percent underweight children relative to 14.5 percent of the latter. How is it possible that the better-nourished infants and children of Senegal respectively die at rates 4.25 and 5.8 times those of Kerala? Likewise, does it make sense that Senegalese mothers giving birth to healthier children die at rates 4.3 times those of Kerala mothers during childbirth?

To make sense of this nonsense, we must look elsewhere. Specifically, we need to examine how the stunting rates are calculated (the procedure for determining underweight children is identical). To classify a child of a given age and sex as stunted, we must compare his or her height to a prespecified standard, set by WHO. In the early 2000s, WHO collected a sample of 8,440 children representing a population of healthy breast-fed infants and young children in Brazil, Ghana, India, Norway, Oman, and the United States. This "reference" population provided the basis for setting the standards.

As expected, when comparing children of a given age and sex even within this healthy sample, heights and weights differed due to genetic differences. Therefore, some criterion was required to identify stunting among these children. In each group, identified by age and sex, WHO defined the bottom 2.14 percent of the children according to height as stunted. The height of the child at 2.14 percentile then became the standard against which children of the same age and sex in other populations were to be compared to identify stunting. An identical procedure was used to set the standard for identifying underweight children.

The key assumption underlying this methodology is that *if properly nourished,* all child populations would produce outcomes identical to the WHO reference population, with only 2.14 percent of the children at the bottom remaining stunted and underweight. Higher rates of stunting would indicate above-normal malnutrition. So the million-dollar question is whether this assumption really holds for the population of children from which the estimate of half of Indian children being stunted is derived.

As it happens, the answer can be found buried in a recent study published by the Government of India (2009a). The latest estimate for stunting in India has been derived from the third National Family Health Survey (NFHS-3), mentioned earlier. The report draws a highly restricted sample from the fuller NFHS-3 sample consisting of *elite* children defined as those "whose mothers and fathers have secondary or higher education, who live in households with electricity, a refrigerator, a TV, and an automobile or truck, who did not have diarrhea or a cough or fever in the two weeks preceding the survey, who were exclusively breastfed if they were less than five months old, and who received complementary foods if they were at least five months old" (Government of India 2009, p. 10).

If the assumption that proper nutrition guarantees the same outcome in every population as in the WHO reference population is valid, the proportion of stunted children in this sample should be 2.14 percent. But the study reports this proportion as above 15 percent. The assumption is violated by a wide margin.

The implication of this and other facts is that Indian children are genetically smaller on average. A competing hypothesis, which says that nutrition improvements may take several generations, fails to explain how, without a genetic advantage, the far poorer sub-Saharan African countries, which lag behind India in almost all vital statistics, could have pulled so far ahead of India in child nutrition. Moreover, the trend of the stunting proportions shown in Figure 5.3 would suggest that nearly all those born in the 1950s and before are stunted. This is as absurd as it gets.

We note here with some puzzlement the uneven treatment of child malnutrition by the prominent activist economist Jean Drèze in his different writings. Thus, in an article in the *Economic and Political Weekly* (Deaton and Drèze 2009), Drèze discusses at length the finding that even the elite Indian children fail to attain the high nutrition levels exhibited by the WHO 2006 population. Yet, when writing in *Outlook* magazine on the same issue, he makes no mention whatsoever of the qualifications this finding implies (Drèze and Sen 2011). In the latter article, the authors begin with two opposite narratives of the post-reform India, a brighter one based on accelerated growth and a gloomy one rooted in poor performance in education and health. In articulating the gloomy narrative, the authors regurgitate the malnutrition indicators that place India below nearly all sub-Saharan African countries without indicating any of the qualifications discussed in Deaton and Drèze (2009).

Adult Nutrition. The story told by the critics about adult malnutrition (as distinct from child malnutrition) is equally suspect. The source of alarm here is the steady decline in per capita calorie consumption in rural India with no clear trend in urban India during the past twenty-five years. Deaton and Drèze (2008), who provide a comprehensive survey of the evidence, point to per capita calorie consumption and the proportion of the population reporting lack of food as sending conflicting signals on hunger. On the one hand, per capita calorie consumption fell from 2,240 in 1983 to between 2,000 and 2,100 in the first half of the 2000s. On the other hand, the proportion of those reporting lack of food fell from 17.3 percent in 1983 to just 2.5 percent in 2004–2005. In addition, per capita protein consumption has declined while per capita fat consumption has risen in both rural and urban areas.

There are several possible explanations for the decline in calorie consumption while the proportion of the population reporting lack of food drops dramatically. One is that increased mechanization in agriculture, improved means of transportation, and improved absorption due to improved epidemiological environment (better child and adult health and better access to safe drinking water) have curtailed the need for calorie consumption. Another possible explanation is a shift from coarse grains, such as millet and sorghum, which are calorie intensive, to finer ones, such as rice and fruits.

Adult weights and heights, which are more direct measures of nutrition, do show steady even if slow improvements. According to the NNMB surveys to which we have previously alluded, the population with below-normal body mass index (BMI) of 18.5 fell from 56 percent to 33 percent for men and from 52 percent to 36 percent for women between 1975–1979 and 2004–2005 (Deaton and Drèze 2009, Table 10). In absolute terms, the proportions of men and women with below-normal BMI prevailing in 2004–2005 are high when seen in an international context. But this is an issue relating to the *level,* not *change,* which is the center of concern of those focusing on increased hunger.

The purpose of pushing back against the critics is not to suggest for a moment that all is well with child and adult nutrition in India. We fully appreciate that despite the progress it has made, India remains very far from the progress made by the developed countries in all aspects of health including child and adult nutrition and therefore has a long way to go.

But this requires a proper assessment of where precisely the greatest deficiencies are so that scarce revenues are spent prudently. Overstating problems has its own hazards: if healthy children are designated as malnourished, we might push them toward obesity and, likewise, if we misdiagnose the problem of a lack of proper balance in diet as one of low calorie consumption, we would erroneously push calorie consumption.

Myth 5.3: The Kerala model has yielded superior education and health outcomes.

Thanks in part to the UNDP advocacy of its policy experience as a role model for development, the "Kerala model" has gained an iconic status in some development circles in both India and abroad. The view in these circles is that the Kerala model has successfully delivered ultra-high achievements in both education and health despite its low incomes and slow growth through redistribution and efficient public spending. But the claim crumbles in the face of careful scrutiny.

True, the evidence is unequivocal that Kerala has the best all-around education and health indicators among the major Indian states. Its literacy rates for both males and females and life expectancy are higher and the rates of infant mortality, maternal mortality, and malnutrition are lower than for all other larger states in India. The superior education and health outcomes in Kerala are not in question.

But the evidence that there is a clearly identifiable Kerala model to which these superior outcomes can be attributed is absent. Authors Richard Franke and Barbara Chasin (1999) offer a definition, but beyond the redistribution of land, it is descriptive of the Kerala experience rather than a set of policies that other states could potentially emulate.[8] As we noted earlier, land redistribution as an instrument of poverty alleviation was well known to Indian planners and was tried all over India but its implementation failed due to political opposition.[9]

Amartya Sen is also said to have talked about a "Kerala model" but George Mathew (2001) has contradicted this: "Dr. Amartya Sen during his recent visit to Kerala repudiated the argument that there is what is called a Kerala model, and disclaimed that he had ever used the term. At best, what has happened is Kerala's experience of development."[10]

There are four observations to be made about Kerala's developmental approach and outcomes.

First, if redistribution has been at the heart of its achievements, as it is widely believed, we should find a relatively low level of and a significantly declining trend in inequality in the state. Yet, according to the 2004–2005 NSSO expenditure survey, Kerala exhibits the highest degree of inequality among the fifteen largest Indian states. It is possible that Kerala had greater success in redistributing land than other states, but that has certainly not translated into a more egalitarian distribution of expenditures than in the rest of the country. Likewise, inequality fails to show a declining trend. Rural and urban inequalities in Kerala did fall between 1983 and 1993–1994 but they rose back in 2004–2005 to levels well above those in 1983. The significant decline in poverty between 1983 and 2004–2005 could not be explained by the trend in inequality.

Second, Kerala began with a huge advantage in literacy over the rest of the country at independence. Since then, it is hard to find anything spectacular or unique in outcomes in Kerala. This is shown in Figure 5.4, which plots the evolution of literacy rates in Kerala, Maharashtra Gujarat, and India. Maharashtra began with a 20 percentage-point disadvantage vis-à-vis Kerala in 1951. By 2011, the disadvantage had been reduced to 11 percentage points. Gujarat began with a 25 percentage-point gap but narrowed it to 15 percentage points. Similar narrowing of the gap can be observed with respect to the India-wide average.

The historical advantage of Kerala can also be observed in the indicators of health. Here we do not have ready access to the data from 1951 but we do have the series on life expectancy and infant mortality rates beginning in the early 1970s.

In Figure 5.5, we show the life expectancy at birth from 1970–1975 to 2001–2005 at five-year intervals in three high-achiever states: Kerala, Maharashtra, and Tamil Nadu. Maharashtra begins with an eight-year disadvantage and Tamil Nadu with a twelve-year disadvantage vis-à-vis Kerala. But the gap narrows to approximately seven years in each case by 2001–2005. A similar story unfolds in the infant mortality rate. The gap of more than forty-five deaths per 1,000 live births vis-à-vis Kerala in Maharashtra and Tamil Nadu in 1971 is reduced to less than twenty in 2009 in each case.

Third, advocates of the Kerala model argue that the state's achievements with respect to poverty, education, and health are to be distinguished from those of other states because it has done so despite its low per capita income and poor growth performance. Clearly, low per capita income and a high Gini coefficient (i.e., unequal distribution of expenditures) and yet low levels of poverty in relation to other states cannot all be true simultaneously. What gives way is the per capita income.

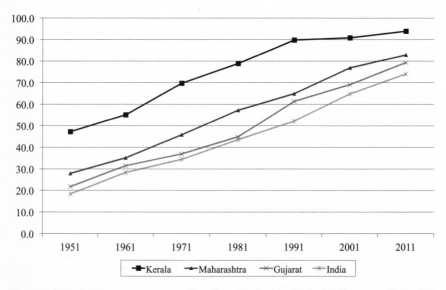

Figure 5.4. Literacy rates in Kerala, Gujarat, Maharashtra, and India, 1951–2011

Source: Authors' construction based on data from the Census of India, various rounds

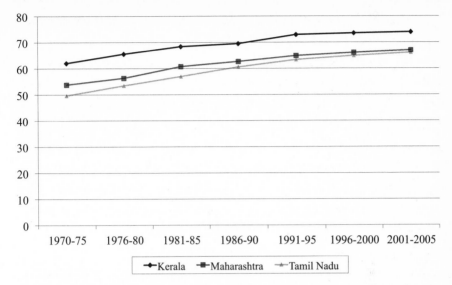

Figure 5.5. Life expectancy at birth in Kerala, Maharashtra, and Tamil Nadu, 1970–2006

Source: Authors' construction based on estimates from Sample Registration Bulletins, Census of India, various issues

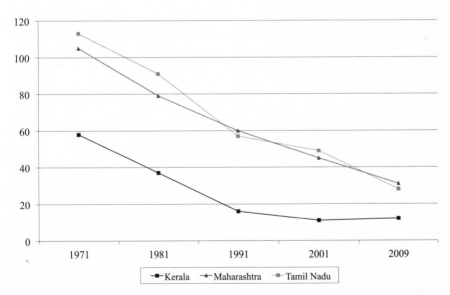

Figure 5.6. Infant mortality rate per 1,000 live births in Kerala, Maharashtra, and Tamil Nadu, 1971–2009

Source: See Figure 5.5

As Chakraborty et al. (2011) show, once the available gross state domestic product (GSDP) data are converted to the common 2004–2005
base and appropriate population series used to obtain *per capita* GSDP,
Kerala consistently ranks among the top five of the largest fifteen states
by this measure beginning in 1980–1981, the year from which the
GSDP series is available on a continuous and consistent basis.[11] The picture is even more dramatic when we consider per capita expenditure.
According to the latest large-scale expenditure survey, conducted in
2009–2010, Kerala tops the list of the larger states ranked by per capita
expenditures in both rural and urban areas. High achievements of Kerala
in poverty alleviation, health, and education are associated with high,
not low, per capita incomes and expenditures.

Finally, the claim by the proponents of the Kerala model that the
state achieved superior health and education outcomes through significantly more activist state interventions also turns out to be implausible.
Once again, at least the available data do not reveal anything out of the
ordinary. During the twenty years from 1991–1992 to 2010–2011 for
which we are able to obtain public-health expenditures data for the
major states, per capita public expenditures on health turn out to be by
far the highest in Goa. Indeed, it is consistently three times the per capita
public health expenditure in Kerala. Excluding Goa, Kerala spends more
than its nearest rival state in eleven out of the twenty years. This may
give some credence to the Kerala model except that the expenditures
themselves are not all that large: except in the recent three or four years,
they rarely exceed 1 percent of the GSDP.

What turn out to be far more impressive for Kerala are the *private*
health expenditures. These data are available for each state for two years
and they are by far the highest of any state (including Goa) in Kerala
both on a per capita basis and as percent of the GSDP. Thus, for example, in 2004–2005 per capita private expenditure in Kerala was 2,663
rupees per annum with the nearest rival, Punjab, spending only 1,112
rupees. In comparison, per capita public expenditures of the two states
in the same year were 280 and 234 rupees, respectively. Good health in
Kerala is being financed predominantly by private expenditures (and this

also may have something to do with the influx of massive remittances from the Middle East, which again would call into question the generally antiglobalization attitudes of the proponents of the Kerala model).

This dominance of the private sector is also observed in education. The NGO Pratham has been conducting extensive surveys of children in school up to sixteen years of age in rural India in recent years. In its latest report (ASER 2010) it finds that, with the exception of two or three tiny northeastern states, Kerala has the highest proportion of students between ages seven and sixteen in private schools in rural areas. At 53 percent, it leads its nearest rival, Haryana, by a margin of 13 percentage points. The conventional and dominant story of Kerala as a state-led success in the postindependence era simply does not stand up to a careful empirical investigation.

When confronted with the evidence contained in our second observation above relating to the lackluster performance of Kerala in terms of the *progress* in the social indicators in the postindependence era, proponents of the Kerala model counter that this comparison is misleading because each percentage-point improvement gets harder as we reach higher and higher levels of achievement. For example, it is much harder to improve literacy from 50 percent to 60 percent than from 20 percent to 30 percent.

But there are at least three reasons why this defense is implausible:

- There is no compelling reason that the going should get rougher as the level of an indicator rises. True, the *scope* for improvement in literacy is less the closer the level of literacy to 100 percent, but this need not translate into slower progress on the margin. Indeed, one can think of many reasons that the going might get easier as the literacy rate rises: the social pressure on a family to impart literacy to its children will rise with the proportion of literate children in its neighborhood. As the level of literacy rises, the pressure on the government to do something about those left behind also rises. Besides, with low levels of literacy, teachers are not easy to find since the handful of the literate are much in demand in other occupations.

- Again, if the Kerala model is that much more effective, it should be able to overcome a higher barrier and still deliver a superior outcome. In effect, resorting to the argument that the performance looks poorer because a higher starting point gives the state a handicap seems like an admission that the model is as mortal as any after all.

- Finally, there is an objective way to test whether the higher starting point was truly a handicap or the Kerala model has indeed been overrated. We can accomplish this by assigning Kerala and the other states the same starting point and then evaluating who wins the race. In Figure 5.7, we depict the progress in literacy in Kerala, Gujarat, Maharashtra, and India with their starting years being 1951, 1981, 1971, and 1981, respectively. These starting years assign the four entities as close a starting literacy rate as data would permit.[12] We depict the literacy rates at the end of three decades since this is as far as we can go for Gujarat and India, whose starting points are both 1981.

Gujarat unambiguously beats Kerala: it starts more than 2 percentage points below Kerala in year 0 but ends up a hair's breadth above it in year 30. Both Maharashtra and India as a whole perform only slightly worse than Kerala. For example, Maharashtra is 1.4 percentage points below Kerala in year 0 and 2 percentage points below it in year 30. India as a whole performs similarly.

The discussion up to this point has focused on the developments in health and education in Kerala in the postindependence era. An interesting and important unanswered question, however, is what accounts for Kerala's having acquired its gigantic lead over much of the rest of India at independence. Even here the conventional story that this was to be attributed to the movements for social justice and social programs by the rulers of Travancore and Cochin is quite incomplete. Careful scrutiny gives way to a more complex explanation that includes important links of Kerala's early success to globalization.

While we have been unable to find reliable accounts of developments in the health sector in pre-independence Kerala, Robin Jeffrey (1992),

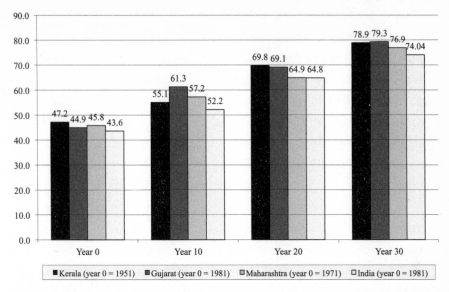

Figure 5.7. Comparing progress in literacy rates in Kerala to those in Gujarat, Maharashtra, and India beginning at approximately the same level

Source: See Figure 5.4

who has spent many years living in various parts of India since the 1960s, offers a detailed account of the socio-economic-political developments that contributed to the spread of literacy in Kerala in the second half of the nineteenth century and first half of the twentieth. Based on his account, four key factors can be highlighted.

First, the rulers in Travancore and Cochin played an important role in the spread of education. Travancore Maharajas began investing in the spread of vernacular primary schools in the 1860s. Maharajas of Cochin followed suit beginning in the 1890s. Their objective was to spread modern knowledge to the widest circle of people through the use of the mother tongue, Malayalam. Children of upper-caste Hindus and Syrian Christians dominated the government schools till the end of the nineteenth century. But by the beginning of the twentieth century, both Travancore and Cochin offered concessions to lower-caste students whose numbers expanded rapidly.

Second, the culture of old Kerala, which included the importance assigned to women by matrilineal tradition among several communities, was conducive to the spread of education. Even before Travancore Maharajas got actively involved in education, an extensive network of village schools had existed. Landed high-caste Hindu and Syrian Christian families supported these schools. The wealth enjoyed by these families allowed them to send their children to schools rather than to work. Nayars and other matrilineal groups sent girls to the schools as well. One measure of the contribution made by this culture of education is that Malabar, the remaining Malayalam-speaking district, which was administered by the Madras presidency and had no princely government to promote education, never fell below third place within the presidency overall and consistently ranked top in female literacy.

Third, caste- and religion-based groups also played some role in the spread of education. Among the upper-caste groups, the Nair Service Society, which was founded in 1914, promoted education through the so-called Nair schools. The Sri Narayana Dharma Paripalana Yogam that the widely revered Sri Narayan Guru founded in 1903 played the same role among the lower-caste Ezhavas, though with less success since the community was much poorer and lacked resources. The Christian missionaries also helped accelerate the process of the spread of education. Protestant missionaries made their debut in Travancore with the arrival of Tobias Ringeltaube in 1806. He quickly got permission from the Maharaja to open a few schools. According to Jeffrey (1992, p. 97), by the middle of the nineteenth century, Travancore had a higher density of Protestant missionaries than any other part of India. They not only actively promoted literacy directly, especially among the lower-caste Nadars, but also greatly influenced the largest Christian group, the Syrian Catholics, who started establishing formal, literacy-oriented schools beginning in the early 1880s.

The fourth and last factor, which rarely is highlighted in the spread of education in Kerala prior to independence, is economic. A necessary condition for all of the above agents of the spread of literacy to succeed was the availability of necessary resources. Those building schools had to have the necessary revenues and the parents sending children to school had to have enough income to make ends meet without their children's labor. To sustain the process, it was also necessary that those acquiring education would have prospects for jobs commensurate with their qualifications.

This is where globalization played a key role. Roman coins commonly found in Kerala testify to its trade links abroad through pepper and cardamom exports going back 2,000 years. Jeffrey (1992) suggests that this trade link is a plausible explanation for the early presence of Jews, Muslims, and Christians—they came to trade and chose to stay: "Long before Britain or America, Kerala was a part of a 'world economic system'" (p. 72).

Beginning in the 1830s, cash crops saw a boom in Kerala. Europeans began establishing plantations to grow crops of interest to Europe and America. First came coffee; after its destruction by a leaf disease in 1880 came tea; and in the 1920s, cashews. Coconut, with its varied uses, turned into the most important crop, with trees springing up everywhere. Jeffrey (1992) quotes the Collector of Malabar in the mid-1930s as reporting to his superiors, "All but the poorest Malabar *ryots* [peasants] have their own compounds of fruit trees" (p. 73). Since coconut could not serve as a staple food, it had to be converted into money and money into food. This contributed in a big way to both the growth of trade as well as the conversion of Kerala into a cash economy. Jeffrey (1992) writes, "In this way, cash-oriented agriculture spread. Before about 1810, Kerala was, to be sure, part of a world market, but few Malayalis had to deal with it directly; but by the 1920s, few Malayalis could avoid it" (p. 73).

The growth of commercial houses and estates created job opportunities for the educated, making education attractive. Cash crops also served as an excellent source of revenues to finance schools for the state as well as larger landowners. Prosperity brought by the spread of cash crops enabled civic organizations to raise funds to open schools as well—an important link of the early spread of education in Kerala to markets and globalization.

The historic origin of preindependence success of Kerala therefore owes as little to the Kerala model as does its postindependence performance.

Myth 5.4: Despite high growth, Gujarat has performed poorly in health and education.

This myth is the mirror image of the previous one, whereby rapid growth in Gujarat is alleged to have not translated into rapid progress in social indicators. The problem once again lies in inference on the basis of the *levels* rather than the progress achieved during the high-growth phase. Gujarat began with low social indicators but its progress has not been poor by any means.[13]

We have already alluded to the superior performance of Gujarat in raising literacy rates in our discussion of the Kerala model. We saw that when we take approximately the same starting level of literacy, as in Figure 5.7, the gains made by Gujarat in three decades exceed those made by Kerala, Maharashtra, and the India-wide average. We may additionally note that when compared with these same entities, Gujarat made by far the largest percentage-point gains in literacy between 1951 and 2011.

This comparison of the gains by Gujarat in literacy carries over to the key indicators of health. Figures 5.8 and 5.9, which show the gains in life expectancy measured in the number of years and decline in infant mortality per 1,000 live births, respectively, illustrate this fact. We have comparable data on life expectancy beginning in 1970–1975 and ending in 2002–2006. The gains of Gujarat over this period at 15.3 years exceed those of Kerala, Maharashtra, and the India-wide average. The available data on infant mortality range from 1971 to 2009. During this period, Gujarat lowered its infant mortality rate by 96 per 1,000 live births relative to 74 for Maharashtra and 46 for Kerala.

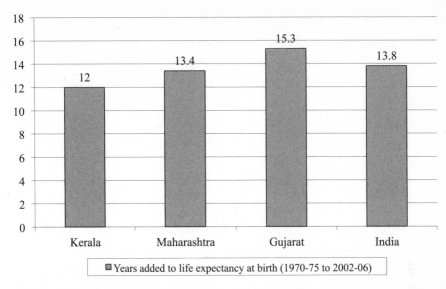

Figure 5.8. Additions to life expectancy in years: 1970–1975 to 2002–2006

Source: See Figure 5.5

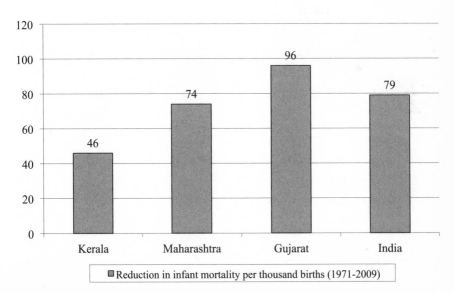

Figure 5.9: Reductions in infant mortality per thousand live births: 1971–2009

Source: See Figure 5.5

Chapter 6

Yet Other Myths

W e have now seen that growth, poverty, inequality, education, and health are the key subjects on which critics have tried to mobilize opposition to reforms. But they have failed. So they have turned to a potpourri of yet other myths. Chief among them are the following four.

Myth 6.1: Reforms have led to increased suicides by Indian farmers.

A common activist objection to liberalization in general and the use of genetically modified seeds in particular has been that they lead to suicides by farmers. The view found its most dramatic expression at the 2003 summit of the World Trade Organization in Cancun, Mexico, where activist farmer Lee Kyung-hae of South Korea climbed the barricade while holding a banner reading "WTO kills farmers" and stabbed himself to death. Recent farmer suicides in India have properly been an emotionally charged issue in India, in particular. The country therefore confronts opposition to reforms and the use of new genetically modified and *Bacillus thuringiensis* (BT) seeds.

Influential journalists such as Sainath (2009) of the newspaper the *Hindu* and activists such as Vandana Shiva (2004) have led the opposition to the new seeds on the grounds that they lead to "agricultural suicides."[1] But the evidence they provide fails to substantiate their case.

Suicide is a complex phenomenon with multiple causes and, in the case of farmer suicides, even the basic facts are treacherous to analyze.

First we look at the problems afflicting the data on suicides, whether overall or among farmers. Next we address whether overall and farmer suicides correlate with Indian reforms generally. We then assess whether the new BT seeds have resulted in accelerated farmer suicides.

At the outset, data on suicides in general and by farmers in particular are not entirely reliable. In the latter case the most commonly used series is also very short. The source on which most scholars rely is the annual publication *Accidental Deaths and Suicides in India* by the National Crime Records Bureau (NCRB), Ministry of Home Affairs. According to Nagaraj (2008), the chiefs of police of all states, union territories, and mega cities furnish data to NCRB, which in turn compiles and publishes them. Although NCRB has published the basic data since 1967, it began to provide details that allow farmer suicides to be identified only in 1995. But the data for 1995 and 1996 are incomplete; the consistent series began in 1997.

Figure 6.1 plots the data reported by Nagaraj (2008). First we observe that since the data begin only in 1997, strictly speaking, we cannot connect suicides to reforms generally. To do so convincingly, we must have the pre-reform data going back to at least the 1970s and 1980s. It is quite remarkable that critics of the Indian reforms have ignored this simple fact and claimed such a link as if farmer suicides today were a new phenomenon (absent prior to their explicit identification by NCRB beginning in 1995).[2]

Second, even if we insisted on trying to forge a connection with whatever little data we do have, we might hypothesize that since major additional reforms took place in the late 1990s and early 2000s and growth accelerated in 2003–2004, we still might make a connection by comparing suicide rates prior to 2003 and later. But whereas the general suicide rates do show a mildly rising trend in the last three years shown, farmer suicides rose in 2004 but fell in 2005 and 2006, dropping below their 2002 level.

Finally and most intriguingly, we may compare the levels of farmer suicides relative to suicides in the general population. At peak, reached

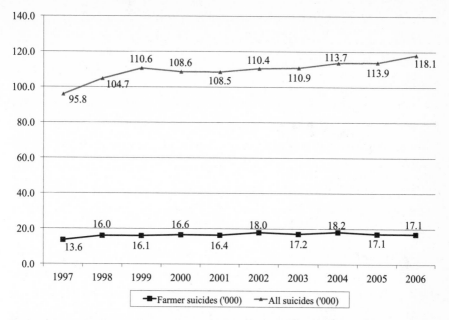

Figure 6.1. Suicides in the general population and among farmers
Source: Authors' construction using data in Nagaraj (2008)

in 2002, they were 16.3 percent of the latter. But at least half of the Indian workforce is engaged in farming. This fact points to a much lower suicide rate per 100,000 individuals for farmers than in the general population. Given this fact, one might well be agitated, less about the farmer suicides than about why the suicide rate in the general population is so much higher and how we could bring it down to the levels prevailing among farmers. On the other hand, the difference is so huge between the measured farmer and non-farmer suicide rates that one may question the validity of the data.[3]

But while there is no evidence for the link between reforms and suicides in general and farmer suicides in particular, it leaves open the narrower and more explosive issue of whether the introduction of BT seeds in cotton in 2002 led to an acceleration of suicides among farmers.

Contrary to what the critics assert, however, it is evident from Figure 6.1 that farmer suicide rates show no accelerating trend from 2002. Yet, according to Gruere, Mehta-Bhatt, and Sengupta (2008, Figure 11), the area under BT cotton expanded from nil in 2002 to more than 3.5 million hectares in 2006. These authors also look at individual states, such as Maharashtra and Andhra Pradesh, and fail to find any correlation between rising trends in farmer suicides and the expansion of the area cultivated under BT cotton.

Gujarat provides the most compelling example from this perspective. It was the first state to adopt BT cotton and the third largest after Maharashtra and Andhra Pradesh. By 2006, 25 percent of its total area under cotton had come under BT cotton. At the same time, it has the lowest numbers of reported farmer suicides at approximately five hundred per year, with the number slightly lower on average during 2003–2006 than in the preceding five years.[4]

Then again, the causes of suicides are many. This is so even in the case of farmer suicides. It is therefore unlikely that a single cause like BT seeds would emerge as the main factor. A study by Deshpande (2002) that examined in depth ninety-nine cases of farmer suicides in Karnataka underlines the need for this caution. Deshpande extensively interviewed the friends and relatives of the victims and considered a long list of proximate causes, including the volume and terms of debt, crop failures, dowry burden, and drinking problems. He did not find a single case in which one reason accounted for the fateful event. On average, there were three or four reasons in each case. Farm-related reasons get cited only approximately 25 percent of the time in suicide. Even more surprisingly, he notes, "Debt burden and the price crash, which have been quite commonly referred as important factors by the media and public personalities, happens to score 6 per cent probability of being one of the prominent reasons for suicides along with other reasons" (p. 2608).

Nonetheless, we may observe that in the few regions where farmer suicides have followed the introduction of BT seeds, the cause could well be that small, highly indebted farmers are bamboozled by salesmen employed by the corporations producing the seeds into buying and using the seeds, using high-cost loans, on the promise that this investment will produce high returns that will relieve the debts under which they labor. This is then a casino-type bet. When that fails, for reasons such as poorly implemented planting or adapting the new seeds to local conditions or simply a bad harvest, the distress rises to a level that prompts a suicide.

It is noteworthy that the earlier green revolution was not a result of privately invented and propagated seeds, and a proper government-financed and -organized extension service for which Dr. M. S. Swaminathan deservedly became famous complemented it. This also meant that the larger farms, with more resources and ability to take the risk of failure used the new seeds, while the small farmers did not.

This time around, in the few regions where farmer suicides have occurred, the small farmers who have been misled by the salesmen peddling the new seeds unscrupulously (much like the salesmen who were peddling risky housing mortgages to undeserving mortgage buyers in the United States and feeding the housing bubble whose collapse forced these victims into distressed sales) are the victims. The answer there appears then to be a regulation of these salesmen and measures, such as the setting up of an extension service for the BT seeds whose cost should be charged to the corporations selling the BT seeds.

Myth 6.2: The post-1991 reforms have led to increased corruption.

While we have seen that the charge that reforms have led to the Gilded Age in India is inappropriate, a separate criticism is that corruption is the result of the reforms: a charge that recurs in other countries that have embraced reforms.

A common refrain of the left-wing critics is that the post-1991 "neoliberal" reforms have led to exponential growth in corruption. For example, in the article "Economic Reforms: Fountain Head of Corruption" in the *New Age Weekly,* the central organ of the Communist Party of India, R. S. Yadav writes:

> The early stage of [the] liberalization process in the 1980s was accompanied by [the] Bofors scandal which for the first time in independent India put up the prime minister and the prime minister's

office in the center of the scandal. After the full fledged adoption of neo-liberal reforms in 1991, the country came across a wave of scams and scandals, every scandal bigger in magnitude, and more bold, and involved people at the helm of governance, administration and industry.[5]

The young among critics such as these are blissfully ignorant of history, while the old probably suffer from amnesia.[6] The near-absence of corruption was among the hallmarks of the Indian political virtue in the 1950s.[7] Corruption broke out not with the liberal reforms of the 1980s, but under the license-permit raj that peaked in the 1970s during the socialist-era policies of Prime Minister Indira Gandhi. With the government controlling the manufacture, distribution, and price of numerous major commodities, bribes became virtually the only means of accessing the latter within a reasonable time frame. Thus, for example, if you wanted a phone, car, or scooter, you had to choose between a many-years-long queue and a bribe. If you were among the lucky few to have a phone, a bribe was still necessary to receive the dial tone. If you wanted an airline ticket or a reserved railway seat, your choice was to take a chance and stand in a long queue or resort to *baksheesh* (i.e., a bribe disguised as a gift). It was no different for a bag of cement. God forbid, if you should have to travel abroad, a many-hours-long queue and unfriendly customs officials would await you upon return. As an entrepreneur, if you wanted an investment or import license or to stop your competitor from getting one, bribing a senior official in the relevant ministry would do.

It was the reforms, initially carried out on an ad hoc basis but made more systemic in 1991, that freed the ordinary citizens and entrepreneurs from their daily travails and humiliations at the hands of the petty government officials. This may not be obvious to the young, who probably do not even know what the license-permit raj was, but those of us who lived through this history know that the reforms bid good-bye to many forms of corruption.

The critical question, then, is: Why have we witnessed so many mega-corruption cases recently? The success of reforms has opened up new opportunities in several areas to make profits. But because the reforms still have not been extended to these new areas, new avenues for corruption of the older variety have now multiplied.

Thus, reforms (which include opening up access to the world markets) and the growth resulting from them have pushed up the prices of scarce resources, such as minerals and land. These price increases have multiplied the scope for government officials (and colluding businessmen) to make vast sums of illegal money through the pre-reform-type arbitrary and opaque allocations of the rights to extract minerals and to acquire and re-sell land.

The 2G-spectrum scam offers a dramatic example of how the success of past reforms (in opening up new opportunities to make profits) and the failure to extend them (to cover these new opportunities) have combined to produce a mega scandal.[8] With the telephone arriving in India in the early 1880s, it took the country 110 years to reach 5 million phones in 1990–1991. But the spectacular success of telecom reforms brought the number to 300 million at the end of 2007–2008, with the rate of expansion reaching 6.25 million per month. This success turned the spectrum on which cell calls travel into a resource worth tens of billions of dollars. That allegedly allowed telecom minister A. Raja to make handsome sums for himself and his friends when allocating the spectrum to his wealthy friends for a small "fee." Had reforms been extended to government procurement and sales policies, Raja would not have had the freedom to allocate the spectrum at a prespecified low price to his friends, with bribes allegedly provided in return.

Therefore, the most effective course of action available to the government to curb corruption is clearly the deepening and the broadening of the reforms to new areas. The reform of the antiquated Land Acquisition Act of 1894, the issuance of land titles that would improve access to credit,[9] transparency in government procurement, and competitive auctions of mineral rights and the telecom spectrum are among such measures.

Myth 6.3: Focus on growth and policies to promote it, such as opening up the country to inward direct investment, crowds out discussion of the really important questions that should concern India because of its poverty.

Of course, the growth strategy was designed precisely to lift the poor and the underprivileged out of poverty. And as we have demonstrated, the strategy did work and helped the poor and the underprivileged once the counterproductive policy framework began to be dismantled and finally growth materialized. So it is astonishing that any serious analyst would claim that we "crowd out" discussion of poverty.

Yet, Jean Drèze and Amartya Sen (1995) have argued:

> Debates on such questions as the details of tax concessions to multinationals, or whether Indians should drink Coca Cola, or whether the private sector should be allowed to operate city buses, tend to "crowd out" the time that is left to discuss the abysmal situation of basic education and elementary health care, or the persistence of debilitating social inequalities, or other issues that have a crucial bearing on the well-being and freedom of the population. (p. vii)

In reviewing this book, Bhagwati (1998) responded sharply:

> Much is wrong here. No one can seriously argue that there is a crowding out when the articulation of Indians is manifest in multiplying newspapers, magazines and books and the expression of a whole spectrum of views on economics and politics; this reviewer has noticed no particular shyness in discussing social issues, including inequality and poverty in India. . . . But, more important, the put-down of attention to multinationals misses the point that India's economic reforms require precisely that India join the Global Age and that India's inward direct investments were ridiculously small in 1991, around $100 million, and that this was an important deficiency that had to be fixed.

The reference to Coca Cola is no better, serving as a cheap shot against multinational investment; but it also betrays the assumption that Coca Cola is drunk by the elite or the Westernized middle class, not by the truly poor. It is more likely, however, that the former derive their caffeine from espresso coffee as well whereas the poor are the ones who must depend on Coke instead! (p. 199)

In fact, we would go further and argue that the inefficiencies caused by pre-reform policies hurt not the rich, but the poor and the lower middle class. This is because the rich manage to insulate themselves against the inefficiencies. Thus, take the Drèze-Sen derision of concern with whether private operators should be allowed to run city buses. Anyone who has had to ride for an hour and a half in a Delhi bus—as Bhagwati did twice a day, from his small sublet in the suburb of Motibagh to Delhi University—will not scoff at the notion that one might improve the service by letting in the private sector; only those who enjoyed high salaries and consulting incomes and drove Fiats could insulate themselves from the question of efficient city bus service. Similarly, if reforms could improve the electricity supply, that would help the poor man who slept on a charpoy and used a small portable fan to cope with the heat of the Delhi summer, by reducing the frequent interruptions in electricity supply that made the fan inoperative. The rich, on the other hand, had their own generators that took over during the interruptions of electricity supply, so they could continue sleeping in their air-conditioned bedrooms.

Myth 6.4: The reforms were forced on India by Bretton Woods institutions captive to the "Washington Consensus."

Yet another populist myth, propagated in the Western media and repeated often by left-wing commentators in India, is that the Bretton Woods institutions that were captive to the so-called Washington Consensus imposed the reforms on India. This is yet another epithet used by Joseph Stiglitz, who was vice president of the World Bank and oversaw its activities in many developing countries.[10]

However, Washington Consensus is nothing but Washington Conceit. Proposals for freer trade worldwide, and for promoting prosperity in India and other developing countries, owed to theoretical and empirical work that was developed in the early 1960s by Indian economists, and then influenced thinking and policy at the World Bank.[11] In one of his early papers written before he started expressing skepticism of free trade, Dani Rodrik said that the World Bank had produced no basic research: he was indeed right.

Reforms as the result of something called the Washington Consensus would have an extra edge in India, where many are keenly aware of sovereignty and, on the intellectual Left, resent the United States.

But it makes no sense to say that the reforms were exogenously "imposed" from Washington, whether by the Bretton Woods institutions or the US Treasury. The crisis in 1991 provided an opportunity to change course. Ever since Bhagwati and Desai (1970) provided the agenda for reform that the post-1991 reforms would begin to implement in earnest, it was *domestic* thinking and writing, and the growing sense that Indian policy makers had shot themselves and the economy in both feet with counterproductive policies that drove home the need for reforms. A significant part of the conditionality attached to the loans secured by India from the Bretton Woods institutions simply underlined what India itself wanted to do. In fact, the Bretton Woods institutions wanted to push further—for example, introducing a proper exit policy for the firms and an end to licensing of consumer goods imports in the early 1990s—but were unsuccessful because of Indian domestic political constraints. These, too, were matters on which many reform-minded economists from India had written for years earlier.

If there is still any doubt about this, just ask: If this was unpalatable and imposed exogenously, why did India not revert back to its bad old ways once the crisis was behind it? In fact, successive governments only reinforced the reforms, though with varying boldness and pace. Panagariya was at the World Bank from 1989 to 1993 and knows firsthand that after the first structural adjustment loan of December 1991, which concluded in December 1992, the World Bank chose to lend to India not because the latter accepted its conditions but because the Bank wanted to stay involved in the country. It was the World Bank that needed India rather than the other way around.[12]

It is pertinent to quote the late Prime Minister Narasimha Rao on this subject since it was during his tenure that the reforms were launched. Rao's reluctance to say almost anything about the reforms is well known. But when asked whether the reforms had been undertaken under pressure from the International Monetary Fund and the World Bank, he is reported to have said:[13]

The reforms initiated by my Government were designed both as a measure to meet an immediate situation as well as a long-term strategy for the country in the changed world conditions.

We thought that these reforms were necessary and this has now been confirmed and has acquired a national consensus cutting across political parties.

However, to say that they were made at the behest of the World Bank and IMF is not correct.

We have evolved a model which is suited to our conditions, which is being termed as the middle way and Market Plus.

India's experience in launching reforms is no different from that of Russia and China. As Padma Desai, a leading economist expert on Russia, has observed, Mikhail Gorbachev decided that the Soviet Union could not go on with the old policy framework under which the country was declining rapidly. Their reformers drew intellectual inspiration from several sources. What did the Washington Consensus have to do with it?

Just as the Indian and Soviet reforms were therefore endogenously arrived at, so were those in China. The Washington Consensus had nothing to do with the reforms in these three major countries.

Part II

The New Challenges: Track I Reforms for Faster and Broader Growth

Chapter 7

Track I and Track II Reforms

Dear Countrymen, to achieve this ambitious target [of doubling India's per capita income in ten years], we have to undertake many important reforms in our economy. At the same time, we need to implement necessary reforms in our administration, our judiciary, in education and in other areas. Reforms are the need of the hour.... To reform is to turn the inevitability of change in the direction of progress. To reform is to improve the life of every citizen. Take, for example, the reforms in the power sector.... These will ... ensure adequate availability of power for increasing production and employment. Similarly, the reforms that we are implementing in the telecom sector will enable us to provide cheaper telephones, mobile phones, and Internet services in all parts of the country. There is no scope for either apprehension or fear about economic reforms. I remember that some people had expressed similar fears even during the Green Revolution. These fears later proved to be baseless....

I urge our farmers, workers, other producers, industrialists, and our intelligentsia to contribute to building a consensus in favor of economic reforms.
   —**Prime Minister Atal Bihari Vajpayee in a speech in Hindi
   from the Red Fort on Independence Day, August 15, 2000**

I n Part I, we emphasized that growth is necessary for alleviating poverty in a country that starts out poor, that growth reduces poverty directly by pulling the poor into gainful employment, and that it facilitates additional poverty reduction by generating revenues that enable the financing of redistributive programs principally aimed at the poor.[1] We also demonstrated that the growth-centered strategy for alleviating poverty, with these double-barreled outcomes reinforcing each other, worked once the reforms introduced significantly since 1991 turned India from a slow-growing economy to a rapidly growing one.

Therefore, the reforms that India has undertaken so far to accelerate growth and to additionally address the plight of the poor through the now-feasible redistributive antipoverty programs have gone some way toward pulling the country out of a state of hopelessness that prevailed until 1980.[2] Yet, the process of reforms remains a work in progress, and a lot more still must be done.

Since independence, Indian planners and politicians have chosen to attack poverty through both growth and redistribution. Because the level of income at independence was extremely low and increased by only a small amount until at least the 1980s due to slow growth, the revenues available for redistribution remained meager. However, with growth having accelerated, especially since 2003–2004, more generous amounts of revenue have accrued to the government, making large-scale redistributive programs, such as the National Rural Employment Guarantee Scheme, possible.

While this is good news, 300 million or more citizens remain below the official poverty line. Moreover, since the official poverty line is itself set at the subsistence level, many among the officially non-poor are far from having a comfortable existence.

Therefore, the need for sustained and accelerated growth, which is progressively more inclusive in its impact, remains acute. Likewise, the redistributive programs must be made more effective even as they expand with the intention of providing greater benefits to the poor.

This strategy calls for future reforms to proceed on two tracks:

- Track I: reforms aimed at accelerating and sustaining growth while making it even more inclusive.
- Track II: reforms to make redistributive programs more effective as their scope widens.[3]

The liberalization program since 1991 has paid off handsomely. India grew at a striking 8.5 percent annual rate during the eight years spanning

2003–2004 to 2010–2011. Therefore, at first blush it may seem that the battle for Track I reforms has already been won and nothing more need be done.[4] This may even be the view of some within the current United Progressive Alliance (UPA) government, which came to power in 2004 and has chosen to focus almost exclusively on the promotion of social programs—Track II policies.

Yet, it would be wrong to think that Track I reforms have been fulfilled. If truth be told, India is far from done on Track I reforms for two broad reasons. First, the potential for growth remains grossly underexploited. The economy remains subject to vast inefficiencies. Removing these inefficiencies offers the opportunity not only to arrest the recent decline in growth but also to push the economy to a double-digit growth trajectory. Second, the poverty reduction that *directly* results from growth, in terms of enhanced wages and employment opportunities per percentage point of growth, can be increased: India can get a larger bang for the buck.

As regards the first issue, productivity remains well below the potential. For instance, according to a 2007 Government of India report, 57 percent of the workers were employed in low-productivity agriculture, which produced only 20 percent of the total output in 2004–2005. And even within industry and services, 84 percent of the workers were employed in enterprises with fewer than ten workers, and these enterprises are generally characterized by low productivity.[5] Employment in larger private-sector enterprises has been extremely low in comparison to other countries such as South Korea, Taiwan, and China and has been growing at best at a snail's pace.

In services, firms with four or fewer workers accounted for 73 percent of the employment but only 35 percent of the value added in 2006–2007. Even more dramatically, approximately 650 of the largest service sector enterprises produced 38 percent of the value added but employed only 2 percent of the workers that same year. Larger firms also show dramatically higher growth: value added grew at the annual rate of 28.2 percent in firms with five or more workers but only 4.5 percent in the smaller firms between 2001–2002 and 2006–2007.[6]

Manufacturing exhibits a similar pattern. The point is best illustrated by comparing the employment patterns in apparel in India and China. In 2005, 90 percent of apparel workers in India were employed in enterprises with eighteen or fewer workers. In comparison, only 2.5 percent of the Chinese apparel workers were in such small enterprises the same year. At the other extreme, India employed 5.3 percent of the apparel workers in enterprises with more than two hundred workers, compared with 56.6 percent in China.[7]

Clearly, huge scope remains for improving efficiency and accelerating the growth rate through progressive expansion of employment in the formal sector. The productivity figures are per worker, of course, rather than for total factor productivity. But total factor productivity is certain to yield the same conclusion because the astonishingly small enterprises are characterized by inefficiencies that should translate into overall inefficiency in that they get much less for the same input than the large enterprises.

Our second reason for continuing with additional Track I reforms is that they would make growth even more inclusive. While all evidence indicates that the acceleration in growth since the 1980s has helped reduce poverty,[8] this effect is far more muted in India than in countries such as South Korea and Taiwan in the 1960s and 1970s and in China more recently.

The key reason for this difference has been the nature of the growth. Whereas growth was driven by rapid expansion of highly productive large-scale firms in labor-intensive sectors, such as apparel, footwear, toys, and light consumer goods, in these other countries, it has been propelled instead in India by capital-intensive and skilled-labor-intensive industries, such as automobiles, two-and three-wheelers, engineering goods, petroleum refining, telecommunications, and software. This difference has reflected itself in a rapid movement of workers out of agriculture into gainful employment in manufacturing and services in South Korea and Taiwan in the 1960s and 1970s, and in China more recently, but in a continued heavy dependence of workers on agriculture in India.

To put the matter concretely, South Korea grew at an annual rate of 8.3 percent between 1965 and 1980. During this period, the proportion of the workforce employed in agriculture in the country fell by 25 percentage points from 59 percent to 34 percent. Simultaneously, the workforce employed in industry rose from 10 percent to 23 percent and in services from 31 percent to 43 percent. Alongside, real wages grew at 11 percent per year.

In sharp contrast, the share of agriculture in employment in India fell proportionately so gradually that, with the workforce growing, the absolute number of workers in this sector actually rose between 1993–1994 and 2004–2005. With the output share of agriculture having shrunk to 20 percent in 2004–2005, an extremely large proportion of the workforce depends on a very small proportion of income. Further Track I reforms are needed to create good jobs for these underemployed workers.

It may be observed that these twin reasons for Track I reforms—accelerating growth and making it more inclusive—are mutually reinforcing. Productivity growth requires moving workers from low-productivity agriculture into high-productivity industry and services and from the informal to the formal sector within industry and services. These same processes would also make growth more inclusive.

We begin the next chapter with a diagnosis of why Indian entrepreneurs have shied away from employing unskilled and low-skilled workers despite their vast numbers in the country and what corrective reforms are required.

Chapter 8

A Multitude of Labor Laws and Their Reform

The time has come for all of us to seriously consider whether the present labor laws, and the machinery for their implementation, need reforms to enable Indian exporters to tap the vast opportunities in the global market. It is my belief that the right kind of labor reforms will simultaneously protect the legitimate interests of the workers, create more employment, and sharpen the competitive edge of Indian exports.

—**Prime Minister Atal Bihari Vajpayee in a speech accompanying the presentation of the National Export Awards, New Delhi, January 21, 1999**

Is it possible that our best intentions for labor are not actually met by laws that sound progressive on paper but end up hurting the very workers they are meant to protect?

—**Prime Minister Manmohan Singh in a speech to trade unions, November 23, 2010**

T ransition from a poor agrarian economy to a modern one typically involves three key transformations: first, movement of workers out of agriculture into industry and services; second, progressive shift of workers from the informal to the formal sector within industry and services; and third, more rapid urbanization, which follows the shift to formal-sector manufacturing and services, which are likely to be in urban areas.

Regarding the last transformation, even if the industry happens to locate itself in or near a region that is rural, it turns the latter urban. The most dramatic example of this is the Pearl River delta in China, which was dominated by farms and villages until as recently as 1985 but has been transformed into a collection of mega-urban centers by the industrialization that followed economic reforms. Prior to that, Singapore went through a similar transformation. Either way, industrialization and modernization go hand in hand with urbanization.

The three transformations were at the heart of the modernization of such countries as South Korea and Taiwan during their fast-growth phases in the 1960s and 1970s. They have also characterized China recently. How does India stack up on these dimensions?

Despite a significant decline in the output share, the employment share of agriculture in India has remained high. Moreover, employment in industry and services also remains predominantly in small, informal firms characterized by low productivity. Consequently and unsurprisingly, urbanization has also proceeded relatively slowly.

Based on the census conducted once every decade, the proportion of urban in total population rose just 14 percentage points in six decades, from 17.3 percent in 1951 to 31.1 percent in 2011. The pace seems to have accelerated in the past decade with a 3.3-percentage-point gain but this is hardly adequate for transition to a modern economy. In contrast, China went from 19 percent urbanized population in 1980 to 45 percent in 2008, representing an average gain of 9.3 percentage points per decade. South Korea urbanized even faster during the 1960s and 1970s.

Flight of the Indian Entrepreneur from Labor

At the heart of this slow progress along all three dimensions is the flight of Indian entrepreneurs in the formal sector from low-skilled labor. It is ironic that in a country with nearly 470 million workers, all evidence indicates extreme and even increasing reluctance of Indian entrepreneurs to employ unskilled workers. The number of workers in *all* private-sector establishments with ten or more workers rose from 7.7 million in 1990–1991 to just 9.8 million in 2007–2008. Employment in private-sector *manufacturing* establishments of ten workers or more rose, on the other hand, only from 4.5 million to 5 million over the same period.[1] This small change has taken place against the backdrop of a much larger number of more than 10 million workers joining the workforce every year. Three key factors are behind this dismal picture.

Slow Growth of Manufacturing

A common feature of the fast-growing low-income countries has been rapid expansion of manufacturing, with the latter pulling unskilled workers from agriculture into gainful employment. This pattern characterized the rapid growth in Taiwan and South Korea in the 1960s and 1970s and in China more recently. Today's industrial economies, such as the United Kingdom, Germany, and the United States, also exhibited a similar pattern when they transformed themselves from primarily agricultural to nonagricultural economies.

But this pattern has failed to emerge in India despite rapid growth. The share of manufacturing in GDP actually fell from 16.8 percent in 1981–1982 to 15.8 percent in 2008–2009. Insofar as manufacturing is often a major source of gainful employment in a low-income but growing economy, its slow growth has been behind the slow movement of the workforce out of agriculture.

Poor Performance of Labor-intensive Manufacturing

Even with a stagnant share of manufacturing, some impetus to gainful employment of the unskilled could have come from a shift in the output composition of organized-sector manufacturing in favor of unskilled-labor-intensive and against capital- and skilled-labor-intensive activities.[2] Unfortunately, this did not happen either.

In a recent study, Das, Wadhwa, and Kalita (2009) analyze precisely this issue, using output and input usage data on ninety-six manufacturing sectors in the organized sector from 1990–1991 to 2003–2004. They identify thirty-one of these industries, such as food and beverages, apparel, textiles manufacture, and manufacture of furniture, as labor-intensive. These sectors accounted for only 12.94 percent of the gross value added in organized manufacturing in 1990–1991. Thus, the labor-intensive sectors were relatively unimportant in overall manufacturing to begin with. But then they remained so: their share rose to 15.9 percent in 2000–2001 and fell back to 12.91 percent in 2003–2004. And in all likelihood, this share has further declined since 2003–2004. In fact, some of the fastest-growing industries between 2003–2004 and 2010–2011 have been automobiles, two-and three-wheelers, petroleum refining, engineering goods, telecommunications, pharmaceuticals, finance, and software. All these industries are either capital-intensive or skilled-labor-intensive.

What about exports? The changes in the composition of merchandise exports of India corroborate the shift in production share toward capital-intensive goods. As Figure 8.1 shows, engineering goods, chemicals and related products, gems and jewelry, and petroleum products, which are either capital-intensive or semi-skilled-labor-intensive, accounted for 41 percent of the total merchandise exports of India in 1990–1991. The share of these products had, however, come to account for 65 percent of the total merchandise exports by 2007–2008. At the other extreme, ready-made garments, which are among the most unskilled-or low-skill-intensive products, saw their share decline from 12 percent to just 6 percent during the same period. Engineering goods and petroleum products, both highly capital-intensive products, witnessed the largest expansion.

Clothing and accessories offer a telling example of the poor showing of India in the world markets for labor-intensive products.[3] These products represent an extremely large world market and formed China's leading exports in the 1980s and 1990s. Indeed, even though electrical and electronic products have emerged as the country's leading exports since the early 2000s, China continues to dominate the market for clothing and accessories. In contrast, India has scarcely been able to keep up with much smaller Bangladesh.

This is evident from Table 8.1, which shows the exports of clothing and accessories by India as percent of those by Bangladesh and China in the 2000s. The exports from India to the United States were approximately the same as those by Bangladesh between 2001 and 2007. As regards the exports to the world as a whole, India had a more than 40 percent lead over Bangladesh in 2002. But it steadily lost ground, with its exports exceeding those of Bangladesh by just 5.7 percent in 2007.

1990-91: Total Merchandise Exports: $18.1 Billion

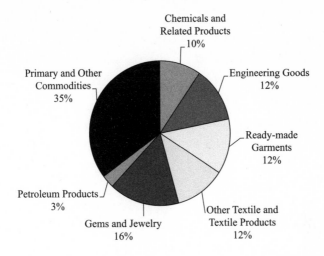

2007-08: Total Merchandise Exports: $163.1 Billion

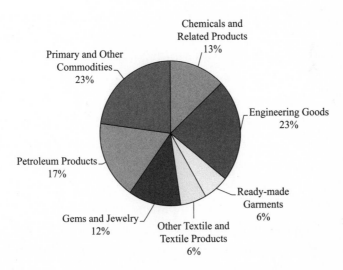

Figure 8.1. Composition of merchandise exports by India in 1990–1991 and 2007–2008

Source: Authors' construction using the statistics from Directorate General of Commercial Intelligence and Statistics

Table 8.1. Exports of clothing and accessories (SITC 84) by India as percent of those by Bangladesh and China

	Bangladesh		China	
Year	USA	World	USA	World
2001	85.9	134.6	33.4	15.0
2002	95.0	143.0	32.1	14.1
2003	100.8	124.6	25.7	12.1
2004	98.8	110.0	23.9	11.2
2005	·117.4	126.5	20.2	11.8
2006	107.4	115.0	18.5	10.0
2007	96.4	105.7	15.4	8.6
2008	N.A.	N.A.	15.3	9.1
2009	N.A.	N.A.	13.8	11.2

Source: Authors' calculations based on the United Nations Commodity trade data

When compared to China, India fares quite poorly in both the US and world markets. Even after the emergence of electronic products as its largest exports, China's lead in clothing and accessories over India has widened considerably. In the US market, India's exports as a proportion of Chinese exports fell from one-third to less than one-seventh between 2001 and 2009. The end to the multifiber arrangement under the Uruguay Round Agreement on Textiles and Clothing clearly exposed the inefficiency of the Indian industry vis-à-vis Bangladesh and China.

High and Rising Capital-intensity in Production

A final avenue to raising gainful employment of the unskilled could have been a shift toward more labor-intensive technologies. But even here, the evidence points to movement away from rather than toward labor. Indian firms use more capital-intensive techniques in production in relation to India's factor endowments to begin with, and technology has moved still further in this direction over the years.

Hasan, Mitra, and Sundaram (2010) show that labor–capital ratios in the vast majority of manufacturing industries in India are lower than in other countries at a similar level of development and with similar factor endowments. Comparing India and China in nineteen manufacturing industries, for example, they show that the capital stock per worker in India is consistently higher in India than in China, in the period 1980–2000. They also find India's growth in capital stock per worker from 1980 to 2000 in these sectors is higher than that in China. It is not surprising, then, that whereas employment in these sectors shows steady growth in China, it has been stagnant in India.[4]

Link to Firm-size Distribution

Ultimately the flight from unskilled labor is at the heart of the unusually heavy concentration of Indian workforce in small firms, especially in the labor-intensive industries. A preponderance of small firms in turn hampers export performance since such firms have no incentive to invest in searching for and developing large markets abroad. Instead, it is far more cost-effective for them to sell their wares in the local market.

In recent important research, Hasan and Jandoc (2012) analyze the firm-size distribution of some major sectors, such as apparel, automobiles, and auto parts, that represent the highly labor- and capital-intensive sectors, respectively.[5] Their work sheds new light on the structure of Indian manufacturing that we have already sketched.

Combining the data on the firms in the organized as well as unorganized manufacturing, Hasan and Jandoc (2012) first show that an astonishing 84 percent of the workers in all manufacturing in India were employed in firms with forty-nine or fewer workers in 2005. Large firms, defined as those employing two hundred or more workers, accounted for only 10.5 percent of manufacturing workforce. In contrast, small- and large-scale firms employed 25 percent and 52 percent of the workers, respectively, in China in the same year.

Upon disaggregation by sectors, Hasan and Jandoc find that the firm-size distribution in India is skewed toward even smaller enterprises in the labor-intensive sectors, with the large firms concentrated in the capital-intensive sectors. Thus, workers in the highly labor-intensive apparel sector are concentrated almost entirely in the small firms, with 92.4

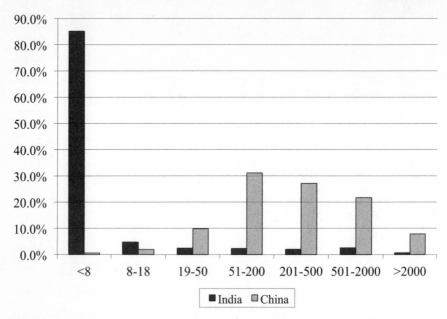

Figure 8.2. Employment share by firm size in apparel in China and India, 2005
Source: Hasan and Jandoc (2010)

percent of workers in firms with fifty or fewer workers. This distribution contrasts sharply with that in China where medium-and large-scale firms account for a gigantic 87.7 percent of the apparel employment (see Figure 8.2). The firm-size distribution in apparel in India also contrasts sharply with the more capital-intensive auto and auto-parts sector within the country, in which large-scale firms employed 50.3 percent of all workers in the sector in 2005 (see Figure 8.3).

The near-absence of medium and large firms in apparel, especially when compared with China, is clearly linked to this sector's poor export performance. The inability to massively capture the export markets in this major sector with comparative advantage is in turn linked to the poor performance of labor-intensive manufacturing and therefore manufacturing in general. The ultimate key to understanding why growth has not been as inclusive in India as in South Korea, Taiwan, and China remains the absence of large-scale firms in the labor-intensive sectors in India.

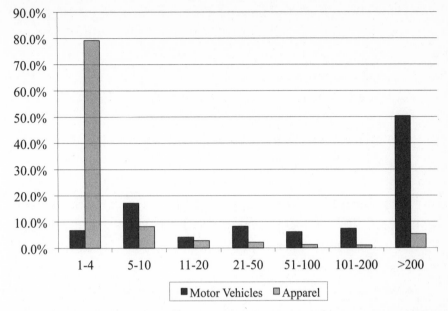

Figure 8.3. Employment shares by firm size in apparel versus motor vehicles and motor parts, 2005

Source: Hasan and Jandoc (2012)

The Neglect of Labor and Land Market Reforms

Why have the reforms so far not done more to produce medium- and large-scale firms in the labor-intensive sectors and hence to create many more well-paid jobs in the economy while boosting exports? The most plausible explanation is that the reforms have been confined principally to product markets (with a limited attention paid to capital-market liberalization). Multiple layers of regulation in the remaining two major factor markets, labor and land, continue to discourage the growth of manufacturing in general and of unskilled-labor-intensive products in particular.

The past reforms have removed four important layers of regulation in the product and capital markets:

- Investment licensing, which prevented large firms from investing outside of the highly capital-intensive "core" industries, has been eliminated

- Protection, which had prevented firms from exploiting large world markets, has been substantially removed from industry and services, though agriculture remains heavily protected
- The door to foreign firms with state-of-the-art know-how and with knowledge of and links to the world market has been opened
- Above all, the reservation of virtually all labor-intensive products for exclusive manufacture by small enterprises has been effectively ended[6]

Many analysts expected that these reforms, especially the last one, would pave the way for the emergence of the large-scale firms in the labor-intensive sectors and lead to a boom in labor-intensive exports. But this did not happen. Why?

Initially the lack of response in apparel, the labor-intensive sector with the largest world market, could have been attributed to the manner in which India had implemented the multifiber export quota. The Indian policy was to give the unused export quota not to existing users but to new applicants. This meant that the existing successful firms could not expand to take advantage of the end to small-scale industries reservation. But with the multifiber-arrangement quotas having ended in 2005 as part of the successful closure of the Uruguay Round on multilateral trade negotiations, this explanation no longer holds.

The true explanation lies instead in the fact that additional layers of regulations and barriers remain that discourage the emergence of large-scale labor-intensive manufacturing in India. The dominant cause is a highly inflexible labor market, which makes the cost of labor in the formal sector excessively high.

In addition, three complementary factors impede the emergence of large-scale labor-intensive manufacturing: the absence of modern bankruptcy laws permitting smooth exit in case of failure; a highly distorted land market; and poor infrastructure. Remarkably, despite the lapse of two decades since economic reforms began in earnest, there has been no attempt whatsoever to undertake the reforms of antiquated labor laws that affect all these issues, with new legislation being generally confined to giving yet more social protections to workers.

A Multitude of Labor Laws

Labor markets in India offer a stark contrast to those in Taiwan, South Korea, and China during their rapid-growth phases. In addition to openness and high savings rates, highly flexible labor markets characterized these latter countries. Unions were absent or weak and for all practical purposes strikes were illegal. Firms also had full rights to hire and fire workers. In contrast, regular workers in the organized sector in India have had legal protections exceeding those in most developed countries and unheard of in the developing world in the early stages of development.

The burden labor laws impose on entrepreneurs cannot be fully appreciated without a detailed discussion of some of the laws, a task we undertake in this section. Under the Indian Constitution, labor is a "concurrent" subject, meaning that both the center and the states can enact laws in this area. Neither has exactly been shy about exercising that right.

Thus the Ministry of Labor lists as many as fifty-two independent central government acts in the area of labor.[7] According to Amit Mitra, former secretary general of the Federation of Indian Chamber of Commerce and industry and now finance minister in the new Mamata Banerjee government in West Bengal,[8] an additional 150 state-level laws exist in India.[9] This count places the total number of labor laws in India at approximately two hundred. Compounding the confusion created by this multitude of laws is the fact that they are not entirely consistent with one another, leading a wit to remark that you cannot implement Indian labor laws 100 percent without violating 20 percent of them.[10]

The 1926 Trade Unions Act requires firms with seven or more workers to allow them to form a trade union.[11] This perhaps gives firms with six or fewer workers the most labor-market flexibility. For instance, the act empowers trade unions to strike and represent their members in labor courts in disputes with the employers. Because union officials can be outsiders, prospects for such disputes rise with the formation of unions. Firms can thus minimize labor-related problems as long as they are smaller than seven workers. The dominance of tiny firms in the apparel sector we saw earlier may well have something to do with this fact.

Factories engaged in manufacturing and employing ten or more workers, regardless of whether these factories use power, are subject to the 1948 Employees' State Insurance Act. State governments may also extend the provisions of the act to other industrial, commercial, or agricultural establishments. For employees, hired at a wage up to 10,000 rupees a month, the act provides benefits related to sickness, maternity, disability, dependents, old-age medical care, funeral, employment injury, and rehabilitation.

On the other hand, manufacturing units, with ten workers using power and with twenty workers even if not using power, are subject to yet another piece of legislation: the 1948 Factories Act. This act limits the maximum hours of work per week to forty-eight; limits work without a day of rest to ten days; requires a paid holiday for each twenty days of work; prohibits the employment of children younger than fifteen; and bans the employment of women for more than nine hours per day and between 7 p.m. and 6 a.m.

The requirements extend to additional demands: the factory premises are to be kept clean, including whitewashing every fourteen months and repainting every five years; proper disposal of waste is mandated; adequate and separate restrooms for men and women are required; and an uninterrupted supply of drinking water must be made available. The act also makes extensive provisions for worker safety, including fencing of machines and moving parts of machines; the use of goggles to protect against excessive light and infrared and ultraviolet radiation; precautions against fire; and limits on the weight permitted to be carried by women and young persons.

Moreover, the mandated requirements rise as the number of employees rises. For example, at 150 workers, lunchrooms must be provided; at 250 workers, a canteen must be available on factory premises. And if the firm employs 30 women, a day-care center must be made available.

Aside from the fact that many of these regulations are costly to implement and increase the cost of hiring more labor, the Factories Act also generates considerable paperwork. For instance, each factory must maintain registers of attendance, of adult workers hired, of the dates of lime washing and painting, of leave granted with wages, provision of health care (in case of persons employed in occupations declared hazardous), and the incidence of accidents. It must also file information to appropriate authorities on half-yearly and annual returns.

Again, all establishments with twenty or more workers, whether in industry or services, are further subject to the 1952 Employees' Provident Fund and Miscellaneous Provisions Act. This act provides three types of benefits: a contributory provident fund, pension benefits to the employees and his family members, and insurance cover including cash support during times of sickness, maternity benefits, payments in case of disability arising from work-related accidents, and medical expenses.[12]

But we have hardly scratched the surface of the labor laws that suffocate Indian entrepreneurs. Indeed, several other legislations impose a variety of requirements, some applying to all establishments and others to those with some threshold number of workers. Often the central legislation gives states the authority to extend the provision of the legislation to establishments not covered by it, which states use unhesitatingly. Among key central legislations are the 1961 Maternity Benefit Act, applicable to all factories, establishments, and shops depending on the state government; the 1948 Minimum Wages Act, which requires state governments to fix the minimum wage in specified employments; the 1965 Payment of Bonus Act, applicable to all firms registered under the 1948 Factories Act and establishments with twenty or more workers; the 1972 Payment of Gratuity Act, applicable to all factories and establishments with ten or more workers; the 1923 Workmen's Compensation Act, which applies to all workers; and the 1946 Industrial Employment (Standing Order) Act, which applies to all industrial establishments with one hundred (in some states fifty) or more workers.

Even if each of these and other central and state legislations are poorly enforced, they imply considerable burden on the smaller firms in terms of paperwork and filing requirements. Indeed, many firms are not even aware of their precise obligations under the large number of central and state legislations. Unwitting noncompliance in one or more areas is inevitable, especially for all but the exceptionally large firms, opening the door to corruption by labor department inspectors.

No discussion of labor laws would be complete, however, without including the 1947 Industrial Disputes Act (IDA). This important legislation covers all industrial disputes regardless of firm size. The disputes typically involve an employer and one or more of his workmen. But the act covers all other disputes as well, such as those arising between two or more workmen or between two or more employers. The act lays down procedures and defines the institutional infrastructure for resolving disputes. It also states the conditions under which employers can alter the tasks assigned to workers, conditions under which they can be laid off or retrenched, and the rules regulating strikes. Several key provisions stack the deck disproportionately against employers and must affect their willingness to hire regular as opposed to contract workers.

First, the IDA confers the power to regulate labor–employer relations on the labor department with jurisdiction over the firm, which is usually in the state where the firm is located. The legislation defines an industrial dispute as *any* dismissal, discharge, termination, or retrenchment of a worker in a firm of any size. The first step in settling a dispute is reconciliation, failing which it is referred to labor courts and tribunals that overwhelmingly rule in favor of workers on the theory that firms have deep pockets and workers do not. An attempt to reform the IDA for its anti-employer bias through alternative legislation in 1950 failed, and no subsequent attempt has been made.

Second, Section 9A of the IDA requires that the employer give three weeks' notice to workers of any change in their working conditions in all industrial establishments with fifty or more workers. These changes may relate to shift work; grade classification; rules of discipline; technological changes impacting the demand for labor; and employment, occupation, process, or department. The workers have a right to object to these changes, which may culminate in an industrial dispute.

Third, and most important, Chapter VB of the IDA effectively makes it impossible for an industrial establishment with one hundred or more workers to lay off or retrench workers even if it is unprofitable and is therefore forced to close the unit. This chapter was first introduced in 1976 and initially applied to industrial establishments with three hundred or more workers. Later a 1982 amendment, which became effective in 1984, reduced the threshold from three hundred to one hundred workers. Establishments subject to the regulation must seek permission from the labor department with jurisdiction over the firm for any layoffs and retrenchment. Concerned labor departments rarely give such permission even when the unit is unprofitable and must be shut down. The owner is effectively required to pay the workers from profits in other operations in case of closure. Few countries have a parallel to this provision in their labor legislations.

The final labor legislation of importance is the 1970 Contract Labor (Regulation and Abolition) Act. Contract workers are indirect employees of an establishment: they are hired, supervised, and paid by a contractor who has in turn contracted with the establishment to deliver certain services in return for a specified compensation. The establishment has no direct responsibility to contract workers; indeed, he need not even know who these workers are. Typically the contractor hires the contract workers for specified tasks and duration. While economic factors justify use of contract workers under many conditions, factories and establishments also prefer contract workers to avoid the burden imposed on them by the onerous labor laws.

The 1970 Contract Labor (Regulation and Abolition) Act attempts to limit this erosion of legislative requirements. It aims to regulate the employment of contract labor in certain establishments and to provide for its abolition under certain circumstances. It applies to establishments employing twenty or more workers and to contractors employing the same number of workers. Several of the provisions in the act are aimed at protecting the interests of the contract worker. But a key provision gives the government with jurisdiction over an establishment the power to prohibit it from using contract labor for work of perennial nature or work that is central to the manufacturing process. The government is also empowered to deny the use of contract labor for a task if other similar establishments use regular workers for that same task. Many states have used this provision to ban the use of contract labor in entire sectors.

Why Skeptics of the Adverse Impact of Labor Laws Are Wrong

The burdensome labor laws explain why entrepreneurs in sectors such as apparel, in which labor costs account for more than 80 percent of the total costs, choose to stay tiny. The costs due to labor legislations progressively rise in discrete steps at seven, ten, twenty, fifty, and one hundred workers. It is not altogether implausible that as the firm size rises from six regular workers toward one hundred, at no point between these two thresholds is the savings in manufacturing costs sufficiently large to pay for the extra costs of satisfying the laws. It may well be that only at a very large scale the cost savings can pay for the costs of labor laws. Under such circumstances, we will end up with either tiny or very large firms, with the middle missing, as has been the case in India to date. But when it comes to the labor-intensive sectors, extremely few firms seem to find it attractive to operate at any scale other than the tiny.

Ajay Shah of the National Institute of Public Finance and Policy tells an interesting story highlighting the dilemma of Indian entrepreneurs considering entry into labor-intensive sectors.[13] Some years ago, he asked a leading Indian industrialist, "You're a smart guy; you saw the [multi-fiber arrangement, or MFA] quota regime going away. Why did you not make a big play for it, given that you were already in yarn and cloth?" The industrialist replied that with low profit margins in apparel, this would be worth his while only if he operated on the scale of 100,000 workers. But this would not be practical in view of India's restrictive labor laws, added the industrialist.

Nonetheless, some analysts remain skeptical of the argument that labor-market rigidities are at the heart of the absence of the midsize and large firms in the labor-intensive sectors. These analysts offer several alternative arguments in support of their position.

They blame a lack of adequate literacy among potential workers. According to them, even the so-called unskilled tasks, such as cutting, sewing, stitching, and packaging garments, require a level of literacy that is lacking in India. This claim is false. For one thing, tailors currently employed in smaller establishments, of which India has plenty, fulfill multiple tasks. They are surely capable of repeatedly performing one or more of these same tasks in a factory setting. Equally, the India-wide gross enrollment ratios in education decisively contradict the claims of insufficient literacy.

Another counterargument relies on the observation that female workers have predominantly populated the large-scale factories in labor-intensive sectors in countries such as China. According to this argument, social attitudes and the legal framework in India do not support the employment of women in large factories.[14] Thus, for instance, families are reluctant to send womenfolk to work in factories, and laws such as the 1948 Factories Act prohibit the employment of women in night shifts that last from 7 p.m. to 6 a.m. Once again, the basic premises behind this argument are faulty. There is no reason why men could not be employed in apparel, footwear, and toy factories. As for the employment of women, while it is desirable to amend the Factories Act to permit them to work night shifts, even under the current law, they could be employed during the day shift with men assigned to night shifts.[15]

Some argue that labor-intensive products, most notably apparel, require just-in-time delivery to export destinations such as the United States and Europe. There is seasonality in demand for clothing and accessories, and the bulk buyers such as Walmart require delivery according to very tight schedules. Such delivery in turn requires first-rate infrastructure. Any delays due to unreliable links between the factory and the port, for example, can result in a loss of the order. Indian infrastructure is simply too unreliable to fulfill such prompt delivery. But while there is some truth in this argument, infrastructure is not a binding constraint everywhere in India. Gujarat has put in place excellent infrastructure including ports that load and unload goods proficiently and expeditiously. While poor infrastructure in some states may contribute, it alone cannot explain the absence of large-scale labor-intensive manufacturing in every state.

Others argue that growing beyond the small size requires access to credit, which most firms aspiring to grow large lack. But this argument is also falsified by the fact that both medium and large firms account for a much larger employment in the capital-intensive sectors, such as motor vehicles and auto parts, than in the labor-intensive sectors, such as apparel (see Figure 8.3). Unless something else, such as the labor laws, has made apparel a riskier business than motor vehicles and vehicle parts, there is no obvious reason why the banks would discriminate in favor of the latter in a labor-abundant country.

It is also argued that when interviewed for business environment surveys, firms rarely point to labor-market rigidities as the key problem. But this phenomenon is wholly misleading; it is the result of what economists call a "selection" problem in the sample of firms surveyed. Midsize and large firms in the labor-intensive sectors, which are likely to complain about the onerous labor laws, simply do not exist and are therefore not represented in the sample. Large firms in the sample surveys also typically come from either the service sectors or the capital-intensive manufacturing sectors. Services firms are not subject to some of the most constraining labor laws, such as Chapter VB of the 1947 Industrial Disputes Act, and therefore are unlikely to point the finger at them. Indeed, many of their employees probably do not even qualify as "workmen" under the 1947 Industrial Disputes Act. As for the large firms in the capital-intensive sectors, their labor costs are less than 10 percent of the total costs and they have high profits per worker, making it worthwhile to bear the costs of labor-market rigidities. They can handle even the problems of layoffs through voluntary retirement in return for golden parachutes. Large firms in the labor-intensive sectors in which labor costs are 80 percent of the total costs and profits per worker are low do not have this option.

Some suggest that while labor laws may be onerous on paper, they are not enforced or that firms can get around them. However, the fact that large firms have chosen not to enter labor-intensive sectors in India while they routinely do so in other comparable countries suggests they are not able to get around these laws in a cost-effective manner. Being able to get around does not mean getting around at low cost. After all, the firms had also learned to get around the import and investment licensing and high trade barriers before reforms began in earnest in 1991. But we now recognize that they did so at a huge cost, that only a few of them were able to do it, and that the country paid a huge cost for the regulations in terms of low growth for four decades.

An example of how rigid laws, combined with an overburdened judiciary, can be highly costly even to large firms in the capital-intensive sectors is provided by the Uttam Nakate case. The following succinct summary of the case from Sanjeev Sanyal (2006) is instructive:

> In August 1983, Nakate was found at 11:40 am sleeping soundly on an iron plate in the factory in Pune where he worked. He had committed three previous misdemeanors but had been let off lightly. This time his employer Bharat Forge began disciplinary proceedings against him, and after five months of hearings, he was found guilty and sacked. But Nakate went to a labor court and pleaded that he was a victim of an unfair trade practice. The court agreed and forced the factory to take him back and pay him 50% of his lost wages. Both parties appealed against this judgment (Natake wanted more money). The case dragged on through the judicial system for another decade and in 1995 another court awarded Nakate more money because he was now too old to be rehired. Bharat Forge eventually had to approach the Supreme Court and in May 2005—more than two decades after the original incident—the apex court finally awarded the employer the right to fire a worker who had been repeatedly caught sleeping on the job. (p. 9)

Surely this "getting around" was a costly affair for Bharat Forge.

A final counterargument offered is that labor-market rigidities apply to only a tiny section of the labor force. In this view, the fact that more than 90 percent of the labor force is in the informal sector or employed informally in the formal sector implies that the bulk of the labor market is highly flexible despite the ill-designed labor laws. However, this is a rather disingenuous argument. After all, the entire debate is about the smallness of Indian firms and, in particular, the absence of medium and large firms in labor-intensive sectors. This argument begs the question of why such a small part of the labor force has found formal employment in India.

In their search for the causes of the near-absence of large-scale firms in the labor-intensive sectors, Hasan and Jandoc (2012) turn to state-level

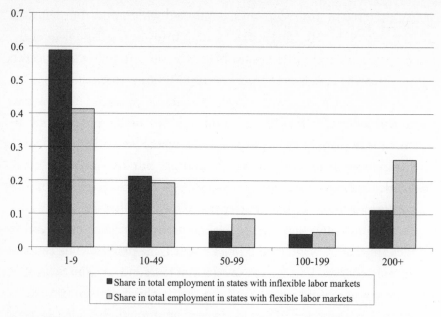

Figure 8.4. Firm-size distribution in labor-intensive manufacturing in states with flexible versus inflexible labor laws
Source: Hasan and Jandoc (2012)

differences in policies and outcomes. They first compare the firm-size distributions of all manufacturing between states with flexible labor regulations and those with inflexible ones and find almost no cross-state differences. However, when they restrict the sample to labor-intensive manufacturing, large-scale firms exhibit proportionately significantly larger shares of employees and small-scale firms a significantly smaller share in states with flexible labor regulations (Figure 8.4). Given that labor laws remain highly restrictive even in the states classified as relatively more flexible, and thus hinder the emergence of medium-and large-scale firms in greater proportion, the existence of these state-level differences is particularly significant.

To be sure that other factors are not behind the state-level differences, Hasan and Jandoc also compare states with good infrastructure to those without. But this comparison yields no real differences in the employment shares of large and small firms across states.

Labor Laws: What Must Be Done?

Almost all labor laws in India are more than four decades old, with the 1970 Contract Labor (Regulation and Abolition) Act being the last major labor legislation passed by an Indian parliament. At the time, these laws perhaps had some rationale in terms of redistribution in favor of the worker. Investment and import licensing gave guaranteed profits to the domestic firms that were lucky enough to get the licenses. Therefore, forcing them to share those profits with the workers through ultrahigh protection to the latter was defensible.

But with the investment and import licensing abolished and trade opened up, domestic firms are subject to intense competition. The same ultrahigh protection to workers in certain dimensions under these circumstances has only prevented the economy from specializing in the goods in which India enjoys comparative advantage. If India is to move its economy toward specialization in labor-intensive products, which is essential to creating far more formal-sector jobs, and therefore for making growth more inclusive, reform of the labor laws is urgent.

Ideally, India needs to reform the labor laws wholesale. But labor legislation is among the toughest to manage politically. So reform may well have to focus first on the most damaging laws on the books. The law in the most urgent need of reform is the 1947 Industrial Disputes Act. This legislation is stacked too heavily against the employers to leave sufficient incentive for a massive expansion of employment-intensive sectors. With the wages in China reaching levels at which it is likely to be forced out of these sectors, India is well positioned to become the world's manufacturing hub. But if the costs of employment remain as they are, that opportunity is likely to be seized by a large number of smaller countries, such as Vietnam and Bangladesh. These countries allow firms to hire and fire workers under reasonable conditions and maintain a balance between the rights of both workers and employers. As a result, large firms in sectors such as apparel can be found aplenty in both countries and both have also seen significantly faster growth of the sector and done extremely well on the export front.

Several changes in the IDA would be enormously helpful. First, the definition of retrenchment for purposes of industrial disputes (in firms of all sizes) needs to be tightened. The IDA defines retrenchment as "the termination by the employer of the service of a workman for any reason whatsoever" other than a punishment inflicted by way of disciplinary action; voluntary retirement; retirement upon reaching the age stipulated in the contract; and termination due to nonrenewal of a contract after it expires or failure of the worker to meet conditions stipulated in the contract. Under this definition, even a discharge of employees due to declining sales or unanticipated change in technology would be interpreted as retrenchment. Debroy (2001) laments that under this definition, Indian courts have even gone on to interpret as retrenchment the discharge of an employee on probation and nonconfirmation of an employee failing a test required for confirmation. The provision has naturally resulted in the multiplication of industrial disputes as well as a disincentive to hire workers. A tighter definition of retrenchment for purposes of industrial disputes would clearly bring down the number of such disputes and encourage more hiring of workers.[16]

Second, the IDA allows every single industrial dispute to go to the labor courts and tribunals. This practice should be replaced by one under which an independent authority is empowered to deliver a time-bound and final verdict in a designated class of cases. At least in cases in which the basis of retrenchment is not in dispute (for example, in the Nakate case), the independent authority can be authorized to give a final verdict within the rules under which retrenchment is permitted.

Third, Section 9A of the IDA, which imposes a heavy burden on an employer wishing to reassign a worker to an alternative task, needs to be replaced by one that gives the employer greater flexibility. Minimally, the employer should be permitted to reassign the worker to a set of prespecified tasks on short notice and without challenge. For example, if a change in technology renders the task of an existing employee redundant, the employer should have a clear right to assign him or her to an alternative task for which he or she is qualified. More broadly, the employer should have the right to reassign workers within a broad set of prespecified tasks.

Fourth, while the IDA prohibits strikes by public utility services without notice, no such restrictions apply to strikes in other industrial establishments except during conciliation or arbitration proceedings. Nor does the law require a secret ballot by trade union members to call a strike. This state of affairs encourages wildcat strikes that can be very harmful to the health of the establishment. Change in the IDA in this regard is necessary.

Fifth, Chapter VB of the 1947 IDA, which makes it nearly impossible to lay off workers in a factory with one hundred or more workers under any circumstances, needs to be repealed. Interestingly, this chapter was added only in 1976; the IDA had existed for twenty-nine years without it, and India needs to return to the pre-1976 IDA. With careful steering, this may be politically doable. For example, the government could begin the process by changing the law for a handful of labor-intensive sectors in which there are only a few large firms in the first place. For instance, if the apparel distributions shown in Figures 8.2 and 8.3 are still valid, repeal of chapter V-B in this sector will impact only a small number of employees who could be exempted. If even this is politically difficult, the initial change could be started with exemption for apparel factories with one hundred to five hundred workers, which account for a tiny proportion of the employment in the sector, making it even easier to exempt the existing employees.

Among other labor laws, the 1948 Factories Act should be revisited to see if it contains provisions that are too onerous for firms with ten or even twenty workers. Our own reading of the act is that small firms are unlikely to have the staff and expertise to understand and ensure fulfillment of the myriad regulations in the act. If this reading is correct, there is a need for an alternative set of fewer and more manageable regulations applicable to firms that employ fewer than fifty workers. Successful large firms often emerge from smaller firms and a case is to be made for giving greater leeway to the latter.

The 1926 Trade Unions Act also needs to be modified. It has led to a proliferation of trade unions in larger firms. Originally this law allowed any seven workers to form a trade union. A 2001 amendment introduced the qualification that those forming the trade unions should minimally include 10 percent of the workforce or one hundred workers. But even this amendment leaves room for a large number of trade unions in larger firms. As a result, we find that the Neyveli Lignite Corporation Limited has as many as fifty trade unions and associations.[17] This organizational feature makes the collective-bargaining process highly problematic since an agreement reached with one union does not automatically apply to another. There needs to be further reform of the act that would limit the number of trade unions to a manageable level.

Is there any way to provide minimal social protections to the myriad workers in the informal sector, often consisting of establishments of fewer than ten workers? Such protection seems impractical in view of their extremely large number. In our view, the solution must be indirect and lies in the labor-market reforms we have proposed, which should accelerate the growth in formal-sector employment, skill creation that will make workers employable in better-paid jobs, and strengthening the Track II redistributive programs (discussed in depth in Part III of this book) that enhanced growth from Track I reforms make possible through increased revenues.

Chapter 9

Land Acquisition

L ike labor, land represents yet another factor that has remained largely untouched by the post-1991 reforms. The antiquated and dysfunctional state of regulations concerning land acquisition creates serious economic inefficiencies.

The 1894 Land Acquisition Act, which lays out key regulations, is more than a century old. Though the act has been amended several times, with the last major amendment in 1984, its basic provisions remain intact and the process of land acquisition continues to be archaic.

At least two issues need to be addressed in the matter of land acquisition. First, if land is to be acquired from a private party, the government must define the "social purpose" for which it can be so acquired. Second, the price at which the owner is to be compensated must be calculated.

The definition of "social purpose" to acquire land is not an exclusively economic issue. In the United States, the Supreme Court recently allowed "taking" private property for social purpose to include building a mall on the grounds that, without the mall, the town would not be able to raise enough revenue to survive. The judgment had the support of liberal (i.e., progressive) judges, such as Justice Stephen Breyer. Yet, there was a hue and cry in several states, and legislation was advanced to overturn the judgment.

Ultimately the decision on what is legitimate social purpose for acquiring land has to be democratically determined. The Indian experience has been disruptive because the government has acquired privately owned land at below-market prices and handed it over to industrialists in Special Economic Zones and for housing projects by private builders and large-scale industrial projects by private businesses. Violence erupted in the case of the Tata Nano project in Singur in West Bengal, which eventually had to be moved to Gujarat, and in the case of the Orissa Steel project proposed by the Korean firm POSCO.

The original intention behind compulsory land acquisition was to prevent a few holdouts from delaying a "socially necessary" project, such as the building of a highway or a railroad. No such acquisition was to be undertaken on a massive scale at less than market-value prices, which amounts to a levy on the private owners whose land was being acquired. This original purpose needs to be restored. Any significant acquisition of land cannot be at less than market prices, especially since this also amounts to a regressive tax whose proceeds typically are shared between the government and the beneficiaries who usually are substantial private parties.

Instead, the current legislation enables a rip-off of private landowners by unscrupulous state governments and large industrialists who offer to bring their projects to these states. For example, as Panagariya (2008b) has recounted, the conflict in Singur, West Bengal, surrounding the Nano car project of Tata Motors had its origins in a secret tripartite agreement in March 2007 between the latter on the one hand and the West Bengal government and West Bengal Industrial Development Corporation on the other. While floating its plans for this small-car project, Tata Motors had pitted the states of Uttarakhand, Himachal Pradesh, and West Bengal against one another in a bidding war. In the end, West Bengal won by promising the company prime land at a throwaway price in Singur, a town just thirty miles northwest of Calcutta, and substantial other subsidies at the cost of the general taxpayer.

The corporation did not finance the extraordinarily cheap land with a subsidy. Instead it forcibly acquired the land for a pittance in the most opaque manner, asking farmers to transfer their land even before it told them the price! The mobilization of farmers by the opposition politician Mamata Banerjee against the heavy-handed tactics of the government and the meager compensation it offered for the land eventually forced Tata Motors out of Singur.[1]

Therefore, there is much to be said for leaving the purchase of land to be undertaken at market prices. Is there still a rationale, which underlies the origin of the forced acquisition legislation, for the government to intervene because some private owners might hold out to extract exorbitant prices? The representatives of business interests as well as landowners have argued that the government must remain involved to resolve this problem. But to our knowledge, this is an infrequent, even rare possibility in practice. In states such as Gujarat, Punjab, and Karnataka, land acquisition for numerous projects has been accomplished smoothly through direct negotiation between private parties. With land costs being a tiny proportion of the total costs, industrialists have been in a good position to make the deal attractive to the sellers.[2]

A slightly different version of this argument is that farmers simply do not want to sell their land. Therefore, no acquisition is possible unless the government is involved in the process. This is a specious argument, as numerous acquisitions in the states of Gujarat, Haryana, Punjab, Tamil Nadu, and Karnataka testify. More interestingly, Sukumaran and Bisoi (2011) report the interesting case in which the chief minister of Karnataka issued a statement on July 27, 2011, that no land acquisition was possible for the POSCO steel project in his state. Soon after, several farmers petitioned the chief minister to reconsider his decision. The petitioning farmers were aware that industrial developers in Karnataka, including the public-sector company NTPC, had paid lucrative prices for the land they acquired and did not want to be deprived of it. Within two days, on July 29, 2011, the chief minister reversed his decision.

Advocates of landowner rights argue that excluding government from land acquisition for private projects would result in the exploitation of landowners by industrialists. They argue that many small farmers do not know the value of their land or the laws governing their rights, leaving them vulnerable. While no one would deny that it is important to protect the rights of the small farmers in land transactions, if recent agitations surrounding the government's own forced acquisition at below-market prices is any guide, landowners do have a keen sense of the value of their land. When the acquisition is done at below-market prices, NGOs in India are quick to get into the act on behalf of the owners. Moreover, mandatory advertisements of the prevailing prices by the buyer of large tracts of land offer a better solution to the imperfect information problem. The problem can also be alleviated through public posting of guidance prices by the relevant revenue departments in the state.

Two arguments have been made against *any* acquisition or purchase of farmland for nonfarm purposes, whether public or private. First, some advocates of farmer interests argue that nothing can compensate the farmers for the loss of their livelihood if their farms are sold. But it surely is possible to invest the proceeds from the sale of land in an annuity that guarantees the farmer an income stream equivalent to what he or she would have generated on average by working the land.[3]

Second, some food-security advocates contend that deploying farmland into alternative uses would undermine India's food security. But the impression that nonagricultural users of land have been diverting much of the land in India from agriculture is false. Based on the latest available data, which relate to the year 2006–2007, nonagricultural uses of land, such as housing, establishments for industry and services, roads, railways, ports, and airports, together account for only 8.4 percent of India's land area. In contrast, the net area under cultivation accounts for 45.8 percent of the total area.[4] Even if we think in terms of expanding the land area under nonagricultural activities by 20 percent, it amounts to raising it by 1.7 percentage points to 10.1 percent of the total land area. In principle, a significant part of this area could come from barren land. But even if all of it were to come from agriculture, it would imply a reduction in area under agriculture from 45.8 percent to 44.1 percent of the total land area. Given that agriculture in India exhibits huge inefficiencies and is characterized by much lower productivity than in countries such as China, there is enormous scope for making up for the small reduction in area by raising productivity. Moreover, there is no reason India cannot count on satisfying a part of its demand for food through imports.

Chapter 10

Infrastructure

T he need for building twenty-first-century infrastructure—multi-
lane highways, all-weather rural roads, railway lines, airports,
ports, telecommunications, well-functioning cities, and electricity—is well recognized. In fact, the theme of infrastructure enhancement
characterizes even the United States today, where the difference among
politicians is over the magnitude of stimulus spending but not over
whether it ought to be on infrastructure, which is widely considered to
be in need of repair: "London Bridge Is Falling Down" is more like a
lament than a nursery rhyme.

India is not afflicted by the "curse" that often arises when infrastructure is built ahead of the growth that would require it. The existence of
roads, for example, does not guarantee that commerce will develop along
them. It is often forgotten, especially in some African countries where aid
agencies and recipient governments wish to spend money on building
roads and ports, that simply building infrastructure will not automatically
generate economic growth that would then give rise to the necessary demand for infrastructure. In such cases, we are putting the cart before the
horse. Fortunately, growth has occurred in India, and the demand for infrastructure is running well ahead of its current supply.[1]

Given this consensus on the need for improved and increased provision of infrastructure along various dimensions, the issues before the
Track I reformers therefore mostly have to do with "how to manage and
deliver." With the possible exception of telecommunications, as in the
developed countries, infrastructure in different sectors and areas will

require the public sector to take the lead even as it seeks the participation of the private sector through public-private partnerships. The main possible difference is that the governments in some developed countries are perhaps more capable than has been the case in India in recent years, necessitating greater participation of the private sector.

The issues are manifold but here we focus only on those that bear on the task of intensifying Track I reforms.[2]

Air Transport

Regarding air transport, progress has been notable in the construction of modern airports in New Delhi, Mumbai, Hyderabad, Ahmedabad, Bangalore, and even some smaller towns, such as Jaipur. At the same time, satisfactory progress has been made in building associated air-transport infrastructure.

The key pending reform in this area concerns Air India, which absorbed more than $10 billion in subsidies in 2010–2011 alone.[3] The government must give serious consideration to privatizing the airline. Jet Airways, which runs a superb international service, provides an excellent model.

Highway Construction

In the construction of highways, while there have been issues of financing, an equally important bottleneck has been the lack of coordination among various arms of the government. Under the National Democratic Alliance (NDA) government, which originally launched in December 2000 the ambitious National Highway Development Program to convert the Golden Quadrilateral highway into four lanes, the issuing of contracts to completion under Phase I of the program was substantially accomplished within just four years.

Despite this excellent beginning, the highway construction program languished under the United Progressive Alliance (UPA) government. The Planning Commission practically banned the National Highway Authority of India from issuing new contracts from early 2005 to at least the end of 2006 on the grounds that the contract the NDA had used was flawed and a new Model Concession Agreement was required.[4] Even after the Planning Commission came out with a new agreement in late 2006, the contracting process could not move forward smoothly.

The situation has subsequently improved only marginally. As late as July 2010, exasperated Road Transport Minister Kamal Nath, who had wanted to accelerate highway building to twenty kilometers per day, stated at a seminar on highways, "When I joined this ministry, everyone told me that the Planning Commission will never let you do it." He went on to describe the commission as "an armchair advisor," noting that the commission was unfamiliar with the ground reality. He elaborated: "Building a road in Kerala is different from building a road in Madhya Pradesh. We must have a concept that is flexible. Public-private partnership for Kerala has to be different from Madhya Pradesh."[5]

Such encounters clearly illustrate the detrimental effect of a lack of coordination among various arms of the government. There is nothing inherently difficult about building roads and bridges. The prime minister should take steps to coordinate the various arms of the government to ensure that the country works coherently to accelerate the road-building program.[6]

Power

Perhaps the infrastructure problem that needs most urgent and concerted attention is power. Power shortage is a critical handicap when India has an ambition to sustain 8–9 percent annual growth. Low-cost electricity is required to keep labor-intensive products competitive due to generally low profit margins in the latter. This would make growth more inclusive, as we demonstrated earlier.

But power is also necessary because in India we must bring electricity to those living in rural areas. The provision of electricity in rural areas is important not only for making day-to-day existence more comfortable but also for stimulating entrepreneurial activity locally.

Although the 2003 Electricity Act initiated a major reform in the power sector, unfortunately, the process appears to have come to a near

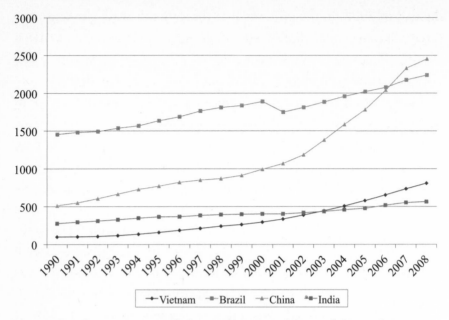

Figure 10.1. Per capita annual electricity consumption in kilowatt hours
Source: World Development Indicators of the World Bank online (accessed November 7, 2012)

standstill with even a reversal (with respect to cross-subsidy in electricity tariffs) under the UPA government. Per capita consumption of electricity is very low and rising extremely slowly. Figure 10.1, which makes some pertinent cross-country comparisons, illustrates this sharply.

The figure shows that both Brazil and China have much higher consumption of electricity in per capita terms than India. Besides, the gap between them and India has steadily widened since 1990. From approximately one-half of China's consumption per capita in 1990, India dropped to less than a quarter of it in 2008. What is even more disappointing is that Vietnam, which consumed a little more than one-third of India's amount in 1990, had reached almost one and a half times India's level by 2008.

Urban Infrastructure

Finally, India also needs to make a concerted effort to build its urban infrastructure. Urbanization is an integral part of modernization, and this requires well-functioning cities. With the possible exception of New Delhi, few Indian cities function well today. Traffic jams, potholed roads, and the absence of a mass rapid-transit system characterize major Indian cities, such as Bangalore and Mumbai. Slow movement in and out of cities in turn contributes to the phenomenon of workers' having to find living space within the city, fueling in turn the growth of slums.

An important source of the problem in Indian cities has been their horizontal nature, a phenomenon reinforced by tight restrictions on the floor-space index, which specifies the maximum floor space that can be created on a plot of given size.[7] Relaxing the floor-space index and, thus, allowing taller buildings can release valuable space for widening the roads and building mass rapid transit aboveground. It can also help build a vibrant city center that minimizes the time lost in going from one office to the other. States that have not yet repealed the Urban Land Ceilings Act of 1976, most notably Maharashtra, need to do so. And above all, issues of uninterrupted water and electricity supply and public health need to be tackled.

Chapter 11

Higher Education

Higher education reforms are necessary in a fast-growing economy, which requires an increasing volume of skilled workers, a steady stream of innovation of new products and processes, and the progressive adaptation of technologies already available from past research in other countries. But these reforms also offer a double dividend because, by improving the educational access of millions of those who aspire to partake of the opportunities opened up by the growth-enhancing post-1991 reforms, they increase the inclusiveness of the growth.

It would be an understatement to say that the higher education system in India is in a crisis. Except for a handful of institutions, the poor quality of instruction in the classroom is a well-known handicap afflicting India whether we consider public or private institutions. True, universities and colleges have an adequate and broadly uniform curriculum and, recognizing the high returns to good college performance, better students manage to do well by mastering it. But the quality of instruction in the classroom is far from satisfactory; indeed it is often poor.

International rankings of universities reflect this situation as well. In the QS World University Rankings released in September 2011, no Indian university including the celebrated Indian Institutes of Technology found a place among even the top two hundred. In contrast, universities from several other Asian countries, such as China, Japan, Hong Kong, Singapore, and Taiwan, managed to be ranked among the top one hundred.

Perhaps even more important, the enrollment ratio in higher education in India is low and rising at a snail's pace. The gross enrollment ratio, which measures the proportion of those in college to college-age population, was 8 percent in China and 10 percent in India in 2000. By 2007, the ratio had shot up to 23 percent in China but crept up to only 13 percent in India. Apparently many students are unable to proceed to higher education, not just due to lack of finances but also due to a shortage of space in colleges and universities.

The comparison with China along both quality and quantity dimensions is especially disturbing since Mao Zedong almost entirely decimated China's higher education system during the Cultural Revolution of 1966–1968. In contrast, India has had an uninterrupted history of modern universities for more than 150 years. The universities of Calcutta, Bombay, and Madras were founded as early as 1857. While the university system in India was considerably strengthened in the early postindependence era, it has languished during the past three decades, precisely the period during which the Chinese have rebuilt theirs.

The problems with India's higher education are many. However, a central problem is an antiquated administrative structure that imparts virtual monopoly to the University Grants Commission (UGC), a statutory body since 1956 at the apex of the system. The UGC determines curricula at various levels, degrees to be awarded, and fees and (indirectly) faculty salaries. Most important of all, it acts as the gatekeeper for the emergence of all universities. Without its approval, no new universities can be started.

There are only two ways that new universities can be started in India: either the UGC deems an existing academic institution, such as a college or research institute, to be a university or the central or a state government passes legislation to establish a new university provided the UGC approves it.

Private colleges are allowed to exist but they must affiliate themselves with a public university to award degrees. Entry of private universities is very difficult and, when they do manage to enter, they must remain unitary: they cannot affiliate colleges to award degrees. Nor are they allowed to open satellite campuses in other states without UGC approval, which involves complex procedures.

This tight control has been maintained in the name of ensuring high standards of education, notwithstanding the fact that the quality of education in public universities leaves much to be desired and is continuously declining.

In contrast, in areas of management and chartered accountancy, which fall outside the purview of the UGC because they award diplomas and certificates and degrees, private institutions have thrived and served the students and the country well. Even in undergraduate engineering institutions, where private entry has been relatively liberal, private institutions have broadly managed to maintain the flow of engineers of adequate quality in sufficiently large numbers to keep India's growth going. It is anybody's guess as to what would have happened to Indian growth had the private engineering colleges and management institutes not expanded at the rapid pace they did to supply the market with qualified engineers and managers.

The same expansion has failed to take place in medical education except in a handful of states, such as Karnataka and Maharashtra, due to the tight control by the Indian Medical Council (IMC), a powerful institution that threatens almost at the drop of a hat to shut down colleges that have existed for decades. The monopolistic working of the IMC, which has an interest in reducing the supply of new doctors, is predictable: the same phenomenon has characterized the American Medical Association, which has long been understood as practicing entry-prevention tactics in several ways. These medical associations can get away with murder, no pun intended, because they can always pretend that if they are not allowed to restrict entry of new doctors through tight regulations, patients will suffer serious consequences. But a developing country like India can ill afford to indulge the IMC.

These issues are particularly salient at the moment in India because, with a demographic transition under way, massive numbers of young Indians are expected to pass through college-going age in the next two decades. The United Nations Population Division estimates that between

2010 and 2025 alone, the population in the twenty- to forty-nine-year-old age group will rise by 131 million in India. The government is short of financial resources to expand universities and colleges at the pace necessary to accommodate this burgeoning young population. Therefore, while it should do as much as it can to expand public-sector higher education, the government needs to drop the pretense that it can serve the country's young men and women well without massive participation of the private sector.

The only educational policy choice before the government, therefore, is for it to end the de facto license-permit raj in this sector and let both for-profit and nonprofit institutions of domestic as well as foreign origin enter the market with ease. The UGC may lay down a set of criteria that private institutions must satisfy, but beyond this, its current gatekeeper role must end.

Again, under the current system, another important problem arises because a committee headed by a retired High Court judge determines the tuition fees even in the private institutions that are allowed to operate. The committee presumably arrives at the fee through cost estimates that include the assumption that the teachers will be given salaries prevailing in similar institutions. Such a fee naturally limits the institution's financial capacity to pay teacher salaries that would be required to attract the best teachers. In effect, the cap on the fees set by the committee also caps the salary the institution can pay its teachers, thereby limiting its ability to get the best teachers. Given the current scarcity of good teachers, it is important that private colleges and universities have the flexibility to attract talented young Indians getting education abroad. But this is not feasible without flexibility in the salaries they can pay. Lifting its control over tuition fees in both public and private universities therefore seems to be a policy change that the UGC must consider.

The common argument that high fees would increase the gap between haves and have-nots is a non sequitur. Good education yields high private returns to the recipient and, unlike primary education, has no obvious externalities. Therefore, there is a good efficiency-based economic case for market-based tuition fees. The equity issue should be separately dealt with through the provision of loans for those qualified for admission to any given institution.

In this regard, excellent analysis and policy proposals, worthy of India's attention, can be found in the recent report by the independent panel on higher education appointed by Great Britain under the chairmanship of Lord Browne.[1] Although Britain abolished its University Grants Committee (after which India's UGC was partially patterned) in 1989, its universities have continued to decline in relation to US universities. Aware of this fact, the country has been actively reforming its higher education system in the past fifteen years. The Browne panel was the latest step in this direction. Its charge was to come up with recommendations to increase investment in education, ensure that the quality of teaching is world-class, and make higher education accessible to anyone with the talent for it.

The Browne report recommended that Britain eliminate the existing tuition fee cap of £3,000 altogether with two key provisions to ensure access. First, students should have to pay no upfront fees, with the government paying to the university up to £6,000 per student. Institutions charging more than £6,000 should be required to pay a progressively rising tax on the margin. The tax should then be used to finance grants to students from low-income backgrounds to meet the living expenses. Second, after graduation, students should be required to begin paying back the costs paid by the government once their income reaches a threshold, recommended at £21,000.

The Browne report argues, correctly in our view, that this package will force greater competition among universities since they can expect higher fees for better education. At the same time, with no fees to pay upfront, it will also give students greater choice and access. The proposed system would give them freedom to join the institution at which they expect the highest net returns. It would also stimulate much-needed investment in higher education.

Consider next the role of foreign universities in raising the quality and supply of higher education in India. The recent effort by Human Resource Development Minister Kapil Sibal to grant entry to foreign universities is to be applauded even as it has led to controversy.[2] A pop-ular objection to the proposal to let foreign universities into India is that, with their deeper pockets, foreign universities will drain distinguished Indian institutions, such as the Indian Institutes of Technology and In-dian Institutes of Management, of their best faculty. This, however, is not a persuasive objection.

First, the best researchers want other best researchers around them. Therefore, moving the faculty from established institutions of excellence is not going to be a cakewalk for foreign universities. This is illustrated by the experience of the Indian School of Business (ISB), an institution that comes the closest to being a world-class foreign educational insti-tution in India. Only four out of approximately thirty of its resident faculty members came from the well-established Indian Institutes of Management.

Second, the key source of faculty for foreign universities will surely be Indian scholars abroad. Of the thirty resident faculty members at the ISB, approximately twenty are recent foreign graduates. An impressive 71,000 Indian graduate students were enrolled during the 2009–2010 academic year in the United States alone and potentially could be tapped to fill faculty positions in India. Likewise, modest incentives can bring many existing senior faculty members at universities abroad to teach on Indian campuses on a part-time basis. The ISB and Indian Institutes of Technology list several world-class Indian scholars abroad among their nonresident faculty.

Third, even if some faculty members leave Indian institutions of ex-cellence to join a foreign university located in India, does it constitute a net loss? After all, they will still be serving Indian students. And the com-petition that such movement will generate might, on balance, benefit rather than harm the country as a whole. Also, the notion that the loss of some will undermine the productivity of the rest reflects the earlier "brain drain" model: today faculty mostly work with faculty of similar specialization in other institutions by e-mail, telephone, and occasional visits and conferences where personal interaction is important. As the economist Frances Cairncross wrote some time ago, we are witnessing the "death of distance"; or, since working in the same area has been called "geography" by the economist Paul Krugman, we might say that geography is history now.

It is anyway highly unlikely that the proposed Foreign Universities Bill will lead to a flood of foreign universities in India. With the large number of safeguards contained in the bill, many are likely to find entry unattractive. For instance, one of the provisions would limit foreign universities to the same fee regulations as domestic unaided private universities. This would automatically limit their ability to pay high faculty salaries, for instance. In all likelihood, the present bill, even if passed without changes, will not bring very many foreign universities to Indian shores and will eventually require amendment.

Chapter 12

Other Track I Reforms

O ur discussion has been confined to several of the most important areas where measures still must be undertaken to broaden
and deepen the Track I reforms that were systematically begun
in 1991. But there are other areas where further reforms would have a
payoff. Among them are reforms in international trade, foreign investment, and agriculture.[1]

Trade liberalization in India, while on course in a slow but sure
process, has come to a standstill since the UPA government came to
power. Although India is now largely quite open to trade in industrial
goods and services, further scope for liberalization in these areas remains.
The top industrial tariff rate, not counting a number of peak tariffs, remains at 10 percent. Because of several rather high peak tariffs, however,
the simple average of industrial tariffs is approximately 12 percent. This
is still high by today's standards; there clearly remains room to bring
these tariffs down further.

Turning to services, India has been wise to finally open multi-brand
retail to foreign direct investment. Given that domestic companies have
been active in this sector for more than five years, we have seen that the
feared injury to small mom-and-pop shops is minuscule: the small and
large happily coexist because they address different needs. At the same
time, the upside potential in terms of developing supply chains and the
expansion of exports through foreign retailers such as Walmart and
Pepsico is high.[2]

Agriculture in India also remains highly protected. Fears that opening to trade might hurt Indian farmers are grossly exaggerated, as was the case prior to 1991 with respect to manufactures. Just as liberalization in manufactures strengthened rather than weakening them, India should benefit from progressive liberalization in agriculture.

But India also needs to move ahead with reforms in agriculture more generally. Several key reforms are necessary both to bring prosperity sooner to the many who continue to be employed in agriculture and to speed up the outward movement of the workforce into industry and services.

First, it is essential to introduce much greater competition in the market for agricultural produce. Somewhat surprisingly, while market reforms have gone a long way in manufacturing and services, progress in agriculture has been limited. Under the original Agricultural Produce Marketing Committees (APMC) Act, the government has had a monopoly over farmers' produce, which it buys from them and sells to wholesalers and retailers. This has proved to be highly inefficient and detrimental to farmers' interests. Reform of the APMC Act has been under way since 2003 but progress has been slow and uneven across states. In particular, some major states such as Uttar Pradesh and West Bengal have yet to introduce it and others such as Punjab, Haryana, and Delhi have introduced only partial reforms. A full-fledged reform would allow farmers to sell their produce directly to whomever they please, including consumers; allow private firms to purchase produce from farmers; and permit farmers to contract to sell their produce directly to contract farming sponsors. If India is to take full advantage of the entry of multiproduct foreign retailers and facilitate the growth of modern agricultural produce supply chains, APMC reform is essential.

Second, India must finally remove all restrictions on interstate movement of grain that prevent the country from functioning as a single market. This will require the repeal of the Essential Commodities Act of 1955, which gives states wide powers to impose restrictions on storage, transport, price, distribution, and processing of agricultural produce.

Third, the Food Corporation of India (FCI), which oversees the country's public distribution system, has turned into a white elephant with 400,000 employees and a highly inefficient storage and distribution network. Rotting and washing off in rain of vast quantities of food grain and leakages through the distribution system are endemic. While we will consider the policy in this area in greater detail in Part III, we may note here that the FCI needs to be greatly downsized, with a large number of its activities transferred to the private sector through various policy initiatives.

Finally, various measures aimed at increasing agricultural productivity are required, including giving land titles to farmers and simplifying the laws relating to renting and selling land. Public investment in extension services to support investment in new seeds and methods of cultivation is required. Without such support, it will be impossible to obtain the productivity gains that genetically modified and BT seeds promise.

Part III

More Effective and Inclusive Redistribution: Track II

Chapter 13

Track II Reforms

Much of the focus of economic reforms in the past decade has been on reducing the role of the government in controlling the Private Sector; controls that hampered entrepreneurial dynamism and often bred corruption. This was necessary. Yet there are many areas, critical areas, that directly affect the quality of life of every citizen, where the government has a role. These include provision of social and physical infrastructure for development, the provision of elementary education and public health, providing drinking water and sanitation.
—**Prime Minister Manmohan Singh, address to the nation,**
New Delhi, June 24, 2004

In principle, growth through Track I reforms, appropriately improved and intensified in ways we just discussed in Part II, will reduce poverty. In turn, the reduction in poverty can also be confidently expected to result in improved clothing, shelter, and other expenditures that an improved standard of living implies. Whether this also translates into adequate improvements in nutrition and health outcomes is less plausible, however, since nothing guarantees that the added expenditures will be devoted to improved nutrition, health, and education.

For instance, nutrition may worsen rather than improve if higher incomes lead to fast food consumption with the result that malnourishment from underconsumption is replaced by malnourishment from the wrong kind of consumption. Thus, the illegal immigrants who come from across the Rio Grande in Mexico to the United States have children who are malnourished because they had sparse diets back home that consisted of a burrito with onions and chili to spice it up, and who now buy doughnuts, hamburgers, and french fries, which they can afford even at their low US wages (which greatly exceed the Mexican wages they left behind), leading to obesity and associated nutritional damage. Poorly informed parents think, as in any poor community worldwide, that fatter children are better than thinner ones.

The answer to this problem is not just more income but also information and education. "Nudging" the poor to spend more virtuously is surely an important part of the overall policy framework if improvements in nutrition and health care are to be assured as poverty declines.[1] Equally, from the outset Indian planners have supplemented poverty-reducing policies with a clear statement of improved nutrition, health care, and education as independent objectives.

Like Track I policies, Track II policies raise issues of design. We shall discuss them at length in the context of specific social objectives in the following chapters. But it is useful here to briefly touch on them in broad terms.

Direct Transfer Versus Wage Employment

One way to use revenues to assist the poor is to boost their purchasing power. Here, there are two options from which to choose: direct transfers or employment in public works at above-market wages.[2] The difference between the two options is that in the former case the transfer is unilateral while in the latter case the beneficiary must work if he is to receive the subsidy implicit in the above-market wage.[3] There are issues of whether the transfer and wage should be paid in cash or in kind and whether they are offered exclusively to the poor or to the entire population, which we consider separately below. In addition, the employment option raises the complex issues of how the workers' labor is to be allocated to various activities and what implications this allocation has for the labor market.

Transfers in Cash Versus Kind

While the purpose of employment schemes and some transfers is to merely transfer minimal purchasing power to the beneficiary, the government may sometimes want to use the transfers to influence the consumption pattern of the beneficiary. For example, it may want the beneficiary to *exclude* certain socially undesirable goods and services, such as alcohol and prostitution, from his consumption basket. Alternatively, it may want him to *include* certain socially desirable goods and services, such as nutritious foods, education, and health services, in it.

In-kind transfers through free distribution or sales at below-market prices of specific commodities are often seen as the instrument of achieving this objective.[4] A moment's reflection should make clear, however, that as long as a private market exists for the commodity in which the transfer is made, the government would in general fail to alter the expenditure pattern of the recipient through the in-kind transfer. Thus, for example, suppose the government makes the transfer by selling a specified quantity of rice at below-market price to the beneficiaries. As long as the price of rice in the private market exceeds the subsidized price, such subsidy will fail to influence the beneficiary's consumption basket. He has the option to sell the subsidized rice at the higher market price and convert the transfer into cash. Cash and in-kind transfers are equivalent in this situation; indeed, cash transfers may have certain advantages over in-kind transfers in terms of administrative costs.[5]

This objection is weakened when in-kind transfer involves a service. For example, if the transfer is available only through a school voucher that bears the name of a specific child, it cannot be readily turned into cash because by definition there is no private market for the purchase and sale of such vouchers. The same can be said of vouchers bearing the names of specific beneficiaries for health-care services.

But even this argument works only if the government has the ability to transparently enforce the use of the vouchers by the beneficiaries. Absent such ability, beneficiaries may still be able to turn the in-kind benefit into cash. For instance, in the case of the education voucher, the parent of a child may make a deal with a school whereby he provides the voucher in return for, say, half of its face value in cash without taking advantage of the school benefit. The school may in turn get full value of the voucher from the government without having to incur the cost of educating the child. Similar deals may be struck between patients and doctors with regard to health-care vouchers.

Public Versus Private Provision

One way the government can successfully alter the consumption pattern at least in the case of services is through their direct provision at subsidized prices, possibly even free of charge. Offering free education in public schools and low-price health care in public hospitals, dispensaries, and primary health-care centers are ways to ensure that the beneficiaries consume what the government deems socially desirable.

This is clearly a viable alternative but often runs into the difficulty that governments are unduly inefficient at providing services. As we shall see, this has clearly been the case in education and health sectors in India with the result that potential beneficiaries have chosen to seek private sources of supply even though they may charge a higher price.

The issue of government provision, of course, also arises in the context of goods. The most notable example of this in India is the public distribution system of food grains whereby the government procures large volumes of grain each year that it in turn sells at subsidized prices to the poor. As we will see, this public provision has been highly inefficient with massive leakages, rampant corruption, and very limited delivery of the subsidy to the intended beneficiaries.

Conditional Versus Unconditional Transfers

An alternative route to influencing the spending patterns of the beneficiaries while still making transfers in cash is to ask the beneficiaries to produce proof of having consumed certain goods and services. This approach is not much different from in-kind transfers and is subject to the same abuse as the latter. If enforcement is weak and corruption endemic, as is the case in India, fake invoices can be obtained inexpensively as proof of having met the conditionality. Like in-kind transfers, conditional transfers are also likely to succeed in altering the beneficiary expenditure pattern only if the government is substantially able to enforce the laws.

Universal Versus Targeted Transfers

A final choice one must make with respect to Track II reforms is whether the intended transfers are targeted to the poor and socially disadvantaged or made universal. The main argument advocates of universal transfers make is that this is the only way to ensure that the poor and disadvantaged groups are not shortchanged and receive the benefits. The human rights groups who strongly favor the rights approach to every social goal also join these advocates.

We have seen no empirical evidence showing that universal transfers are either necessary or sufficient to ensure that all those in need receive the intended benefits. For a long time, the public distribution system for food grains in India was universal. But dissatisfaction with its reach to the poor led to a switch to the current, more targeted system. It is simply not clear why reverting to a universal system will now work better. More important, if the objective is to bring food security, health, and education to the poor, at the current state of economic development, revenues are grossly inadequate to run universal programs that could then make substantial contribution per individual. We could either bring marginal benefits to all or substantial benefits to the bottom 30 percent or 40 percent of the population. The argument that the poor are not easily identified is also no longer valid. For example, the National Rural Employment Guarantee Scheme has surely identified the rural poor.

Our Preferred Strategy

There is general agreement on the objectives of social policy. All analysts favor speedy delivery of basic needs with respect to food, clothing, shelter, education, and health care to the poor and socially disadvantaged. Any differences relate to the approach to be taken to achieve this goal.

Our preferred policy mix consists of unconditional cash transfers for most needs, vouchers for elementary education, and insurance for major illnesses with government covering the premiums. We also favor targeted rather than universal coverage. Finally, the provision may be a mixture of private and public, with the beneficiary having the sole decision-making power to choose between them. Let us briefly explain why.

In principle, an approach that assigns a prominent role to the government could deliver on the desired goal. The government could offer employment in the public works programs at a prespecified wage to combat poverty and provide socially desirable goods, such as food, health care, education, and even shelter, free of charge or at subsidized prices to the beneficiaries. It could bear not only the financial burden associated with the employment program and provision of food, education, and health but also take on the responsibility of their delivery.

But the success of this approach is predicated on the government's ability to run public works programs efficiently and to deliver the goods and services efficiently. In our discussions in the following chapters, we will repeatedly see that at least the Indian government has had an extremely poor track record in delivery. The task is especially compounded by the existence of endemic corruption at all levels. Therefore, we will repeatedly lean in favor of an approach that minimizes the role of the government or at least requires it to compete with private-sector providers on equal terms. In turn, this choice translates into a reliance on cash transfers for most needs, education vouchers in the case of elementary education, and insurance for major illnesses, with the government paying the premium. An extremely important benefit is that this approach empowers the beneficiary rather than the provider. Armed with the cash, voucher, and insurance, the beneficiary decides whether he or she would choose a private or public provider and which one from within the two groups. Government provision does exactly the opposite: it leaves the beneficiary at the mercy of the provider, who wields all the power.

We also favor targeted instead of universal programs. The concern that targeting may exclude many among the poor and disadvantaged from accessing the benefits is readily addressed by applying exclusion rather than inclusion criteria to identify the beneficiaries. That is to say, unless identified as ineligible according to certain criteria, each individual may be considered eligible for the benefits. Exclusion criteria may include the ownership of a motorcycle, a scooter, a car, a specified amount of land, or other similar assets. Because all these vehicles require registration in India and revenue records identify land ownership, these are verifiable criteria. This approach would naturally result in a larger proportion of beneficiaries than what would be suggested by a reasonable set of inclusion criteria but would ensure that all the poor and disadvantaged are included. At the same time, a substantial exclusion will prevent the social expenditures from being spread too thinly and thus being diluted.

Finally, it will be best to make the transfers unconditional except in the cases of elementary education and major illnesses. We lean in favor of vouchers for education and insurance for major illnesses. Given the limited administrative ability of the Indian government at all levels, adding conditions to the transfers will only result in corruption without delivering the desired outcome. The objective of influencing the consumption basket except in the case of elementary education and major illnesses should, instead, be pursued through alternative instruments. For example, nutrition improvement can be achieved through requiring fortification of key foods and informing the public on the necessity of nutritious foods and the dangers of alcohol, tobacco, and cigarette consumption. Education being a social goal, vouchers offer the best com-
n_____ _____ between empowering the beneficiary and ensuring that the _____ _____ education do get used for that purpose. It _____ ransfer the voucher or to sell in the open _____ to large-scale corruption. Likewise, insur- _____ ive instrument of assisting poor families in _____ s less likely to be abused.

Chapter 14

Attacking Poverty by Guaranteeing Employment

T he principal instrument of direct attack on poverty in India has been schemes providing employment to the poor in the rural areas. While the central and state governments have sponsored a variety of these schemes over the past decades, the central government-sponsored scheme launched under the National Rural Employment Guarantee Act (NREGA) of 2005 eclipses them all in magnitude and scope.[1] Implemented over the entire country, this scheme is the principal vehicle for placing minimum purchasing power in the hands of rural households today. Therefore, we must examine the weaknesses in its design and functioning, and suggest reforms that would achieve the scheme's objective at lower cost and with greater effectiveness.

The NREGA has been implemented in three distinct phases. Under Phase I, which began February 2, 2006, it was implemented in the two hundred poorest districts nationwide. Under Phase II, an additional 130 districts were covered beginning April 1, 2007. The remaining 274 districts came under the scheme as part of Phase III, implemented with effect from April 1, 2008. Therefore, the scheme has been in operation over the entire country for four full financial years ending on March 31, 2012.

The broad contours of the NREGA are easily defined. The program guarantees one member of every rural household, whether poor or not, 100 days' worth of unskilled manual employment at a wage no less than that specified by the central government. Originally specified at 60 rupees per day, the wage was revised to 100 rupees per day in January 2009. Beginning January 1, 2011, the wage has been linked to the consumer price index.[2]

If an applicant is not provided employment within fifteen days of seeking it, the state is obliged to compensate him or her at a rate no less than one-fourth of the specified rate for the first thirty days and at no less than half of the wage rate for the rest of the period. The state is required to bear the burden of this compensation. At least one-third of the beneficiaries are required to be women who have registered and have requested work.

Labor hired as a part of the program is to be employed in public works and other activities specified in the legislation, such as water conservation and water harvesting; drought proofing, including forestation and tree planting; irrigation canals; land development; flood control; and rural connectivity. The cost of the material component of projects including skilled and semiskilled workers is capped at 40 percent of the total cost. The central government covers only 75 percent of the material cost, with the state having to fund the remaining 25 percent. The legislation makes very detailed provisions for creating the implementation machinery at the center, state, district, block, and village levels.

The closest parallel to the NREGA in developed countries is the massive employment program overseen by the Works Progress Administration (renamed Works Projects Administration or WPA in 1939) under President Franklin Roosevelt in the United States. The WPA employed millions of unskilled workers to carry out public works projects that included the construction of roads and public buildings. The scale of the program can be judged by the initial appropriation of the WPA at $4.9 billion in 1935, which amounted to a gigantic 6.7 percent of the GDP in that year.

Table 14.1 reports the key achievements of the NREGA in terms of financial and physical indicators, as officially reported. Beginning with the total expenditure of 88.2 billion rupees ($1.9 billion) in 2006–2007, the program spent a total of 393.8 billion rupees ($8.6 billion) in 2010–2011. Of this, approximately two-thirds was spent on wages and the rest went to materials.[3] The number of households benefiting from the pro-

Table 14.1. Key achievements of the NREGA as officially reported

Item	2006–2007	2007–2008	2008–2009	2009–2010	2010–2011
Financial					
Total amount spent (billion nominal rupees)	88.2	158.6	272.5	379.1	393.8
Of which wages (billion nominal rupees)	58.4	107.4	182.0	255.8	256.9
Percent share of wages in the total	66.2	67.7	66.8	67.5	65.2
Physical					
Households receiving employment	21.0	33.9	45.5	52.5	55.0
Person days of work done (billion)	0.91	1.44	2.16	2.84	2.57
Percent share of Scheduled Castes and Tribes	61.0	57.0	53.7	51.2	51.5
Percent share of women in the work done	41.0	43.0	47.9	48.1	47.7
Average person days per household employed	43.3	42.5	47.5	54.1	46.7

Source: For years 2006–2007 and 2007–2008, see www.nrega.net/csd/Forest/field-initia tives/Sustainable%20Developemnt.pdf (accessed November 18, 2011) and for the last three years, see "DMU Report" at http://nrega.nic.in/netnrega/home.aspx (accessed November 18, 2011)

gram rose from 21 million to 55 million over the same period. After the program peaked in 2009–2010, the total person days and person days per week declined slightly to 2.57 billion and 46.7 days, respectively, in 2010–2011. Clearly the average person days per household receiving employment under the program is well below the maximum one hundred days offered under the program.

Going by just the wages paid, the NREGA program placed 4,671 rupees per household on average in 2010–2011 in the hands of the households covered by the program. But this average masks one key implication of Table 14.1: the Scheduled Castes and Scheduled Tribes benefited disproportionately from the program. According to the 2001 census, the Scheduled Castes and Tribes account for 24.4 percent of the

Indian population. But their share in the days worked in 2010–2011, shown in Table 14.1, was 51.5 percent. If we assume that the distribution of households by caste in the beneficiary population mirrors that in the general population, we would conclude that the Scheduled Caste (SC) and Scheduled Tribe (ST) households received 2.2 times the average sum or approximately 10,275 rupees per household in 2010–2011. Of course, to the extent that the SC and ST households were represented more than proportionately among the beneficiary households, this figure would be lower. Whatever one assumes, the data do seem to point to a proportionately larger part of the benefit going to the SC and ST households that also happen to have a higher incidence of poverty.

Pitfalls of the Scheme and the Superiority of Cash Transfers

Few critics would consider the scheme so counterproductive as to advocate its elimination even if no other antipoverty scheme replaced it. Indeed, most would agree that the NREGA has done more to transfer purchasing power to the poor than almost all existing redistribution programs, which include food, fertilizer, water, and electricity subsidies and even education and health expenditures. Even accepting that the NREGA is subject to significant leakages as the money flows from the center all the way down to the actual beneficiary, and that it has contributed to larger fiscal deficits and inflation and has adversely impacted economic activity by distorting the labor market, it is to be viewed positively vis-à-vis a situation without the NREGA insofar as it has placed a significant sum of money in the hands of poor households, at least going by the official statistics reported in Table 14.1.

But the picture looks much bleaker when we instead compare the situation with the NREGA to the one in which it is replaced by an *alternative* policy of making direct transfers to poor households. Advantages of such a transfer scheme over the NREGA are many, with almost no disadvantages.

First and foremost, transfers will virtually eliminate the leakages. The precise volume of leakages under the NREGA is not known but even the proponents of the scheme do not deny that they are significant. A study by Sharma (2009), jointly sponsored by the National Council on Applied Economic Research and the Public-Interest Foundation, observed that leakages in Jharkhand, Orissa, and Uttar Pradesh went up to "one-third to half of the stipulated wages," adding that since the leakages are disguised through the addition of fictitious names to the muster rolls, employment generation is also overstated. Sharma (2009) writes, "All three states have what is referred to as the PC or 'percentage' system in which bribes have to be paid according to fixed percentages to the whole hierarchy of staff up to the block level, and sometimes going higher" (p. 128, footnote 7). For Orissa, Sharma is able to provide more precise estimates. He notes, "The study estimates that only 58 percent of wages disbursed in sample works during the first two years of the program reached workers listed in the muster rolls, the proportion being only 26 percent in KBK [Kalahandi Balangir Koraput] region" (p. 129, footnote 8).

Cash transfers should substantially eliminate these leakages. Advances in technology now allow an official in New Delhi to deposit money into the bank account of the beneficiaries held in a distant village, using just a few keystrokes. The states of Rajasthan and Karnataka have recently experimented with cash transfers to widows and the elderly with strikingly positive results. Summarizing their study of these experiences, "Small But Effective: India's Targeted Unconditional Cash Transfers," Dutta, Howes, and Murgai (2010) note:

India's approach to social security stresses the provision of subsidized food and public works. Targeted, unconditional cash transfers are little used, and have been hardly evaluated. An evaluation of cash transfers for the elderly and widows, based on the national household survey data and surveys on social pension utilization in two [states], Karnataka and Rajasthan, reveals that these social pension schemes work reasonably well. Levels of leakage are low, funds flow disproportionately to poorer rather than richer households, and there is strong evidence that the funds reach vulnerable individuals. A comparison with the public distribution system reveals that the main strength of the social pensions scheme is its relatively low level of leakage.

The authors are careful to note that the study is not decisive, since it relates to small-scale programs. Nevertheless, it greatly strengthens the case for giving cash transfers a further play rather than acquiescing to knee-jerk assertions by critics that they are not feasible or that they, too, will be subject to corruption equal to that in the existing schemes. The central government, which has repeatedly shied away from carrying out proper pilot projects, needs to evaluate the feasibility of the cash transfers on a larger scale.

Second, even assuming equal volume of leakages as under the NREGA, which is highly implausible, cash transfers will place a greater volume of purchasing power in the hands of the poor for other reasons. Thus, while NREGA gives the beneficiary a wage that is higher than what would prevail in the market absent this scheme, it takes away his or her labor in return. Under a cash transfer, the beneficiary will receive the equivalent amount of public money and will also get to keep his labor, for which he can earn additional wage in the market. Moreover, NREGA ends up spending 35 percent of the expenditures on materials. Under cash transfers, these funds will be available for distribution to the poor.

Furthermore, cash transfers will not suffer from an important regressive feature plaguing the NREGA. The NREGA provides that the labor of a worker can be used in the

> provision of irrigation facility, horticulture plantation and land development facilities to land owned by households belonging to the Scheduled Castes and the Scheduled Tribes or below poverty line families or to beneficiaries of land reforms or to the beneficiaries under the Indira Awas Yojana of the Government of India or that of the small farmers or marginal farmers as defined in the Agriculture Debt Waiver and Debt Relief Scheme, 2008.[4]

Surely most workers offering their labor under the program are even poorer than some of the entities entitled to or benefiting from their free labor under this provision. In contrast, under a cash transfer, the workers retain the right to sell their labor at the market wage.

Then again, NREGA has also led to severe distortions in the labor market that cash transfers would avoid. Three such distortions are worth emphasizing. One, by diverting a fraction of the labor force from its productive private-sector deployment to public works projects, it has replaced genuine value added by projects likely to be of dubious value. Because NREGA funds can be accessed only for prespecified activities considered to serve public interest, local authorities have an incentive to come up with projects fitting this list even when the social return on them is low, possibly even minuscule. Normally it is the social return that drives the search for resources to finance a project. But NREGA reverses this process: the availability of the funds drives the search for projects.

Unsurprisingly, therefore, available studies have recorded projects of zero or even negative social value being undertaken under the scheme. Reporting on the quality of assets created, Sharma (2009) states,

> It is difficult to argue emphatically about the quality of assets that have been created because very little information is available on them, but a few examples provided here underscore the problems in terms of the quality of these assets. Ponds were dug in a drought-prone area with scanty rainfall, soil was sandy and had no water retention power and others were without water (Haryana). But, some had become like swimming pools due to heavy expenditure incurred on material and masonry works. (p. 125)

He goes on to add, "A lot of money was spent on digging ponds without conceptualizing factors like catchment area, sources of recharging, technical sanctions, and preparation of detailed estimates. Assets created in Karnataka were not according to specification and quantities executed were not as per the technical sanction." He notes similar problems in road projects in Orissa, Tripura, West Bengal, and other states.

The NREGA also poses the risk of perverse choice of input mix in agriculture through increased market wage. Just as high effective labor costs of operating in the formal economy have led the firms to opt for capital-intensive products and technologies, a NREGA-induced hike in rural wages will lead to premature shift in favor of capital-intensive farm products and techniques. While the current empirical evidence on this is limited to press reports, it is only a matter of time before more systematic corroborative evidence should emerge.

Finally, there is likely to be another detrimental long-term impact of NREGA on economic development. Given that the primary purpose of public works is to generate employment and the creation of an asset is largely incidental, the work effort demanded by them is likely to be leisurely.[5] In turn, this would have an adverse impact on the work culture. Eventually work effort is likely to decline even in private employments paying the same wage as the public works.[6]

In a similar vein, since public projects discourage the use of any machinery, save simple implements such as shovels, and exclusively provide manual and unskilled work, they offer the workers no scope for skill creation. A yet more detrimental developmental impact is likely to be added disincentive for migration. Because public works under NREGA are confined to rural areas, they require presence in the rural areas and slow down a process of income-improving emigration that is already moving at a snail's pace. A cash transfer that the household can receive even as one of its members migrates to work elsewhere does not suffer from this pitfall.

Chapter 15

Adult Nutrition and Food Security

P olicy initiatives to secure nutritional improvement also raise serious questions. Unlike the concern with the poor alone, this issue is seen as cutting across all classes of the population. In particular, with adult nutrition in mind, many civil society groups now demand an expansion of the public distribution system through right-to-food legislation that would guarantee an adequate quantity of food grains at highly subsidized prices to all the country's citizens.

Calorie Consumption Versus Hunger

The concern for adult nutrition has originated primarily in the steady decline recorded in per capita calorie consumption (though a decline in protein intake is also an issue). A 1996 report on nutrition by the National Sample Survey Organization provides some of the early documentation of this trend.[1] Additional data appear in similar follow-up reports.[2] The long-term trend is one of declining calorie consumption in both rural and urban areas, though the trend is steadier in rural areas. Protein intake has shown similar patterns in rural and urban areas, though the intake of fats has steadily climbed. Figures 15.1 and 15.2 depict these movements graphically.

The trends in calorie consumption and protein and fat intake reflect a shift away from cereals (Deaton and Drèze, 2009, Table 4) to other lower-calorie, lower-protein, more fatty and sugary foods. Such a shift in diet due to increased income from a very low level is likely. Finer

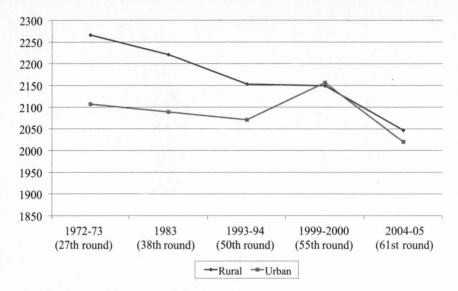

Figure 15.1. Average calorie intake per person per day
Source: Drawn using the data in NSSO (2007a, p. v)

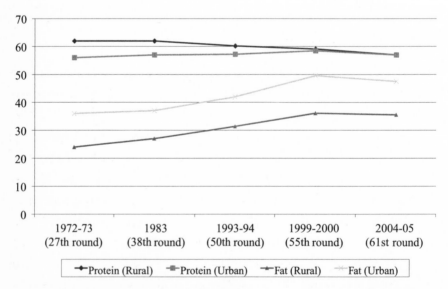

Figure 15.2. Grams of protein and fat intake per person per day on average
Source: Drawn using the data in NSSO (2007a, p. v)

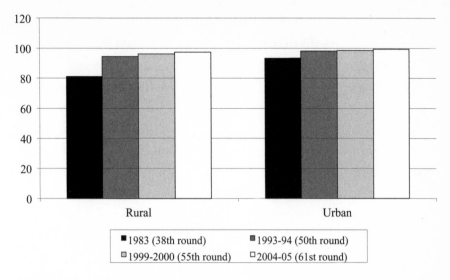

Figure 15.3. Percent of respondents stating they had enough to eat on all days of the year

Source: NSSO (2001b and 2007b)

grains, white flour, rice, fruits, and oily foods replace coarse grains and whole-wheat flour. Consumption of fruits, fried products, and desserts has seen a steady rise in the past few decades.

While activists interpret the trend in calorie consumption as a decisive indication of increased hunger, other evidence seriously questions such a conclusion. Thus, when directly asked whether they had enough to eat every day of the year, successive rounds of the expenditure surveys of the National Sample Survey Organization show increasing proportions of the respondents answering in the affirmative. In the 1983 expenditures survey, only 81.1 percent of the respondents in the rural areas and 93.3 percent in the urban areas stated that they had enough food every day of the year. But by 2004–2005, these percentages had risen to 97.4 and 99.4 percent, respectively.[3] Figure 15.3 depicts these trends in rural and urban India.

Conceptually, the rising trend in the proportion of the population stating that it had enough to eat throughout the year can be reconciled with the declining trend in calorie consumption once we recognize the factors that explain why there may be a decline in the need for calorie consumption. For example, greater mechanization in agriculture, improved means of transportation, and a shift away from traditional physically challenging jobs may have reduced the need for physical activity. Likewise, better absorption of food made possible by improved epidemiological environment (better child and adult health and better access to safe drinking water) may have lowered the needed calorie consumption to produce a given amount of energy. Hence, the inference that declining calorie consumption implies increasing malnourishment is not warranted.

Indeed, the interpretation that the decline in calorie consumption represents increased malnourishment is also contradicted by the weight and height trends of adults. According to the National Nutrition Monitoring Bureau surveys, the proportion of people with below-normal body mass index (BMI) fell from 56 percent during 1975–1979 to 33 percent during 2004–2005 for men and from 52 percent to 36 percent for women during the same period (Deaton and Drèze, 2009, Table 10). Deaton and Drèze (2009) also analyze the data on the heights of different cohorts of men and women collected by the second and third rounds of the National Family Health Survey and conclude that later-born adult men and women are taller. They calculate that the rate of increase of height is 0.56 centimeter per decade for men and 0.18 centimeter per decade for women. Thus, even if India continues to do poorly in international comparisons, all trends point to improving and not worsening adult nutrition.

Parenthetically, we note here our puzzlement at the implicit endorsement by Deaton and Drèze (2009, p. 45) of the argument that the declining calorie consumption represents rising poverty.[4] While the declining trends in both calorie consumption and protein intake can be sources of concern, surely poverty is not to be measured by the ex post calorie consumption. It must be measured instead by how many calories the individuals are able to afford *ex ante*. The policy response greatly depends on which measure of poverty we choose.

If we measured poverty by the ex post calorie consumption, we would be tempted to offer free food to Bollywood actresses trying to stay slim on low-calorie diets! If, however, we measured poverty, correctly in our view, by the amount of calories the individual is able to afford *ex ante,* we would be spared the obvious policy mistakes. Thus, if the decline in calorie consumption turns out to be the result of lack of affordability, the solution would be to improve the purchasing power of the citizenry through growth and redistribution. If instead the decline took place despite sufficient purchasing power and therefore due to ill-informed decision-making, we would want to supply better information, undertake persuasive advertising to "nudge" people into healthy eating, and pass laws requiring fortification of major foods by necessary nutrients.

Regrettably, the dominant view today, aggressively pushed by activists in India and around the world and by influential international organizations, such as the World Health Organization, Food and Agricultural Organization, and the World Bank, is that the decline in calorie consumption represents increased poverty and therefore increased hunger. The fact that more and more people in India are able to afford increased rather than reduced food purchases over time and that the decline in calorie consumption has occurred across all individuals, whether they be rich or poor and whether they be residents in rural or urban areas (Deaton and Drèze 2009, pp. 45–47 and Figures 1 and 2), would suggest, however, that something other than purchasing power—for example, reduced need for calorie consumption due to the various factors detailed here—is behind the change. But the increased-hunger school has conveniently ignored this inconvenient truth.

Pitfalls of the Right-to-Food Bill

This diagnosis of malnutrition, that it is due not to poverty and hunger but rather to unhealthy consumption, also implies that the current reliance on the right-to-food legislation, and implementation of further expansion of public distribution of food grains, is misguided.

A bill to this effect has just been approved by the cabinet and soon will be tabled in the Parliament. The bill would provide subsidized grain through the public distribution system to 75 percent of the rural and 50 percent of the urban population. Specified criteria exclude 25 percent

of the rural and 50 percent of the urban population from receiving subsidized food. A minimum of 46 percent of the households in the rural
and 28 percent in the urban areas must be priority (i.e., poor) households. The remaining households not falling under the exclusion criteria
are designated "general" households. Under the bill, the government
would supply 7 kilograms of millet, wheat, or rice per person per month
at the prices of 1, 2, and 3 rupees per kilogram, respectively, to priority
households. With five persons per household, the quantity of subsidized
grain would amount to 35 kilograms per household. The bill also proposes to give a minimum of 3 kilograms of millet, wheat, or rice per person per month at prices not exceeding 50 percent of the respective
support prices to general households.

In the case of many beneficiaries who may already be consuming adequate grains with malnutrition, reflecting a lack of balanced diet, as we
have argued, such an objective itself is questionable. But even accepting
that the increase in grains consumption is a desirable goal, it is unlikely
that the proposed program would accomplish it. Given that a private
market for food grains offers significantly higher prices than the subsidized prices under the bill, beneficiaries will have the option to buy
grains at low prices from the public distribution system and sell it on the
private market for cash at a profit.[5] There is no guarantee, therefore, that
the program will encourage increased consumption of food grains if the
beneficiaries do not see the need for it. Indeed, non-priority beneficiaries
(the general households in terms of the definition used in the bill), who
would receive only partial supplies from the public distribution system,
are likely to cut their purchases kilogram-for-kilogram from the private
market. This argument is reinforced by the fact that the ongoing decline
in the consumption of calories from cereals has taken place in the presence of an extensive public distribution system providing subsidized
wheat and rice.

Indeed, the subsidy structure in the bill makes it unviable at the implementation level.[6] Recognizing that the absolute subsidy per kilogram
is the largest in rice, the eligible households would stand to maximize
the implicit transfer to them by buying rice and no other grain from the

public distribution system. By reselling this rice on the private market, they would be able to convert this maximized in-kind subsidy into cash. They would then be free to spend the proceeds as they wish. Of course, with all eligible households buying rice for their entire permitted quotas, the government distribution system will simply fail to procure enough rice. Thus, there is a clear mismatch in the bill between the objective of pushing calorie consumption and the instrument chosen.

When we add to these considerations the high delivery costs of the public distribution system, the right-to-food bill makes even less sense. Waste, leakage, and theft in the public distribution system have been widely documented. The system lacks adequate warehouse facilities, with vast volumes of grain stored in the open. Rains frequently wash off large proportions of these stocks. Parts of stock go unused for sufficiently long to rot. Pests and rats take their share as well. Finally, there are significant leakages as grain moves from procurement by the center to distribution to the states, districts, villages, and eventually the actual beneficiaries.

A recent study by Jha and Ramaswami (2011) estimates that in 2004–2005, 70 percent of the poor received no grain through the public distribution system (exclusion error) while 70 percent of those who did receive it were non-poor (inclusion error). They also estimate that as much as 55 percent of the grain supplied through the public distribution system leaked out along the distribution chain, with only 45 percent actually sold to beneficiaries through fair-price shops. The share of food subsidy received by the poor turned out to be an astonishingly low 10.5 percent.

Many proponents of the right-to-food bill offer ensuring inclusion of all poor as the key justification for universal or nearly universal coverage (Drèze and Khera 2010; Himanshu and Sen 2011). They base this argument on the evidence of large exclusions of the poor from the current targeted rather than universal public distribution system. But even this justification for yet further expansion of an already broken system fails to stand up to close scrutiny. In his excellent analysis, Svedberg (2012) makes this point forcefully and it is worthwhile to quote him at some length:

The evidence in support of universality as an efficient method for eliminating, or even notably reducing, exclusion errors, is not altogether convincing. Before 1997, the PDS [Public Distribution System] was in principle universal, but large proportions of poor households were either effectively excluded, or purchased very small amounts of subsidized grains. On the basis of 1993–94 NSS data, Dutta and Ramaswami (2001) found that the poorest household quintile, on average, managed to purchase about 10% and 20% of the PDS grains allowed in Maharashtra and Andhra Pradesh, respectively. Other evaluations of the pre-1997 PDS also report blunt de facto targeting of poor households (Jha 1992; Ahluwalia 1993; Howes and Jha 1992, 1994; Dev and Suryanarayana 1991; Parikh 1994).

One may also gauge the extent to which universality reduces exclusion errors by consulting more recent estimates from Tamil Nadu, the only state that opted for a universal PDS after 1997. In 2004–2005, about 80 percent of the households in the three lowest Monthly Percapita Expenditure deciles in Tamil Nadu reported consumption of PDS rice, but practically no wheat. This share is more than twice as high as the all-India figure (National Sample Survey Organization 2007c), but it still reflects substantial exclusion of poor households. To have a right to purchase subsidized grains is obviously not sufficient for eliminating exclusion; the system has to be known, attractive, and accessible as well, and ensuring this costs money.

So, the right-to-food bill can be expected to neither boost grain consumption nor target the poor significantly better than the current system. It may result in some transfer of purchasing power to some of the poor but only at a huge cost in relation to the benefit accrued. Add to this the fact that for the vast proportion of the population, calorie consumption may not even be the main factor in poor nutrition. Instead, the key deficiency is most likely a lack of proper balance in diet: for example, the malnourished families should be shifting their diet to more milk and fruits rather than consuming additional quantities of grain, on which the right-to-food bill has focused.

A Better Way

Significant gains in efficiency can be achieved by replacing the public distribution system by cash transfers. The argument against such transfers that the beneficiaries might spend the money on something other than grains is spurious. As argued above, such an outcome is also readily achievable under in-kind transfers by selling the grain in the open market. The advantage of cash transfers is that they would greatly minimize the leakage along the distribution chain and also eliminate the huge waste that characterizes the public distribution system.

Once the issues of transfer of purchasing power and the right basket of consumption are separated, the focus of policy can shift to ensuring that consumers make the right consumption choices. This would require two sets of measures. One set of measures would inform and then "nudge" the public in several ways toward a more nourishing diet. The second set of measures, which is more likely to produce results, would aim at getting wholesalers and retailers to fortify various foods with necessary nutrients. The Food Safety and Standards Authority of India can play an important role in implementing this set of measures.

Of course, even though demand can be shifted toward dairy products, fruits, vegetables, fish, and meat, policy must also be directed to ensure increased availability of these items. Here Track I and Track II reforms come squarely together. The availability of products needed to promote good nutrition depends on both domestic production and imports. It is surprising, however, that discussions on food security, which focus on enhancing the availability of various food items over time, rarely mention imports.[7] This omission has often resulted in India's failure to fully exploit the benefits of imports. For example, the key component of "food inflation" from 2008–2009 to 2010–2011 has been milk. Clearly, easing the imports through a reduced tariff on powdered milk could have greatly alleviated the shortage of this critical item. But the government did not take advantage of this channel.

As for domestic production, there is in fact critical need for raising productivity on the farm as well as along the supply chain, for nearly every agricultural commodity. Per hectare yields in India are lower than in most of the comparable countries in most crops. Likewise, vast volumes of fruits and vegetables perish in transit as the produce makes its way from the farm to the final consumer. The agricultural economist Ashok Gulati reminds us that water tables in the original Green Revolution states of Punjab, Haryana and western Uttar Pradesh have been falling at rates of almost a foot per year.[8] Therefore, the effort to enhance yields has to move to the eastern part of the country, which has an abundant water supply. Gulati cites the successful Chinese experience with hybrid rice varieties, noting that it produces almost 200 million tons of paddy from 29 million hectares, compared with India's 150 million tons from 44 million hectares.

A key element in improving productivity is to reform the laws on sales and rental of agricultural land. Over the years, land holdings have shrunk in size with the result that today more than 80 percent of the land holdings are less than two hectares and more than 60 percent are less than one hectare. Only 6.5 percent of the holdings are four hectares or larger. Ease of sales and rental will help consolidate holdings. Flexible rental laws that allow the owner and the tiller to negotiate and sign formal agreements will provide better security to the tiller and provide the necessary incentive for making productivity-enhancing investments in land.

Improvements in the supply chain also require the development of contract farming, infrastructure, and organized retail. Contract farming can establish a direct link between the farmer and the processor of the produce, thereby cutting all intermediaries and minimizing waste. It can also ensure a good price to the farmer. Infrastructure development includes the provision of uninterrupted supply of electricity at reasonable prices and road and railway transport. The former allows the development of cold storage while the latter permits rapid movement of produce from the producer to the consumer. Moreover, organized retail has the capacity to develop efficient supply chains.

Finally, agricultural productivity increases today depend additionally on a new Green Revolution. The old Green Revolution was based on the new seeds invented under the leadership of Dr. Norman Borlaug and spread in India under the scientific leadership of Dr. Swaminathan.

Today they depend on the adoption and absorption of the genetically modified and BT (*Bacillus thuringiensis* or natural insecticide) seeds and agricultural crops, such as cotton and brinjal (eggplant). Some NGOs have objected to these as Frankenstein foods, though scientific evidence does not support such fears. The Environment Ministry has handled this issue ineptly, going back on the genetically modified and BT innovations after meeting the NGOs in public without scientists who could respond to these fears. India cannot afford to forgo the new Second Green Revolution in this way. Otherwise, it will have also replaced the highly improbable Frankenstein by the certain Grim Reaper as scarcity overtakes plenitude in the production of food grains and crops.

Chapter 16

Reforming Health Care

W e argued in Part II that, contrary to common assertions, India has made definite, if inadequate, progress in areas such as life expectancy, infant mortality, and maternal mortality when compared with countries with similar levels of income. The common impression of India's failure in this area results from the low levels with which India started. But as far as improvements are concerned, steady progress has been made. Moreover, when health indicators such as those relating to child nutrition show below-average progress, their scientific foundation turns out to be shaky.

Of course, being still a poor country, India has hardly won the battle against ill health. There remains vast scope for improvement along all dimensions of health. Reforms are necessary in five key areas: public health, routine health care, care involving hospitalization or outpatient surgeries, human resources, and oversight of the health system.

Preventive Public Health

Public health services, which constitute a classic case of a public good, fall into two categories: *population-wide* environmental services that reduce exposure to and spread of disease, and *clinical* services, such as screening and vaccination that prevent the spread of diseases from one individual to another.[1] Because the benefits of public health services are spread over a wide population and once provided, the services become available to all at no additional cost, the market typically fails to supply them in adequate volume.

For example, the cost of disinfecting a swamp to prevent the spread of vector-borne disease such as malaria or dengue fever may be minuscule in relation to the combined benefit to households living around the swamp, but no single household will find it attractive to undertake this cost. This is because each household will count on other households to take action and on "free riding" its benefits. If the group involved is small, its members may be able to solve the "collective action" problem by coming together and making small contributions to cover the cost. But typically this is not the case.

Intervention is also likely to be required when the benefits of an action to an individual are large but still fall short of the total benefits to the society as a whole, as is the case with vaccination. Because vaccination of one individual lowers the chances of others around him or her contracting the same disease, fewer people will take vaccines on their own than are socially desirable. For example, a school-age child who has not been vaccinated against tuberculosis is at risk of contracting the disease. And yet, since the vaccine itself is not costless in view of possible reaction, many students (or their parents) may opt out of it, thereby placing other students at the school at risk.

Nonetheless, the central, state, and local governments in India have done a regretfully poor job of supplying public health services. Drainage systems, the supply of drinking water, and general standards of hygiene in public places remain extremely poor. A bout of monsoon rains is often enough to create conditions conducive to the quick spread of communicable diseases. While the governments have run some effective campaigns against specific communicable diseases, such as smallpox, polio, and Guinea worm disease, their record in providing day-to-day public health services has been disappointing.

In part, the undersupply of public health services may reflect inadequate public expenditures on health in general. But the problem has been exacerbated by political-economy factors, which have biased the allocation of health expenditures in favor of medical services rather than public health.

Thus DasGupta et al. (2009) have carefully analyzed this problem and note that Sri Lanka has been able to provide public health services at a satisfactory level by spending only 0.2 percent of the GDP. They attribute the neglect of public health services in India to an organizational change immediately following independence. Following the recommendation of the 1946 Bhore Committee report, the central government and all states except Tamil Nadu merged the medical and public health services into a single department. Later, as per the Jungalwalla Committee report of 1967, they also combined the medical and public health cadres into a single cadre. The combined effect of these changes was the neglect of public health services in favor of medical services whose proponents, the well-organized doctors' lobby, have more prestige with the public and carry much greater clout.

According to DasGupta et al. (2009), Tamil Nadu, which retained public health services under a separate department, has been more successful in improving health outcomes than other states. But the evidence in this regard is mixed. Tamil Nadu does come out on top in terms of vaccination. But its performance along other indicators, while generally among the top five out of the fifteen larger states, is less compelling. Nevertheless, there is some merit in the argument Dasgupta et al. (2009) make. In principle, establishing a separate agency entrusted with public health services with its own budget should help boost the provision of these services.

Two additional public health measures are worth implementing. First, governments at all levels must carry out regular campaigns to inform the public of the benefits of a healthy local environment.[2] When people live in neighborhoods with unhygienic conditions for several years, even decades, they become so used to the unhealthy conditions that they do not even notice them. Demonstrating that cleaner conditions are possible and are both healthier and nicer may go some distance toward generating beneficial public action at the individual level.

Second, it is important to make the Food Safety and Standards Authority of India (FSSAI), established under the 2006 Food Safety and Standards Act, more effective. The Authority lays down science-based standards for articles of food and regulates their manufacture, storage, distribution, sale, and imports. But the implementation of these standards requires the consolidation of food supply chains. Currently the supplies come from innumerable and unknown sources and are distributed by as many retailers spread over a vast territory. It is not possible for any administrative unit to monitor these small units all across the country. Consolidation is required at the processing and wholesale stages, which will pave the way for the emergence of branded products, even though the retail distribution continues to consist mainly of small shopkeepers. From this perspective, the recent reform opening multi-brand retail to foreign retail chains, such as Walmart and Tesco, is a step in the right direction. As large buyers of processed foods, these retailers can potentially help consolidate food processing and introduce and popularize branded products meeting FSSAI standards.

Routine Health Care

Let us next turn to health care, which we shall divide into two categories: routine health care and major illnesses. The former involves ailments such as cold, cough, fever, and minor injuries. These ailments afflict nearly all, often several times a year, and are not hugely expensive to treat per episode. Major illnesses, including those requiring prolonged treatment at home, surgeries on an outpatient basis, and hospitalization, occur with unpredictable frequency and are costly per episode.[3]

Setting aside considerations of poverty for the moment, the case for free public provision of, or subsidy on, routine health care is extremely weak. Routine health care directly benefits the recipient of the service with no significant positive or negative implications for the rest of the population. Therefore, the arguments for government intervention, such as those applying to vaccination or cleaning of the swamps discussed earlier, do not apply here.

An argument for government provision is, however, made by some on the alternative grounds of asymmetric information. These analysts argue that the patient is unable to assess the quality and price of the service, so that private providers may dupe the patient into paying high prices for worthless service. Government provision of the service can overcome this problem.

But this argument has at best limited force when it comes to routine health care since repeated interactions with the provider and conversations with other patients provide the patient an opportunity to observe and assess the quality and price of the service. Moreover, even if one accepts the information asymmetry as a serious issue, it is far from clear that the Indian government has the ability to deliver high-quality routine care at a reasonable price. According to a National Sample Survey Organization (2006, p. H-2) survey conducted during January–June, 2004—the latest such survey available—81 percent of urban and 78 percent of rural patients in India sought private providers for non-hospitalized care in preference to the government subcenters and primary health-care centers in rural areas and government dispensaries and hospitals in urban areas.

In their important work, Das and Hammer (2007) provide even more direct evidence questioning the ability of the public sector to provide quality service. They show that although the public sector employs well-qualified doctors and pays them relatively high salaries, this hardly translates into quality care. The benefits of better qualifications of these doctors over those in the private sector are offset by a lack of effort on their part to fully apply their knowledge to providing patient care. The government may be able to use its access to public money to hire better doctors but it cannot make them deliver better service.

A different case for government intervention is sometimes made on the grounds that better health service improves the ability of individuals to work and therefore helps produce a healthier workforce. But once again, this increase in productivity should generate private benefits to the recipients of the service in terms of higher wages. Therefore, this argument also falls short of providing a persuasive case for intervention by the government.

In the ultimate analysis, the principal plausible justification for government intervention in providing routine outpatient care stems from poverty. A large chunk of the population at the bottom of the income distribution in India is too poor to afford even a minimum socially acceptable level of health care. To the extent that financial resources permit it, a modern welfare state must strive to provide a minimum level of health care to those unable to afford it. This view is reflected in the aim to provide access to "comprehensive primary health care" in the National Rural Health Mission, launched in 2005.

The key policy question, however, is whether such care is provided through the government *provision* of outpatient care or by other means. We noted in Part I that India had begun to build up the primary health-care infrastructure as early as the 1960s following the recommendations of the Health Survey and Planning Committee (Mudaliar Committee 1961). But nearly fifty years of efforts in building this infrastructure have not led to the provision of effective health care in rural India. As just noted, no more than one-fifth of the rural patients seek routine outpatient care at public health facilities. The remaining four-fifths of the patients go to rural medical providers who are largely unqualified providers of routine health care in rural India.

Given the government's inability to deliver the service after a half century of efforts, alternative models must be given a chance. In our view, the best course is to place the financial power to buy health services in the hands of the patients: give cash transfers to the poor to meet their routine health-care expenses. The government can continue to provide services but its facilities must compete against the private providers and meet all their costs from the revenues they earn by charging the patients. Once the poor are given the financial resources, public health-care facilities will be justified in charging for their services, which will enable them to recover their costs. This will force market discipline on the government facilities while giving patients a greater choice of providers.

An important question in this context is whether the transfers should be contingent on meeting certain requirements or given unconditionally. According to the bulk of the empirical evidence from Latin American countries such as Mexico and Brazil, requirements such as regular medical checkups are useful devices to ensure that the financial transfer is spent as intended. Nevertheless, the benefits of the conditional approach must be weighed against the corruption they are likely to engender in Indian conditions. Given the extreme shortage of doctors, certification of regular checkups could itself turn into a business. Doctors would extract a part of the transfer from patients just for providing certification. Therefore, it is our view that the best course is to make transfers to the poor without conditions, perhaps to the senior-most female member of the household. This way, households may even be encouraged to maintain a healthy lifestyle to avoid visits to the doctor, thereby releasing the funds for expenditures on items such as milk and fruits that improve the body's natural immunity.

It is easy to see that if the government were to opt for cash transfers, it could accomplish its objectives well within the current fiscal constraints. Make the generous assumption that the transfers will be given to the entire bottom half of the population—to approximately 600 million individuals. Assume further a cash transfer of 500 rupees per individual. These figures imply 300 billion rupees at 2010–2011 prices in total expenditure. With a GDP of 79 trillion rupees at market prices in 2010–2011, the transfer amounts to 0.38 percent of the GDP. Even doubling the transfer to 1,000 rupees can be accomplished for less than 0.8 percent of the GDP.

Major Illnesses

Major illnesses, in which we include childbirth and maternity care as well as prolonged illnesses even when they are treated at home, differ from routine health-care in two important respects: their frequency is much lower but the cost per episode is high, and their frequency, as well as the magnitude of the associated expense at the individual level, is unpredictable.[4]

These characteristics make the market for the care of major illnesses a perfect candidate for insurance. In common with other insurance markets, we face the adverse selection problem: those already hit by an illness or suffering from a prolonged illness would seek insurance while those in good health would avoid it. The common solution to the problem is group insurance. Since the poor in India cannot afford the insurance premiums, the government will have to foot the bill.

A beginning in this direction has been made in recent years. Stimulated by the opening of insurance to the private sector, including 26 percent foreign direct investment in 2001, a nascent private market for insurance has been emerging. Within this context, the government has also tried to address the needs of the poor by requiring private entrants to issue a specific proportion of their policies to the rural populations. This provision has led some private insurers to team up with self-help groups such as SEWA to insure entire groups in rural regions. One scheme along these lines, Yeshasvini Cooperative Farmers Health Care Scheme in Karnataka, was launched in 2003 and covered approximately 3 million farmers against the risk of expensive surgeries. The scheme is funded partially by premiums and partially by government subsidy. Members receive medical services for listed procedures at approved public and private hospitals and nursing homes, which numbered 462 in 2010–2011.[5]

A far more ambitious scheme aimed at the poor is the Rashtriya Swasthya Bima Yojana (RSBY), launched by the Indian government on April 1, 2008. The scheme is funded in 3:1 ratio by the central and state governments and is available to households below the poverty line. Under the scheme, the government pays the premium for five members of each covered poor household and issues the family a smart card that can be used to access approved public and private hospitals. A long list of illnesses requiring hospitalization is covered up to a maximum expenditure of 30,000 rupees per year for a family of five. As of December 8, 2011, 25.6 million smart cards were in circulation across twenty-three states.[6] State governments have introduced similar schemes; these include Arogyasri in Andhra Pradesh, Vajpayee Scheme in Karnataka, and Kalainger Scheme in Tamil Nadu.

In our view, these schemes are on the right track. They target the poor, cover major illnesses, carry significant but fiscally manageable coverage, and allow private and public providers to compete for patients. They also seem scalable. The operation of several schemes rather than a single national one allows for experimentation according to local needs as well.

The eventual fiscal costs would depend on who is covered and the benefit provided. As an example, suppose we make the generous assumption that half of the population in India is poor. This implies coverage to 600 million individuals at the state's expense. Making the further generous assumption that 5 percent of the individuals require hospitalization in any year, which is higher than the current rates, insurance will have to pay for 30 million hospitalizations per year. Assuming the cost of hospitalization on average is 10,000 rupees at 2010–2011 prices, the total expense would be 300 billion rupees. With a GDP of 78,779.47 billion rupees, this represents 0.38 percent of the GDP. Assuming five members per household, it is thus possible to provide coverage of 50,000 rupees per household for less than 0.4 percent of the GDP.

The provision of *universal* health coverage by the state has been proposed by civil society groups, which have now captured not just the National Advisory Council headed by Congress President Sonia Gandhi as well as the Planning Commission. Thus, a recent report by a high-level expert group appointed by the Planning Commission (2011), consisting of relatively few economists and chaired by a medical doctor turned activist, recommends a national health package accessible to all Indian citizens free of charge by 2022.[7] It is our view that before jumping on this "right-to-health" bandwagon, the government must take a hard look at the rationale behind it and, more important, at the government's ability to provide universal coverage.

Astonishingly, the expert group report provides no satisfactory rationale for its proposals for a package equally available to all. Nor does it document how it proposes to transform the public health infrastructure from its current debilitated state to a level that would attract rather than repel patients from seeking hospitalized as well as non-hospitalized care in the rural as well as urban areas. We find ourselves largely agreeing with the scathing critique of the report by Rao (2012), who pointedly comments, "The HLEG [high-level expert group] report neither recognizes the problems, constraints and compulsions of the departments of health at the national, state and district levels, nor offers any solutions on how to deal with them" (p. 16).

Finally, insofar as universal coverage is being increasingly connected to the recognition of the associated social goal as a legal right, the government must take a cautious view of such proposals. When universal coverage is close to reality, as, for example, in elementary education (see the next chapter), its recognition as a right may be a useful instrument of solidifying access to all. But when it is a distant goal, such recognition can be costly and counterproductive.

Human Resources

India faces a critical shortage of health-related human resources including doctors, nurse practitioners, nurses, midwives, pharmacists, and other health workers. Unqualified providers currently dominate the private sector, especially in rural areas. Improvements in access to health care, growth in population, and growth in personal income can be expected to further expand the demand for these personnel. On the supply side, shortages of medical personnel in the rest of the world due to aging populations are likely to accelerate the exit of these personnel from India. Therefore, in the absence of a major push to expand the supply, India will face massive shortages of medical personnel. Unfortunately, the problem does not seem to be on the radar screen of policy makers.

The need for rapid expansion in two areas is particularly acute. First, rural medical providers (RMPs) serve much of rural India. These practitioners have picked up some rudimentary skills either as employees in hospitals or while working as assistants to doctors but lack true qualifications for the job they do. Replacing the RMPs with proper doctors with MBBS (Bachelor of Medicine, Bachelor of Surgery) degrees in a short period is an unrealistic goal even if it is desirable in the long run. Therefore, India needs to create a cadre equivalent to nurse practitioners in the United States. Even a one-year training program for the current RMPs may lead to a significant improvement in service and reduce risk to the patients.

Second, the expansion of the number of qualified MBBS doctors must begin right away. Recall that the Medical Council of India has treated medical education as its fiefdom. Its members are rumored to

Table 16.1. Medical colleges and MBBS seats with states arranged in ascending order of population per MBBS seat

State	Number of medical colleges	Number of seats	Population per seat
Karnataka	41	5625	10868
Kerala	23	2800	11924
Tamil Nadu	40	4815	14982
Andhra Pradesh	37	4850	17457
Maharashtra	41	4860	23122
Punjab	10	1145	24196
Gujarat	19	2380	25371
Haryana	5	600	42255
West Bengal	14	1850	49377
Rajasthan	10	1300	52785
Madhya Pradesh	12	1370	52991
Orissa	6	750	55930
Assam	4	526	59257
Uttar Pradesh	25	2899	68845
Bihar	10	660	157280
India	335	40335	30004

Note: Population in the last column is taken from Census 2011.
Source: Indian Medical Council, www.mciindia.org (accessed August 8, 2011)

have extracted large bribes for authorizing new medical colleges and for letting existing colleges stay open.

The result of this tight control and associated corruption has been an overall shortage of doctors with MBBS. Only politically powerful and well-connected entrepreneurs, often politicians themselves, have been successful in getting approval for the opening of medical colleges in a handful of the states, especially Karnataka and Maharashtra. Table 16.1 graphically brings out this point. Maharashtra and the four southern states currently account for 54 percent of medical colleges and 57 percent of MBBS seats in all of India. To dramatize the contrast, there is one MBBS seat per 157,280 people in Bihar, compared with one per 10,868 people in Karnataka.

India clearly needs to loosen the stranglehold of the Indian Medical Council on the expansion of medical colleges.

Oversight of the Health System

During the six decades since independence, health services in India have operated under a largely regulation-free environment. This has allowed health services to grow rapidly, with competition keeping the prices of not just everyday outpatient care but also surgical procedures relatively low. Absence of medical malpractice suits also has helped control costs. Likewise, the provision of only process and not product patents on medicines until 2005 has greatly facilitated the growth of a low-cost medicine industry.

This absence of regulation is by no means without cost. Reports of sales of fake medicines and their use by private providers as well as government-run hospitals are commonplace. RMPs and many providers in urban areas lack the required qualifications. Many hospitals and nursing homes are known to operate without a license or registration. Likewise, many diagnostic facilities exhibit poor standards.

Should India turn to regulation to combat these deficiencies? Our view is that a move toward systematic and substantial regulation at this point is premature. Once introduced, regulation in India has a way of quickly turning into a license-permit raj. Therefore, India must move cautiously in this direction. For now it may be best to go after egregious cases of malpractice and rely on informal oversight by NGOs and committees consisting of medical professionals and representatives of citizens at the village, block, district, and city levels. Regulation may be introduced gradually as medical services expand in the organized sector. But even then such regulation initially will be best left to local jurisdictions so that its design takes into account local conditions and constraints. Only after a sizeable organized sector emerges nationwide should full-fledged national-level regulation be considered.

Chapter 17

Elementary Education

B ecause higher education is critical to growth even while con-
tributing to inclusion, its discussion belongs to Track I policies
and was therefore taken up in Part II. In contrast, elementary education, though helpful in promoting and sustaining growth, is an important social objective in itself. Therefore, we consider it here as a part
of Track II reforms.

Elementary education consists of primary (grades one through five)
and middle (grades six through eight) school education. Here we first
offer a brief review of progress toward universalizing elementary education and of the effectiveness of private versus public schools. We then
follow up on the key policy issues for which the 2009 Right to Education Act provides the context.

Progress So Far

The Indian Constitution, which came into effect on January 26, 1950,
stated in one of its directive principles of state policy, "The State shall
endeavor to provide, within a period of ten years from the commencement of this Constitution, for free and compulsory education for all children until they complete the age of fourteen years." But this goal proved
to be overly ambitious in view of the country's meager financial and
physical resources, and the target date was repeatedly deferred, first to
1970 and then to 1980, 1990, and 2000.[1] It was not until the 86th Constitution (86th Amendment) Act of 2002 that education for children

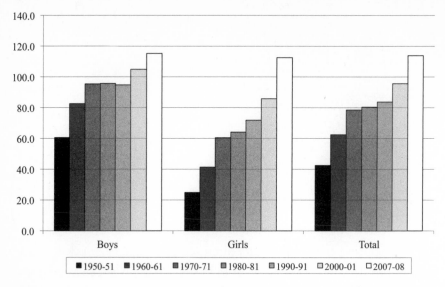

Figure 17.1. Gross enrollment ratios (grades one through five) for boys and girls

between ages six and fourteen was promoted from a directive principle of the policy to a fundamental right. Even then the lack of financial resources held up the implementing legislation.

In the end, the Right of Children to Free and Compulsory Education Act of 2009 (or Right to Education Act for short) was passed in August 2009 and brought into force on April 1, 2010. Provisions of this act have been highly controversial.

Figures 17.1 and 17.2 show the gross enrollment ratio (GER) in primary (grades one through five) and middle (grades six through eight), respectively, by decade beginning in 1950–1951 and ending in 2007–2008, the latest year for which we have data. As previously noted, the GER measures the number of students enrolled at a particular educational level as a percentage of the population in the age group normally associated with that level. Because some students enrolled at the specified level may be older or younger than the typical age group, the ratio can exceed 100.

Figure 17.1 shows the enrollment ratios in primary education for girls, boys, and boys and girls combined. It may be noted that the ratio

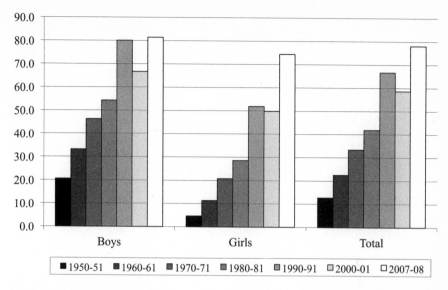

Figure 17.2. Gross enrollment ratios (grades six through eight) for boys and girls

remained below 100 for both boys and girls until 1990–1991 (fifth bar from left). Even in 2000–2001, it reached 100 only for boys and it almost certainly did not imply the inclusion of all boys in the age group six to eleven, because those enrolled included children older than eleven years and younger than six. As many as forty years after the original deadline in the Constitution, the government lacked the resources to achieve universal education even at the primary level.

Enrollment ratios in middle school consistently have been distinctly below those at the primary level and well below 100 even in 2007–2008 (Figure 17.2). Of course, this feature partially reflects the fact that many children ages eleven to fourteen are enrolled in primary school. This inference is supported by the enrollment ratios for grades one through eight combined, shown in Figure 17.3.

Progress has been made across all social groups including the Scheduled Castes and Scheduled Tribes. We show the enrollment ratios for boys and girls combined in these groups for grades one through eight as a whole in Figure 17.4. For both the Scheduled Castes and Tribes, the

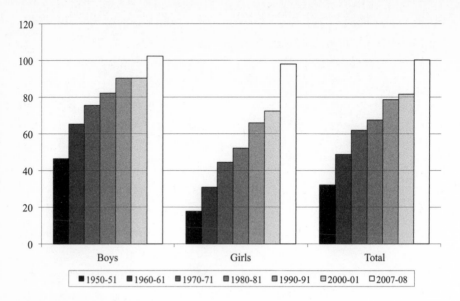

Figure 17.3. Gross enrollment ratio (grades one through eight)

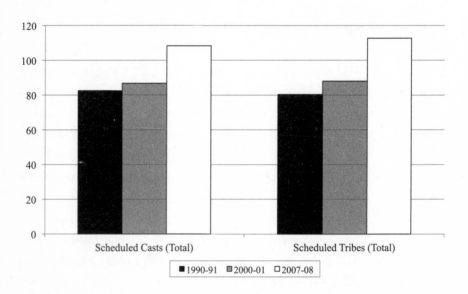

Figure 17.4. Gross enrollment ratios for Scheduled Castes and Tribes, boys and girls

Source data for Figures 17.1 to 17.4: www.educationforallinindia.com/ses.html (accessed December 12, 2011)

ratios had crossed the mark of 100 percent in 2007–2008. Thus, outcomes have improved across the board.

That most children ages six to fourteen are now in school is further corroborated by the annual surveys conducted in rural areas by the NGO Pratham. According to its latest survey, summarized in the report *Aser 2010,* the percentage of children ages six to fourteen not enrolled in school fell from 6.6 percent in 2005 to 3.5 in 2010 in rural India. The proportion of girls not enrolled fell from 11.2 to 5.9 percent over the same period.

These trends show the power of growth directly and through enhanced revenues to support social goals. Given the increasing role private schools have played in elementary education, the direct role of growth in its spread cannot be denied.[2] At the same time, the government has been able to expand public schools more rapidly, thanks to enhanced revenues. The government effort became particularly intense after the launch of the Sarva Shiksha Abhiyan (SSA; universal education movement) in November 2000. It is on the strength of this expansion in both private and public sectors that the Indian government was able to adopt free and compulsory elementary education as a fundamental right beginning on April 1, 2010.

Public Versus Private Schools

It is important to discuss the effectiveness of private schools, which have become an increasingly important part of India's elementary education landscape, in relation to that of public schools. These schools represent a wide range in terms of physical infrastructure and other resources, formal training of teachers, and tuition.

At one extreme, we have a small proportion of elite government-recognized schools, which offer excellent infrastructure, trained teachers, low student–teacher ratios, and very high tuition fees. This set of schools attracts talented students from elite families and produces outcomes superior to those of public schools. At the other extreme, we have a large number of "unrecognized" schools with relatively poor infrastructure, untrained teachers, and low tuition fees. These schools exist in both rural areas and in poor neighborhoods and slums in the cities. The number of private schools now ranges in the hundreds of thousands across India.

According to available evidence, even the low-end unrecognized schools have produced outcomes superior to those of their public counterparts operating in the same geographical area. They have done this while paying salaries to teachers that are a small fraction of public-school salaries. Compared to the latter, they are also generally poorly equipped in terms of playgrounds, classroom space, and libraries. The single most important key to their success has been the accountability of teachers. Public schoolteachers are state employees and are almost entirely immune from layoffs under any circumstances. Therefore, unless they feel morally obligated to teach their pupils, they have no incentive to carry out their assigned duties with any degree of sincerity. Teachers in private school do not enjoy such immunity and can be shown the door if they fail to deliver minimum outcomes. The result has been a far greater incidence in the public schools of teacher absenteeism and poor performance by the teachers when present in the classroom.

Muralidharan and Kremer (2006), who collected a nationally representative sample from rural India in 2003, estimate that 28 percent of the rural children in India had access to fee-charging private primary schools in the village where they lived that year. They show that children in these schools exhibited higher attendance rates and test scores than in government schools. Private school teachers were 2 to 8 percentage points less likely to be absent and 6 to 9 percentage points more likely to be teaching when present than government schoolteachers. Muralidharan and Kremer also report that private schoolteachers received salaries that were typically one-fifth and sometimes as low as one-tenth of those received by government schoolteachers.

The authors point to the head teacher's ability to discipline the teachers under him as the key reason for lower absenteeism in private schools. They note that out of 3,000 government schools they surveyed, only one head teacher had dismissed a teacher for repeated absences. In the private sector, they found thirty-five such cases in just six hundred schools surveyed.

Tooley and Dixon (undated), who undertook a census of primary and secondary schools in one of the poorest areas of Delhi, Shahdara, in

2004–2005, report very similar findings. They found a total of 275 schools in the area, of which 27 percent were government owned; 7 percent private but government aided; 38 percent private, unaided, and recognized; and 28 percent private, unaided, and unrecognized. The last two categories, accounting for 66 percent of the total number of schools, represented entirely private schools.

Tooley and Dixon state that upon unannounced visits, their researchers found 38 percent of teachers teaching in government schools, compared with 70 percent in private schools. They tested 3,500 students and found that compared to their government-school counterparts, students in unrecognized private schools scored on average 72 percent higher in mathematics, 83 percent higher in Hindi, and 246 percent higher in English. Students in the recognized private schools did even better. The private-school advantage was maintained after controlling for background variables.

Tooley and Dixon further report that the government teachers earned seven times as much as teachers in private unrecognized schools. Though class sizes were larger in the government schools, the salary per pupil in them remained two and a half times that of private unrecognized schools. Yet, surprisingly, the teachers in unaided schools reported that they were no less satisfied than their counterparts in government schools in terms of salaries, holidays, or social standing.[3]

Against this background, we may examine the current elementary education policy of the Indian government. The key features of this policy are now enshrined in the 2009 Right to Education (RTE) Act and the model rules that elaborate upon several of the provisions in the act. (We provide the salient features of the RTE Act in Appendix 3.)

Problems with the 2009 Right to Education Act

At one level, the RTE Act is quite pernicious. Potentially, it can do to elementary education what we found the 1947 Industrial Disputes Act (IDA) to have done to manufacturing: enforce standards of protection that end up hurting the very population it is intended to protect while bringing significant benefits to a lucky few. On the one hand, the IDA has provided ultrahigh protection to workers lucky enough to land a handful of the jobs in the organized sector. On the other hand, it has been destructive of organized-sector labor-intensive manufacturing and therefore well-paid manufacturing jobs. As our discussion below suggests, if implemented as provided, the RTE Act would similarly end the access of millions of poor children to decent private elementary education while giving a select few access to the country's best private schools.

The RTE Act provides that every child between six and fourteen years of age has the right to free and compulsory elementary education. The "right" is given to the child, while the burden of "compulsion" falls on the state government (or the central government in the case of the union territories) and on the local government, such as the municipal corporation in the city and *panchayat* in the village.

Given that universal elementary education is now within India's grasp, this provision is clearly welcome. Yet, the simultaneous requirement that local governments proactively pursue every child in their jurisdiction to place him or her in school is quite unrealistic.[4] For one thing, state and local governments in India lack the capacity to enforce such a requirement. And besides, given the high levels of poverty, there are bound to be cases, especially in rural areas and among the tribes, in which families are so poor that they need children to work to help them get two square meals a day.

The RTE Act further requires all unaided private schools to reserve 25 percent of the seats in grade one for children from weaker sections and disadvantaged groups in the neighborhood. Under the act, the government must reimburse the school at the per student rate that it spends in public schools.

It should be obvious that this provision does not advance in any way the right to education since it crowds out one-for-one the students from other sections of the society in favor of the students admitted from weaker and socially disadvantaged families. Therefore, it is purely a redistribution measure that gives the children from weak and disadvantaged families access to high-quality private schools. While this is a worthy objective, its promotion as a right-to-education measure misleads.

There are other downsides of the provision. It essentially amounts to a cross-subsidy. Reimbursement at per student expenditure in public education will fall short of the actual expense in the high-quality private schools. This will raise the cost to fee-paying students and discourage the entry of new high-quality private schools on the margin. A more efficient instrument would be for the government to offer to cover the entire fee of the selected students, from the general budget. Alternatively, it could offer the children vouchers worth the per capita expenditure in public schools and then have them find the private school of their choice willing to admit them in return for the voucher. This would encourage rather than discourage the emergence of private schools.

The government's approach to promote equality in the manner it has chosen raises other questions. The poor and disadvantaged who are nevertheless rich or lucky enough to live in areas where quality private schools exist will gain access to such schools. But the poorest among the poor, who live in poor neighborhoods and remote villages where quality private schools do not exist, get nothing at all. Indeed, as we discuss below, another provision in the RTE Act positively hurts them. Thus, the act effectively divides the underprivileged themselves into beneficiaries and victims.

Finally, there is a real danger that implementing the provision will lead to wholesale interference in the admission process by influential politicians and bureaucrats. The government must first devise the means to identify the weak and disadvantaged families. It must then match the children from these families with the schools. Given that no admission tests are permitted under the act (see Appendix 3), there would seem to be no obvious alternative transparent mechanism for this matching other than a lottery. But one and a half years into the implementation phase, the mechanisms are far from clear.

However, the most pernicious provision of the act involves setting minimum norms and standards for all schools. These take the form not of outcomes, such as achievements of children in reading, writing, and problem-solving, but instead physical amenities in the school. They include a student–teacher ratio of thirty for primary and thirty-five for middle-level education; an all-weather building with one classroom per teacher, a kitchen for midday meals, and a playground; a well-equipped library; games and sports equipment; and more. All schools are required to achieve these norms by March 31, 2013.

At the fee they charge, the vast majority of the low-end unrecognized schools will not be able to meet these norms and standards.[5] At the same time, the poor families they serve cannot pay significantly higher fees. Therefore, if this provision is implemented, the impact will almost surely be a closure of many of these schools. Alternatively, it will create a large-scale inspector raj in elementary education whereby government inspectors will falsely certify that the school meets the prescribed norms and standards in exchange for an appropriate bribe.

If the first of these outcomes is what is realized, it is doubtful that the government will be able to provide the displaced children seats in schools that meet the prescribed norms and standards and have the qualified teachers as stipulated in the RTE Act. Indeed, there is a good chance that rather than bring more children into the fold of elementary education, the RTE Act will wind up forcing some of the children currently enrolled in low-end private schools out of the education system altogether.

Several other provisions of the RTE Act and model rules are problematic as well. According to the latter, scales of pay and allowances, medical facilities, pension, gratuity, provident fund, and other prescribed benefits of teachers are to be those applicable to regular teachers. Once again, the vast majority of unrecognized schools will go bust if they have to pay these salaries since the children they serve come from poor families.

Ironically, while guaranteeing teachers in all schools much higher salaries and benefits than most private schools currently can afford, the RTE Act stops well short of providing effective measures to force the teachers to perform their duties. It simply prescribes "disciplinary action under the service rules applicable" to the teacher for failure to perform his or her duties. Such disciplinary actions have done precious little to discourage teachers from shirking their duties in the past and surely won't do so in the future.

The RTE Act stipulates that no child can be required to pass any board examination until completing the elementary examination with automatic promotion to the next grade guaranteed. At one level, this measure is intended to bring down the dropout rate, but the other side of the coin is that it can potentially kill the value of education altogether. In a system that grants diplomas without passing a single board examination and everyone has the diploma in view of the compulsory education, its value to a potential employer is hard to assess. Absent examinations, it will also become nearly impossible to measure the progress in improving the quality of education over time.

Finally, the RTE Act also prohibits schools from subjecting either the child or the parent to any kind of screening procedure for admission purposes. While there is some merit in this provision, especially the prohibition on the screening of parents, it is not clear how else schools would make their admission decisions. Once testing of children is outlawed, the scope for arbitrariness in admissions is likely to rise unless the government forces schools to do admissions by random assignments among applicants. That is, however, an unlikely prospect.

India: Past and Future

While our analysis has continually related Indian experience on growth and its impact on poverty to other developing countries, we now return to Indian policy performance and prospects. Recall that by the 1980s, Indian economic performance was widely seen to be abysmal. India's per capita income had grown by a paltry 1.5 percent annually; the country therefore also failed to attack poverty and the (mis)fortunes of the underprivileged. The economic dimension of Prime Minister Jawaharlal Nehru's tryst with destiny remained elusive.

The counterproductive policy framework, most visible in the license-and-permit raj, had made India a laughingstock around the world. Could anyone take seriously a country that would not let companies expand license capacity and would prevent diversification of production? These are only two of the many irrational restrictions that undermined initiatives as if India had suddenly turned into the Soviet Union. These astonishingly foolish policies, and the abysmal growth rate that they entailed, were crying out to be changed, so that India would finally begin to fulfill Nehru's dream of his country's economic destiny.

Having been converted to the view that India could not go on the way it had, Prime Minister Narasimha Rao enlisted Dr. Manmohan Singh (the current prime minister) as his finance minister. Together this team quickly dismantled investment and import licensing, and opened the economy from virtual autarky to significant openness to direct foreign investment. Other reforms followed shortly. Tariff barriers were slashed; direct and indirect taxes were streamlined; private entry into airlines and telecommunications was permitted; private domestic and foreign entry into banking and finance was increased; and the reservation of a large number of products for exclusive manufacture by small enterprises was largely abolished. These were real, not symbolic, actions with a huge impact.[1]

Growth accelerated and poverty began to fall significantly. And as we have demonstrated (Myth 3.3), the fortunes of the Scheduled Castes and Scheduled Tribes also registered improvement. Increased prosperity went hand in hand, pretty much as it had been hypothesized when the Plans began in India over half a century ago, with the goals of reducing poverty and uplifting the underprivileged. Even on the inequality front, to which the freewheeling critics shifted in retreat, the evidence is mixed, to say the least. Rather than join the bandwagon against reforms, the question now is: How does India broaden and intensify them so that it may improve upon even growth-centric Track I reforms, thereby getting yet better results on all dimensions?

In fact, the increased revenues that have followed the Track I reforms have meant that India can now genuinely expand social spending to finally begin what we have called Track II reforms in earnest. These reforms take the shape of health care, education, and transfers of income directly or via employment in public works. Indian reforms are now Track I reforms, which as our analysis in Part II showed require further changes to induce greater growth and still greater impact on poverty, as well as Track II reforms, which we have analyzed in depth in Part III. We are confident that if the government implements the reforms we have outlined in Parts II and III, we can be optimistic about India's medium- and long-term prospects.

Misplaced Pessimism

Before we consider the medium-and long-term prospects, however, we must address the current pessimism that afflicts the vast majority of commentators on the future course of the Indian economy. Some of this pessimism reflects worries about the short-term consequences of the post-2008 crisis. But the fact is that virtually every economy, certainly China, Japan, the European Union, and even the United States, has suffered from the crisis. India is not leading the crisis-impacted decline and has indeed gone on to recover faster than most other countries.

Pessimism has also gripped many observers of India in the wake of the approximately 2 percentage-point decline in the growth rate in the financial year 2011–2012, two years after the country had fully recovered from the financial crisis. Many commentators have expressed the view that we are now witnessing the beginning of the end of the Indian growth story. But these commentators greatly overstate their case.

What we have witnessed is a short-term decline originating in two transitory factors: thirteen consecutive hikes in the interest rates by the Reserve Bank of India (RBI), the country's central bank, and policy paralysis in the central government. The interest rate hikes originated in persistent inflation while policy paralysis resulted from every central ministry freezing up prudentially in response to an outbreak of massive corruption scandals.

Both factors have already begun to go into remission. The RBI has begun to ease up, allowing the interest rate to decline. Moreover, the paralysis has yielded to yet more reforms. As Panagariya (2012b) details, Prime Minister Singh has seized the initiative from the Congress Party leadership to reclaim his legacy as a reformer and announced a series of liberalizing steps, including opening multibrand retail to direct foreign investment (DFI) up to 51 percent and substantially reducing the diesel subsidy. He has also opened civil aviation to DFI up to 49 percent and raised the DFI cap in broadcasting from 49 percent to 74 percent. The prime minister has even announced his decision to introduce cash subsidies, as advocated in this book and in Panagariya (2008a, 2012c).

Indeed, pessimists who base their fears on the reforms' having come to a standstill misread both history and current developments. The reforms had come to a standstill as far back as May 2004, when the United Progress Alliance first came to power. But the decline in the growth rate is quite recent. Besides, even prior to the announcements of the measures just noted, we had begun to see slight progress in the reforms. Reversing its 2004 decision, the government recently deregulated gasoline prices, a much-awaited measure to improve efficiency as well as to contain the fiscal deficit. In a similar vein, it had successfully abolished the

51 percent FDI cap on single-brand retail, leading the Swedish retail furniture giant IKEA to announce plans to invest nearly $2 billion in India.

Some commentators argue that coalition politics in India has led to paralysis. But this argument is not borne out by evidence. Whereas Prime Minister Rajiv Gandhi could implement only small reforms despite a three-fourths majority in the Lower House of the Parliament during the second half of the 1980s, Prime Minister Narasimha Rao under a minority government and Prime Minister Vajpayee under a coalition government were able to introduce far-reaching reforms during the 1990s and early 2000s. Besides, with the emerging consensus on the importance of growth as the essential stepping-stone to combating poverty and advancing other social agendas, the road to reform is likely to be smoother instead of rougher.

Optimism in the Medium and Long Run

Therefore, we are not shaken in our optimism for India's prospects for the medium and long term. Perhaps we are biased in our optimism: we were economic theorists and later turned to policy analysis that would help transform India and the world. If we were pessimists, this shift would be irrational: Unless we expected that we could change the world, why turn to policy analysis? But bias aside, we can provide objective reasons why we believe that good days lie ahead for India.

Public Opinion

1. There is little doubt that Indian reforms are irreversible and can only go forward. A large number of young Indians are conscious of the benefits that reforms have brought to them and to the country. There is no politically important constituency that can thrive on anti-reform rhetoric in the years to come. It is telling that so many political parties tried to organize protests against the September 2012 package of reforms that included the opening of multibrand retail to foreign investment and cut the diesel subsidy but failed to mobilize public support.

2. Many have also noticed that the anticorruption mass movement, led by activist Anna Hazare and several social activists, is far bigger than the Occupy Wall Street demonstrations. But what sets it apart is that it is against corruption, *not* against reforms. In fact, more reforms (extended to new areas, such as mining rights) rather than less are what the demonstrators have called for.

3. Besides, as we have argued at length when dissecting the numerous anti-reform myths that the critics repeat ad nauseam, the critiques rarely go beyond assertions, and increasingly, the refutation that we and others provide are being read and the old anti-reformers are now losing the iconic status that in the past was accorded readily to our prominent intellectuals.

Objective Arguments

But if public opinion will not sabotage the reform process, what do "objective" factors tell us about India's growth prospects? Here, too, three fundamental facts work to India's advantage.

1. Growth depends on two underlying factors: savings (or investment) and the productivity of the investment. The Soviet Union had phenomenal savings rates but little productivity, so it went steadily downhill despite its "blood, sweat, and tears." The East Asian economies had phenomenal savings rates but also high productivity, so they grew at "miraculous" rates. Fortunately, India's savings rate has steadily risen. It is already 32 percent to 33 percent of GDP and is expected to rise further.

2. As for productivity, India has profited, and will continue to profit, from two factors. First, India has steadily opened up to the world economy. There is ample evidence that openness pays dividends. The second factor is India's diaspora, which brings dividends through a variety of channels. Working in senior positions in numerous large companies in the United States, the diaspora bring these companies to the shores of India, linking the country to the latest technologies. There are also synergies

between Bangalore and Silicon Valley. Indian entrepreneurs are also a source of vast remittances that now amount to more than $50 billion annually. The presence of the highly professional and successful diaspora in the developed world has also promoted a friendly image of India, translating, for example, in the Indo–US nuclear cooperation deal. Finally, with their analysis and advocacy, the diaspora have kept pressure in favor of continued reforms.

4. Ironically, the recent slowdown in the economy has suddenly refocused the attention of one and all on growth. From the times when 5.5 percent growth was viewed as an impressive achievement, India has arrived to the point where the drop to this rate in the first two quarters of 2012 was seen as a disaster. Even many traditional skeptics who argue that higher growth does not help the poor have begun to complain that the declining growth is hurting them. In turn, Prime Minister Singh has been able to successfully use the occasion to convince Congress President Sonia Gandhi that there is no alternative to Track I reforms for the revival of growth, which alone can yield the steadily rising stream of revenues necessary to finance the Track II reforms that have been her sole focus in recent years. The return of Track I reforms is, of course, a major source of optimism for us.

India–China Comparisons

Finally, how will Indian growth fare compared to China's? Amartya Sen thinks this is a "stupid" question.[2] We reject this view. China's huge growth rate has produced for China dividends in international politics. It gives China an advantage over India in influencing economic outcomes in its favor. So, where does India stand vis-à-vis China?[3]

1. China has been rapidly increasing its defense spending. It is trying to match its "hard power" to the "soft power" that its phe-

nomenal growth rates have earned it. But this has gone with its increasingly aggressive behavior in the East China Sea, in the South China Sea, and in its activities in the regions surrounding India. India is thus constrained to react by spending more on its defenses. Which country will be damaged more by this developing rivalry and defense spending remains to be seen.

2. China has been growing very fast, so its demand for labor in Guangdong and nearby provinces on the east coast has been rising rapidly as well. But its labor supply is not rising anywhere as fast because of its one-child policy and the restraints on rural migration to the urban areas including export processing zones. So, wages have been rising, with China transitioning from a Marxian reserve army of labor available at a constant real wage to a situation of rising wages with growth. This slows down growth as well. By contrast, India is behind the curve and its demographics imply that it will have an ample supply of young labor, which can place India on the growth trajectory of the earlier China with abundant labor.

3. China's authoritarian regime, compared to India's democracy, leads to two important consequences that militate in India's favor. First, China is fearful of *samizdat*:[4] it cannot afford to have software develop to a point where the people can communicate freely and even dare to undermine political control. The result is that the PC (the personal computer, and all that it implies today) is incompatible with the CP (the Communist Party). But much technical progress comes through software developments. So, India, which is a freewheeling democracy like the United States, has an enormous advantage over China.

4. The other implication of China's authoritarianism is that as the bourgeoisie develops and seeks political rights, China faces a real dilemma. Will the country respond to these demands in the fashion of the suppression at Tiananmen Square, or will the authorities be accommodating? In the former case, China will surely implode at some stage. The Chinese future therefore has

a big question mark on it. By contrast, India will continue to move along, albeit at a slightly less hectic pace, with its "agitation and response" model, whereby grievances are aired and government responds. Slower but surer. And after all, democracy must be judged not just instrumentally, in terms of its economic consequences, but also as an end in itself.

Acknowledgments

In the course of finalizing this book, we benefited greatly from the comments by several panelists and participants at a prepublication discussion of the book that the National Council on Applied Economic Research (NCAER) and the Columbia Program on Indian Economic Policies jointly organized at the India International Centre in New Delhi on January 5, 2012. Our thanks go to Rajesh Chadha, Senior NCAER Fellow, who organized that event and oversaw its efficient execution.

The event brought together two panels, one consisting of intellectuals from various fields and the other composed of a group of leading journalists from Indian and Western newspapers. The comments and critiques we received at this meeting have resulted in many revisions.

In particular, we are grateful to Bibek Debroy (professor, Centre for Policy Research), Jay Panda (member, Lok Sabha), Manish Sabharwal (CEO, TeamLease), and Shekhar Shah (director general, NCAER), who spoke on the first panel, and Vikas Bajaj (*New York Times*), Sunil Jain (*Financial Express*), James Lamont (*Financial Times*), and T. N Ninan (*Business Standard*), who served on the second panel. Bina Agarwal (Institute of Economic Growth), Bornali Bhandari (NCAER), Rajesh Chadha (NCAER), Shashanka Bhide (NCAER), Rana Hasan (Asian Development Bank), Vijay Joshi (Oxford University), and Deepak Mishra (World Bank) offered additional comments from the floor.

The eminent historian Ramachandra Guha read all the chapters in Part I and provided detailed comments that have led to many improvements in the final draft. We also received positive feedback from Ashoka Mody of the International Monetary Fund and Swagato Ganguly of the *Times of India,* who read parts of the book.

A rather generous input came from a young scholar, Manish Kumar from Bihar. He researched virtually all publicly available volumes of speeches by Prime Ministers Jawaharlal Nehru, Indira Gandhi, P. V. Narasimha Rao, Atal Bihari Vajapyee, and Manmohan Singh and provided us literally dozens of pages' worth of quotations to choose from. We are deeply indebted to him.

Zeenat Nazir, Shivam Srivastava, and May Yang provided excellent research assistance at various stages of the work.

The book generously draws on the scientific research undertaken by a number of leading scholars of the Indian economy as a part of the Program on Indian Economic Policies under the joint auspices of the School of International and Public Affairs (SIPA) and the Institute for Social and Economic Research and Policy (ISERP) at Columbia University. The program has been funded by a substantial grant from the Templeton Foundation. While the views expressed in the book are solely ours, we take this opportunity to thank the Templeton Foundation for funding the program and the ISERP staff, especially Michael Falco, Michael Higgins, Shelley Klein, Carmen Morillo, Andrew Ratanatharthorn, and Kristen Van Leuven, for their excellent logistical support.

Most of all, we acknowledge the splendid support that the Council on Foreign Relations provided to one of us (Bhagwati) for the research of this book. CFR President Richard N. Hass, Director of Studies James M. Lindsay, and Director of Maurice R. Greenberg Center for Economic Studies Sebastian Mallaby provided insightful comments on our manuscript, while Amy Baker and Patricia Dorff assisted with publication formalities.

Socialism Under Nehru

Now, it is well known, and we have often stressed this, that production is perhaps one of the most important things before us today: that is, adding to the wealth of the country. We cannot overlook other things. Nevertheless, production comes first, and I am prepared to say that everything that we do should be judged from the point of view of production first of all. If nationalization adds to production, we shall have nationalization at every step. If it does not, let us see how to bring it about in order not to impede production. That is the essential thing.

—**Prime Minister Jawaharlal Nehru in Constituent Assembly** (**Legislative**), **February 17, 1948**

Nehru was a pragmatist first and a socialist second. The policy framework that emerged under him resulted principally from the objective of self-sufficiency. In Nehru's conception, the pursuit of self-sufficiency meant progressive reduction in the dependence on the external markets for either the sales of Indian goods abroad or the purchase of foreign goods to satisfy domestic needs.[1] India having just emerged from the colonial rule, this seemed an eminently reasonable objective.

Yet, what is reasonable is not necessarily rational. Self-sufficiency became an argument for import substitution and policies (such as protection) directed at promoting it.[2] It meant the recalibration of the production basket to domestic needs. If India needed bicycles, it must produce bicycles as well as the steel going into them. If it needed fertilizer, it must produce fertilizer and the chemicals going into them. And, of course, it must also produce the machines necessary to produce the bicycles, steel, fertilizers, and chemicals.

There being general agreement at the time that the private sector lacked resources to invest in the heavy-industry sectors consisting of such items as steel and machinery, it was also decided that the public sector would enter them in a major way.[3]

But reinforcing this argument for the public sector's expansion was Nehru's political belief in the desirability of progressive expansion of the public sector. In this regard he was a Fabian socialist who did not favor "painful" nationalization but relied instead on a progressive and "painless" shift in investment over time to yield a larger share of the public sector in production in the economy. It was a policy of painless, "asymptotic" achievement of an economy dominated by public ownership of the means of production.

The last argument explains why the public sector was viewed not just as *substituting* for the private sector that could not undertake expansion in the favored import-substituting sectors. In fact, the goal of expanding the public sector relative to the private sector progressively over time also led to the policy of *reserving* certain sectors exclusively for the public sector. In turn, that meant that government monopolies were created, which had unfortunate consequences for efficiency since eliminating domestic competition would be joined later by eliminating import competition as well.

In addition, one can detect some concern, starting in Nehru's administration, that the planners had to direct investment selectively to sectors—that there were social payoffs in some sectors and not in others. This meant that sectoral quantities in the planning exercises were increasingly taken as not just indicative but as firm targets, to be implemented by a licensing system that would restrain investment in the less-favored sectors.[4] Therefore, investment licensing for large firms was adopted to allocate private investments according to the national priorities.

On the external front, the policy regime during the 1950s was remarkably open. Tariffs were low, and though import licensing had been inherited from the Second World War–era controls, licenses were leisurely issued. Consumer goods imports were allowed and the importer did not have to be the actual user.[5] On the foreign investment front,

Nehru fought off the domestic private industry, leftist parties, and radical socialists within the Congress to maintain and promote a liberal
regime. He refused to nationalize the foreign firms and accorded them
national status. He also permitted the repatriation of profits and dividends of foreign companies abroad. As late as the early 1960s, the
government actively sought foreign investment in heavy electrical equipment, fertilizer, and synthetic rubber, sectors in which the public sector
had been active.

Investment licensing also remained relatively liberal with the decisions on the applications made without undue delay in the 1950s. This
is partially evidenced by the near-absence of complaints by private entrepreneurs and also the rapid expansion of the private sector. The share
of the public sector in the total investment in the First Five-Year Plan
was 46 percent. The Second Plan set the explicit goal of raising this share
to 61 percent. But because private-sector investment greatly exceeded
its projected level, the plan fell well short (54 percent) of the target in
proportionate terms even while substantially achieving it in absolute
terms. The Third Plan sought to push the share to 64 percent but once
again fell short at approximately 50 percent.

The key factor behind tightening the import and investment licensing regimes was not ideological, but the balance of payments crisis in
1957–1958. That crisis led the finance ministry to introduce foreign-
exchange budgeting beginning in the second half of 1958. This required
estimating the expected availability of foreign exchange in each forthcoming six-month period and then allocating it across various uses.
Hereon, each investment-license application had to provide sufficient
technical details to allow the evaluation of the foreign-exchange burden
it would impose for machinery and raw material imports. The license
was issued only if the product it sought to produce was judged to be
sufficiently important to justify the allocation of the needed foreign
exchange.

While the grip of the license-permit raj became significantly tighter
during the first half of the 1960s, radical socialists within the Congress
and outside had at best limited salience while Nehru lived. Indeed, toward the end of his administration, several right-of-center politicians

gained influence in the Congress organization while hard-core socialists, such as Krishna Menon and K. D. Malviya, were forced out of the union cabinet.

The "second phase" of socialism under Indira Gandhi, the "accidental" prime minister, was unfortunately far less pragmatic, as we note in the text: it changed the course of Indian policy until the reforms began in earnest in 1991.

Appendix 2

Measuring Inequality:
The Gini Coefficient

The Gini coefficient is the most common measure of the distribution of expenditure, income, wealth or another attribute within a given population. Since it is common to speak in terms of income distribution among households within a population, we explain the measure in terms of inequality of income across households. The value of Gini varies between 0 and 1, with 0 representing a situation of perfect equality, such that income is identical across all households, and 1 representing a situation of extreme inequality whereby all income is concentrated in a single household. Between 0 and 1, higher values of the Gini are associated with higher levels of inequality.

The logic behind the Gini and its limitations can be explained with the help of the Lorenz curve (explained below), shown in Figure A2.1. On the horizontal axis, we arrange the households in the rising order of their incomes. Therefore, the household with the lowest income is the nearest to the origin and the one with the highest income is the farthest. We "normalize" the total number of households to 100. On the vertical axis, we measure the cumulative incomes of households as percent of the total income of the population. The curve representing the cumulative percentage incomes of households, depicted by OAO' in Figure A2.1, is called the Lorenz curve. A point on the Lorenz curve represents the percentage of the total income by households up to that point. The Lorenz curve originates at the origin since 0 percent of the households account for 0 percent of the population income. Likewise, the curve terminates at a point showing the values of 100 on both horizontal and

| 215 |

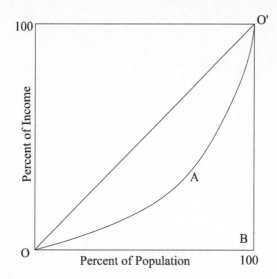

Figure A2.1. The Lorenz curve

vertical axes since 100 percent of the households must account for 100 percent of the population income.

The Gini coefficient equals the area between the diagonal OO' and the Lorenz curve divided by the triangle OBO'. It is immediately obvious that if the Lorenz curve coincides with the diagonal OO', the Gini coefficient becomes 0 since the area between the diagonal and the Lorenz curve is zero in this case. Alternatively, if the Lorenz curve coincides with triangle OBO', the Gini coefficient becomes 1. In this case, the area between the Lorenz curve and the diagonal is triangle OBO' and its ratio to triangle OBO' is 1. In all other cases, the value of the Gini coefficient is strictly between 0 and 1.

In the first of the above extreme cases in which the Lorenz curve coincides with the diagonal, the income is identical across all households. Identical distribution implies that the bottom 10 percent of the households account for 10 percent of the total income, the bottom 20 percent for 20 percent of the income, and so on. These points are of course on the diagonal. In the second extreme case in which the Lorenz curve coincides with triangle OBO', the distribution is the most unequal it can be. The most unequal distribution implies that all income is concentrated in one household. This means that all households ex-

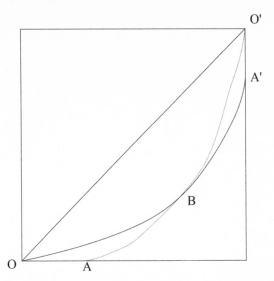

Figure A2.2. Two Lorenz curves with the same value of the Gini coefficient

cept one have zero income so that the Lorenz curve coincides with the horizontal axis except when we get to the last household, at which point the curve coincides with the vertical axis. The Lorenz curve is thus represented by triangle OBO'. The lower the share of the households at the bottom, the closer is the Lorenz curve to the horizontal axis at the bottom. Likewise, the larger the share of the households at the top, the closer is the Lorenz curve to the vertical axis at the top. Both these factors pull the Lorenz curve away from the diagonal. Therefore, the more unequal the distribution, the farther the Lorenz curve is from the diagonal and therefore the closer is the value of the Gini coefficient to 1.

Finally, observe that any given value of the Gini coefficient is consistent with infinitely many shapes of the Lorenz curve, so that the frequent references to Gini coefficients across time or regions as measures of inequality must be handled with care. Figure A2.2 illustrates this point. Here we draw two Lorenz curves, OBA'O' as a solid line and OABO' as a dotted line. Because the area between the Lorenz curve and the diagonal is the same in the two cases, the value of the Gini coefficient associated with them is the same. Yet the two Lorenz curves represent very different distributions of income. The dotted curve shows a large proportion of the bottom households as having no income and hence is associated with a significant volume of abject poverty. The solid line exhibits less poverty at the bottom but is characterized with a high degree of concentration at the top. Most observers would find the distribution represented by the solid line far more acceptable than that represented by the dotted line, though both are associated with the same value of the Gini coefficient.

Key Provisions of the Right to Education Act, 2009

- All children older than six years and younger than fourteen years have the legal right to free education.
- The state government and the central government in a union territory in combination with the local authority (municipal corporation, municipal council, *zila parishad, nagar panchayat,* or *panchayat,* as the case may be) have the obligation to provide every child between six and fourteen years of age elementary education meeting *specified norms and standards* by April 1, 2013.
- Specified norms and standards that schools must meet include
  - » Student–teacher ratios of thirty at primary and thirty-five at middle level (to be enforced by the local authority beginning October 1, 2010)
  - » Provision of all-weather building consisting of one classroom per teacher, kitchen where midday meals can be cooked, separate toilets for boys and girls, and a playground
  - » Library with newspapers, magazines, and books on all subjects
  - » Availability of games and sports equipment
  - » 800 instructional hours per academic year at primary and 1,000 hours at the middle level
- Duties of the local authority include
  - » Ensuring the availability of a neighborhood school by March 31, 2013

> » Maintaining records of children up to the age of fourteen years residing within its jurisdiction
> » Ensuring and monitoring admission, attendance, and completion of elementary education by every child residing within its jurisdiction
> » Ensuring admission of children of migrant families

- Every school must achieve the specified norms and standards by March 31, 2013, failing which it will be shut down.
- No new schools should be established without recognition certificate from the authority appointed by the state or central government and every unrecognized school must get recognition within the time stipulated from this authority.
- No child or parent can be subject to any kind of screening procedure for purposes of admission.
- No child can be held back, expelled, and required to pass the board examination until the completion of elementary education.
- No donation or capitation fee at the time of admission is permitted.
- Private schools will have to take 25 percent of their class in grade one from the weaker section and the disadvantaged group of the society and provide free compulsory education until the completion of elementary education. Government will fund education of these children at the rate of per child expenditure in public schools.
- Every teacher is required to attain minimum qualification specified by a centrally appointed authority by March 31, 2015.
- The state government or local authority will set the terms and conditions of service and salary and allowances of teachers.
- No teacher is to engage in private tuition or private teaching activity.
- A teacher will be duty-bound to
  - » Maintain regularity and punctuality in attending school
  - » Complete entire curriculum within the specified time
  - » Assess the learning ability of each child and accordingly, supplement additional instructions as required

» Hold regular meetings with parents and guardians and apprise them about attendance, ability to learn, progress made in learning, and any other relevant information about the child

» A teacher in default of duties is liable to disciplinary action under the service rules applicable to him or her

Prime Ministers of India

Prime Minister	Dates	Party	Coalition
Jawaharlal Nehru	August 15, 1947–May 27, 1964	Indian National Congress	
Gulzari Lal Nanda (Interim)	May 27, 1964–June 9, 1964	Indian National Congress	
Lal Bahadur Shastri	June 9, 1964–January 11, 1966	Indian National Congress	
Gulzari Lal Nanda (Interim)	January 11, 1966–January 24, 1966	Indian National Congress	
Indira Gandhi	January 24, 1966–March 24, 1977	Indian National Congress	
Morarji Desai	March 24, 197–July 28, 1979	Indian National Congress (O)	Janata Party (minority)
Choudhary Charan Singh	July 28, 1979–January 14, 1980	Bharatiya Lok Dal	Janata Party (minority)
Indira Gandhi	January 14, 1980–October 31, 1984	Indian National Congress (I)	
Rajiv Gandhi	October 31, 1984–December 2, 1989	Indian National Congress (I)	
Vishwanath Pratap Singh	December 2, 1989–November 10, 1990	Janata Dal	National Front (minority)

(continues)

(continued)

Prime Minister	Dates	Party	Coalition
Chandra Shekhar	November 10, 1990–June 21, 1991	Samajwadi Janata Party (minority)	
P. V. Narasimha Rao	June 21, 1991–May 16, 1996	Indian National Congress (I) (minority)	
Atal Behari Vajpayee	May 16, 1996–June 1, 1996	Bharatiya Janata Party (minority)	
H. D. Deve Gowda	June 1, 1996–April 21, 1997	Janata Dal	United Front (minority)
Inder Kumar Gujral	April 21, 1997–March 19, 1998	Janata Dal	United Front (minority)
Atal Bihari Vajpayee	March 19, 1998–May 22, 2004	Bharatiya Janata Party	National Democratic Alliance
Dr. Manmohan Singh	May 22, 2004–present	Indian National Congress	United Progressive Alliance (minority)

Notes

Preface

1. In the end, it turned out that *private* savings would also rise as opportunities increased for profitable investment, as demonstrated in the East Asian experience we touch upon below. This undercuts arguments based entirely on the ability to tax to raise *public* savings.

2. Nearly all developmental economists in the West in the 1950s and early 1960s were rooting for India's success: these included the pioneers of development economics, such as Paul Rosenstein-Rodan. Their "love affair" with India was manifest in their writings and their willingness to work in India through programs that brought in many Western economists, the most prominent example being MIT's program, which brought MIT economists Richard Eckaus and Louis Lefeber, and Ian Little (Oxford), Brian Reddaway (Cambridge), and Trevor Swan (Australian National University) to work in New Delhi. Others included George Rosen and Wilfred Malenbaum.

3. Thus, China's autarky was a result of Marxist aversion to integration into the world economy, as was the case also with the Soviet Union. In India's case, autarky reflected erroneous economic doctrines rather than ideological politics.

4. There has been discussion whether the foreign aid inflow adversely affected domestic savings effort. But extensive analysis by Bhagwati and Srinivasan (1975) concludes otherwise.

5. See Bhagwati, "The Miracle That Did Happen: Understanding East Asia in Comparative Perspective," 1996; reprinted in Bhagwati

(1999). The stark contrast in the productivity-of-investment of the Soviet Union and of East Asia, which we note in the text, is what made many observers critical of Paul Krugman's argument that East Asia would go the way of the Soviet Union because capital accumulation would lead to diminishing returns in East Asia. In the end, what caused East Asia to collapse, not gradually as the Krugman argument would imply but sharply and dramatically, was huge capital inflows after premature and ill-advised freeing of capital flows and the subsequent outflow of capital.

6. Panagariya (2008, Chapters 2–4) provides extensive documentation of regulatory policies during the first three decades of Indian development.

7. This meant that a manufacturer licensed to produce 100,000 cars was forbidden from using a part of his authorized production capacity to produce trucks.

8. Of course, in economic theory, economists can demonstrate that market losses are compatible with social gains. But while some Indian economists, such as Amartya Sen in the early 1980s, argued this way, the losses in the public-sector enterprises simply reflected inefficient production resulting from the monopoly positions they enjoyed, and the political overstaffing that they were typically subjected to. This unpleasant reality was captured well by John Kenneth Galbraith, who had been ambassador to India under President John Kennedy, when he described the situation as one of "post office socialism."

9. Many empirical studies underlie the positive relationship between growth and openness, using postwar data for a much wider range of developing and developed countries. See, in particular, Panagariya (2004). Admittedly this study only establishes correlations, leaving open the issue as to whether trade explains growth or the other way around. But it does establish that policies that bottle up trade will also bottle up growth. Moreover, other studies, most notably Frankel and Rose (2002), establish causation running from trade to per capita incomes.

10. Panagariya (2008, Chapter 6) compares the experiences of India and South Korea in the 1960s and 1970s, arguing that trade openness was crucial to the latter's success while autarkic trade policies proved fatal to the efficiency of investments and therefore growth in the former.

11. Panagariya (2011c) has recently revisited the Taiwanese miracle of the 1960s and 1970s, countering each of the many critiques of authors such as Rodrik (1995) and Wade (1990) and showing that trade openness complemented by a set of market-friendly domestic policies along the lines described in the text above was central to it.

12. See Chapter 6.

13. The phrase appears to have been coined by a former journalist, Joshua Cooper Ramos, writing in 2004 at the Foreign Policy Center in England.

14. For other economic reasons that China's growth rate should slow down as labor becomes scarce, see also Bhagwati (2011a).

15. The East Asian and Indian experiences diverge on freedom of capital flows. East Asia crashed by freeing capital flows; India was saved by prudence in that regard. That India was right in its prudence, as was China, is generally conceded now. The IMF's embrace of capital account convertibility, which led it to denounce Bhagwati (1998) for his noting the asymmetry between the case for free trade and for free capital flows that he argued for in a much-cited essay in *Foreign Affairs,* has now been renounced. See Bhagwati's posting on the *World Affairs Journal* blog, March 9, 2011; this has been revised and posted on his Columbia University website as "IMF Does *Mea Culpa* After All," April 15, 2011 (www.columbia.edu/~jb38).

16. See Chapter 3.

17. See Bhagwati (1988).

18. Obviously this is not the problem in a few countries, such as Saudi Arabia in the Middle East, which have money coming out of their ears. But Allah often afflicts them with a different problem: the "resource curse."

19. See Chapter 8.

Introduction: The Tryst

1. Winston Churchill was among the orators whose speeches were his own handiwork; as Lord Birkenhead remarked, "Winston has spent the best years of his life writing impromptu speeches." By contrast, John F. Kennedy flew to great heights on wings supplied by Ted Sorenson.

2. It is interesting, for example, that President Barack Obama is notorious for the use of the teleprompter even though he won the White House with stirring speeches. This also means that he mispronounces names wherever he goes, obviously because his speechwriters do not take care to rehearse the names included in the speeches. He did this several times, including in the address he gave to the Indian Parliament, leading the Members of Parliament to warn Bhagwati, who addressed the Parliament a few weeks later, to avoid reading a speech and to speak extempore and from the heart, with wit and humor. Obama was mispronouncing names during his visit to Japan as well. One can only dread the prospect of his battling with the tonalities of Chinese names!

3. Italics added. That electoral democracy without institutions such as an independent judiciary and a free press would be hollow was not a thought that would have been foreign to Nehru's *Weltanschauung*.

4. We have written extensively on the subject elsewhere. See, in particular, Bhagwati (2011), Panagariya (2011e, 2011g), and Gupta and Panagariya (2011a, 2011b, and 2012).

Chapter 1: Indian Socialism and the Myths of Growth and Poverty

1. We provide historical details corroborating this proposition in Appendix 1.

2. See Bhagwati and Desai (1975).

3. "Socialism" under Jawaharlal Nehru is set out in greater depth in Appendix 1, while "socialism" under Indira Gandhi is discussed immediately below in the text. The former was like a medium Merlot, while the latter was a full-bodied Cabernet Sauvignon.

Chapter 2: Myths About the Early Development Strategy

1. For further details, see Chakrabarty (1992).

2. We say more on redistribution below. Our quote from the first five-year plan, however, has it right. Redistribution was not regarded as a strategy that could take us far, given the extent of the poverty. The

principal strategy had to be "growing the pie." Also, among the social objectives was not just poverty reduction, which was an overarching objective, but also, for example, prevention of concentrated economic power that, in the wrongheaded way in which it was pursued, wound up detracting gratuitously from the poverty-reduction objective.

3. Thus, when it comes to stating the party's key economic objective, the document describes it as: "Further broadening and deepening of economic reforms, based on a self-reliant approach, for sustained double-digit GDP growth rate to achieve complete eradication of poverty and unemployment" and also to end "regional and social disparities; and bridge the urban-rural divide" (from the BJP *Vision Document*; www .indian-elections.com/partymanifestoes/party-manifestoes04/bjp.html; accessed September 11, 2011).

4. As we document below, these are not cursory side remarks but get full-length treatment in the Plan documents. There are also program evaluation reports, which address the progress and the shortfalls in reaching targets in these areas. We might add that even the membership of the Planning Commission, which was quite a prestigious affair at the time, included Shrimati Durgabai Deshmukh, who was a child widow and an articulate and effective advocate for women's issues. There was also a health portfolio in the cabinet and the incumbent was another remarkable woman, Rajkumari Amrit Kaur.

5. See Nundy (2005) for further details.

6. Whether the revenues would have resulted in intended outcomes is a question that remains pertinent today. We consider this question in the recent context in Part III.

7. See Balachandran (2010) for details.

8. See Government of India (2005), p. 48.

9. We do not mean to imply that resources are a sufficient condition of improving health. They are, however, a necessary condition. How best to use the resources to get a good, if not the best, bang for the buck is an extremely important issue today. We return to this issue in depth in Part IV.

10. The underlying growth models used in the two plans were different, however. The First Five-Year Plan essentially worked with the "flow"

Harrod-Domar model, whereas the Second reflected the "structural," "putty-clay" model associated with the Soviet economist Feldman and the Indian statistician Professor Prasanta Chandra Mahalanobis.

11. Bhagwati produced two substantial papers, one on income distribution estimates for India, and one on the cross-country income distributions, when he worked for Pitambar Pant. The argument in the text was in the latter paper. Produced in the early 1960s before the advent of photocopy machines and computers, these two "cyclostyled" papers were not preserved by Bhagwati due to a lack of storage space since he lived in different temporary locations. But they may still be gathering dust on the shelves in the Planning Commission or in the Indian Statistical Institute in Calcutta.

12. Specifically, Haq (1972) wrote (as quoted in Sau, 1972, p. 1572), "It appears that within a period of less than two decades, China has eradicated the worst forms of poverty; it has full employment, universal literacy and adequate health facilities; it suffers from no obvious malnutrition or squalor. What's more, it was my impression that China has achieved this at fairly modest rates of growth." Haq's statements about standing economic theory "on its head" and the "GNP rat race" are nothing but rhetorical hand waving, of course. Economic theory has well-known models that lead even to immiserisation from growth (e.g., Bhagwati's 1958 model). It would be nice also to know which rats Haq has in mind!

13. Later, some anti-growth-strategy economists in India would shift to Kerala as their icon of development. And when "Kerala Shining" became hard to argue plausibly, this group shifted to citing Bangladesh. On this issue, we will draw below on the claims to that effect by Amartya Sen (2011) recently and refutations thereof by Panagariya (2011a, 2011b).

14. The private final consumption expenditure is estimated at 1999–2000 prices from the National Account Statistics (NAS). It consists of gross national product net of gross capital formation and current government spending. The average expenditures estimated by the National Sample Surveys are generally below the NAS expenditures.

15. Note that Myth 2.3 declares that growth is not *necessary* for alleviating poverty, whereas Myth 2.4 claims that growth is not *sufficient* to do so.

16. Maybe Haq was thinking of his native Pakistan, where the army, as we know now, was siphoning off the entire gains from aid and more than the gains from growth. But then one cannot help wondering why he went back from the US to join the cabinet under Zia's military dictatorship. In fairness to Haq, it should be added that the world divides into those, like Solzhenitsyn, who confront dictatorships and those, like Tvardovsky, who work for reforms from within. The latter edited *Novy Mir* and in fact managed to publish Solzhenitsyn's *One Day in the Life of Ivan Denisovich* in *Novy Mir* in November 1962, A fascinating account of Solzhenitsyn's subsequent assault on Tvardovsky on this issue and a spirited defense of Tvardovsky appears in Vladimir Laksin, *Solzhenitsyn, Tvardovsaky, and Novy Mir* (Cambridge, MA: MIT Press, 1980).

17. See Sau (1972) and Ranadive (1973).

18. The quotation can be found in Ranadive (1973), p. 834.

19. This additional effect through easing of the revenue constraint was precisely what Bhagwati (1988) had pointed out almost a quarter century ago in the Vikram Sarabhai Lecture, in Ahmedabad, on "Poverty and Public Policy." Evidently, if the revenues are spent instead on other purposes, this additional effect on helping the poor will not follow.

20. See the detailed evidence on South Korea in Panagariya (2008a, Chapter 6) and on Taiwan in Panagariya (2011c). The same can be argued for China, whose phenomenal growth in the Guangdong province helped increase the demand for labor dramatically, raising wages and improving labor standards.

21. See Dehejia and Panagariya (2012) for further elaboration on this point.

22. Mukim and Panagariya (2012) provide systematic charts relating per capita incomes to poverty levels.

23. Establishing causation that is beyond objection by econometricians on a relationship that does not lend itself to setting up a randomized experiment, as is the case with most of the important issues of

macro-level economic policy, is a very difficult task. But evidence from Cain, Hasan, and Mitra (2012) and Mukim and Panagariya (2012) suggests a link between per capita income and poverty. We note as an aside that while many micro-level programs on which many recent development economists like to concentrate do lend themselves to the randomized trials approach, the integral sum of their importance to development policy is far exceeded by that of macro-level policy issues, such as those relating to international trade.

Chapter 3: Reforms and Their Impact on Growth and Poverty

1. Marathe (1989, Chapter 4), who retired as secretary of industry in 1980, offers a fascinating insider's account of policy-making during this period. He states, "By the early seventies there was sufficient evidence and a corresponding awareness of the inadequacy or ineffectiveness of some of the main elements of the industrial policy and particularly of the decision-making and administrative apparatus. The objective of 'growth with social justice' . . . was beginning to run into difficulties. It was increasingly evident that there was a conflict between the number of individually desirable objectives of policy, . . . and that the system seemed incapable of resolving these conflicts with the result that in actual practice there was neither adequate growth nor was there a discernible move towards greater social justice" (pp. 91–92). Later in the chapter, referring to the liberalizing measures during 1975–1976, the author states, "By far the most important reason why this phase of liberalization did not add up to much was that there was an unwillingness at the political level to recognize or accept that a change in direction was needed. . . . In the words of a distinguished civil servant who had retired by then, the attempt was 'to go by stealth' and necessarily, therefore, the amount of good that could be done had to be modest" (p. 100).

2. Bhagwati has suggested two additional factors helping the cause of the reforms. First, the growing Indian diaspora consisted of the families of nearly all influential bureaucrats and politicians. They brought home to these leaders that India's policies were so bad that India had become

a laughingstock. Second and related, these leaders, who thought Indian civilization entitled them to a superiority complex, faced the problem that the country's dismal economic performance produced an inferior status. The worst psychological situation is where a superiority complex confronts an inferior status. The dissonance that follows was obviously a strong spur to reform.

3. The details of these policy changes are set out in Panagariya (2008a, Chapters 2–5).

4. Rodrik and Subramanian (2005) further develop this point. Srinivasan (2005) offers a scathing critique of these authors.

5. The discussion below also draws on Panagariya (2004; 2008a, Chapter 1), among others.

6. In reporting the latter of these two periods, the year 1991–1992 is excluded because this was the crisis year for which the reforms could not be blamed. If we include 1991–1992, we should also include the high-growth years of 1988–1991, as done in Figure 3.1, which culminated in the 1991 crisis due to the fiscal expansion that partially fueled growth in the late 1980s.

7. We may mention here the earlier work of Wallack (2003), which tries to divide the years between 1951–52 and 2001–2002 into two or more periods based on statistically significant differences in growth rates. She finds one such breakpoint, which is 1980–1981 if we consider the GDP series, and 1987–1988 if we consider the GNP series. Given that the GDP and GNP growth-rate series are virtually identical, the vast differences between the cutoff points in the two series indicate extreme sensitivity of her statistical method to small variations in the data. In contrast, the method used by Ghate and Wright is robust.

8. See Panagariya (2004) for details.

9. Data for India usually relate to its fiscal year, which begins April 1 and ends March 31. Therefore, a year such as 1990–1991 refers to the period from April 1, 1990, to March 31, 1991.

10. Two additional contributions in a vein similar to Rodrik (2003) and Rodrik and Subramanian (2005) are Kohli (2006) and Nayyar (2006). Panagariya (2008a, pp. 16–21) provides a critique of each of these contributions.

11. Starting in 1973–1974, India began conducting large-scale expenditure surveys approximately every five years. Figure 3.2 is based on poverty estimates derived from those surveys. The only missing survey is that conducted in 1999–2000. Due to a sample design change, poverty estimates derived from this survey are not fully comparable to those from the other surveys.

12. The annual percentage-point reduction in poverty was 1.44 from 2004–2005 to 2009–2010. This compares with the annual percentage-point reduction of 0.85 from 1983 to 1993–1994, 0.77 from 1993–1994 to 2004–2005. and only 0.98 from 1993–1994 to 2009–2010.

13. For example, in the op-ed "Two Decades of a Misplaced Idea" in the newspaper *Mint* (September 16, 2011), the anti-reform commentator Himnashu argues that if the reforms are judged by what they have done for the poor, the results are at best mixed. He then cites the following numbers based on the revised, higher official poverty line: "The number of absolute poor in the country, which was 404.9 million in 1993–94 and 406.6 million in 2004–05 has come down marginally to 397 million by 2009–10."

14. For example, in its *1999 Annual Review of Development Effectiveness,* the World Bank (1999, p. 1) noted, "The number of poor people living on less than US$1 a day rose from 1,197 million in 1987 to 1,214 million in 1998. Excluding China, there are 100 million more poor people in developing countries than a decade ago."

15. In fact, the World Bank was being increasingly taken over by populist economists and non-economists, especially under President James Wolfensohn when it adopted the practice of aggressively highlighting the absolute number of poor. Wolfensohn's trusted consultants among the economists were also anti-growth and anti-reforms economists such as Joseph Stiglitz (who was also the World Bank chief economist and vice president) and Amartya Sen. See, for example, Wolfensohn and Stiglitz (1999) and Sen and Wolfensohn (1999).

16. We assume here a uniform increase in the population across rich and poor and no movement into and out of poverty. Insofar as population growth might be faster among the poor than the rich, the number

of poor in the additional population of 374 million may turn out to be even larger than in the text.

17. The question of compensation is a valid one. Those whose lands are taken for eminent domain, that is, for a social purpose, need to be compensated. This also raises questions as to what is a valid "social purpose," which individuals must be compensated, and by how much.

18. The term "Dalit" refers to untouchable castes that are included among the Scheduled Castes by the Indian Constitution.

19. For the document with the statement by the National Campaign on Dalit Human Rights, see www.publications.parliament.uk/pa /cm201011/cmselect/cmintdev/writev/616/m02.htm (accessed June 3, 2011). The statement by Bidwai can be found in the article "Equity, Not Growth, Is the Key," at www.mydigitalfc.com/op-ed/equity-not-growth-key-359 (accessed June 3, 2011).

20. See Das et al. (2011).

21. Thorat and Dubey (2012) also note the larger decline in poverty among the socially disadvantaged groups relative to the overall population.

22. These surveys identify the ownership of proprietary and partnership enterprises by social group, though not of cooperative and corporate enterprises. Therefore, it is possible to study the evolution of entrepreneurship by social groups within the proprietary and partnership enterprises.

23. In the case of the Scheduled Tribe–owned enterprises, value added as well as the number of workers employed grows faster than the corresponding average growth for all groups taken together. Therefore, shares of the Scheduled Tribe–owned enterprises in the value added and the number of workers employed grew larger between 2001–2002 and 2006–2007. For the Scheduled Castes, the growth in value added is slightly below the average for all groups and that for workers significantly above it. Consequently, despite healthy growth, its share shows a tiny decline in value added and a rise in the number of workers employed.

24. See www.globalpost.com/dispatch/news/regions/asia-pacific/india /110421/india-untouchable-dalit-business-entrepreneur (accessed November 10, 2012).

25. The following discussion draws heavily on Panagariya (2012a).

26. Not only was Professor D. T. Lakdawala a leading scholar of poverty, he also stood on the broad shoulders of such stalwarts as Pitamber Pant, once handpicked by Prime Minister Jawaharlal Nehru to head the Perspective Planning Division of the Planning Commission, and V. M. Dandekar and Nilakant Rath, both pioneering scholars of poverty in postindependence India. Although Professor Lakdawala passed away before the report of his committee was submitted, the latter was largely the result of his work with other committee members.

27. Our discussion of this myth is substantially borrowed from Bhagwati and Panagariya (2012).

Chapter 4: Reforms and Inequality

1. Thus, economists' salaries are particularly high owing to the opportunities they enjoy outside of academia. Hence, there are resentments by academics from lesser-paid disciplines, such as anthropology, philosophy, and comparative literature. An inside joke is that if you wanted academic signatures on an anti-liberal or anti-establishment petition, you were assured of many signatures if you went to these lower-paid departments: their resentments would prompt them to sign any such petition in huge numbers!

2. They use not the Gini measure, which is explained in Appendix 2, but what economists know as the Theil index. The latter has the advantage that it allows overall inequality in a population to be broken down into inequality within and across subpopulations. For example, it allows inequality among households within a country to be broken down into inequality among households within states and that across states. Like the Gini coefficient, the Theil index varies between 0 and 1.

3. Some analysts rest their assertion of a large increase in inequality on the grounds that the NSS expenditure surveys, on which all estimates of expenditure inequality are based, are characterized by a systematic underreporting at the top of the distribution relative to the bottom end

and that this underreporting has gotten worse over time. But without some hard evidence, we cannot be sure that this is true.

4. Some identify the precise period of the high point of the American Gilded Age as 1869–1877, which coincided with the administration of President Ulysses Grant, with many writers including 1878–1889 as well.

5. The Progressive Era prompted several writers, such as Upton Sinclair, to write novels about the abysmal social conditions afflicting the poor. These writers were called the "muckrakers."

6. Cf. www.pbs.org/wgbh/amex/carnegie/gildedage.html (accessed November 10, 2012).

7. See Panagariya (2011d).

8. The businessmen who profit thus are "cronies" of the politicians who favor them. But of course, the bribes that are involved need not go to cronies.

Chapter 5: Reforms and Their Impact on Health and Education

1. In the op-ed mentioned earlier, Amartya Sen (2011) puts the matter thus: "India's per-capita income is now comfortably more than double that of Bangladesh. How well is India's income advantage reflected in our lead in those things that really matter? I fear not very well—indeed not well at all." Sen also cites an op-ed by Jean Drèze (2004) titled "Bangladesh Shows the Way," which implies that Bangladesh has moved ahead of India in health outcomes. Most recently, the themes of these articles have been repeated in Drèze and Sen (2011).

2. For example, see the recent attack by Drèze and Sen (2011) on the health achievements of India relative to those of Bangladesh and other South Asian countries.

3. We may also add that in terms of the United Nations Human Development Index (HDI), India ranks ahead of Bangladesh by ten places. It may be recalled in this context that it was Amartya Sen, a leading proponent of the view that Bangladesh has outdone India in terms of

human development, who helped the UN Development Programme design the HDI. Oddly, as Panagariya (2011b) points out, Sen (2011) neglects to cite this statistic in his critique of India in relation to Bangladesh. Indeed, any references to the index remain conspicuously missing even from Drèze and Sen (2011), which was published after Panagariya (2011b).

4. It is odd that authors disparaging India often applaud Bangladesh for doing well in health outcomes despite its lower per capita income but gloss over the much larger per capita income gap India suffers vis-à-vis China.

5. See "An 'Annie Hall' Moment: A Nobel Prize–Winning Economist Spouts Off, and a Chinese Survivor Sets Him Straight," *Wall Street Journal,* February 21, 2005; www.parrikar.org/misc/amartya-wsj.pdf (accessed March 3, 2012). According to the report, speaking in Hong Kong, Sen had argued that while China had made great strides in medicine during the Cultural Revolution, the move to a privatized system in recent years had made the system less fair and efficient. It so happened, however, that the audience included a Hong Kong banker, Weijian Shan, who had lived through the Cultural Revolution and had been one of Mao's "barefoot doctors." The report notes that Shan was surprised by Sen's comments and went on to state to the audience, "I observed with my own eyes the total absence of medicine in some parts of China. The system was totally unsustainable. We used to admire India." He added that when he observed medical school graduates in Taiwan serving in the countryside in the 1980s during a visit there, he thought, "China ought to copy Taiwan." Shan further stated that had Mao's medicine system been made optional, "nobody would have opted for it."

6. The post is at http://blogs.ei.columbia.edu/2011/03/24/india-is-booming-so-why-are-nearly-half-of-its-children-malnourished-part-1 (accessed September 21, 2011).

7. There is a third measure of child nutrition known as wasting, which measures weight for height. The problem with this measure is that even if the height-for-age and weight-for-age measures are showing improvements, it will show deterioration if the former improvement is suffi-

ciently faster. Because of this strange characteristic, we do not discuss this measure.

8. The interested reader may look up the details and references in the entry "Kerala model" in Wikipedia (accessed September 23, 2011).

9. The nature of the redistribution in different parts of the country depended on the land tenure system in place. The different land tenure systems came from different ideas and philosophies of the British in the different presidencies, as brilliantly documented by the historian Eric Stokes.

10. An early influential case study of Kerala in this context was done by the Center for Development Studies at Thiruvananthapuram for the Department of Economic and Social Affairs of the United Nations (1975).

11. For consistency over time, Uttar Pradesh, Madhya Pradesh, and Bihar are defined to include Uttarakhand, Chhattisgarh, and Jharkhand, respectively, in these data. The latter three states were carved out of their mother states in 2000.

12. Unfortunately, there remains one small element of non-comparability due to the fact that the literacy rates for years 1951, 1961, and 1971 relate to rates for the above-five-years of population while those for subsequent years to above-seven-years population. This means the starting-year literacy rates for Kerala and Maharashtra were calculated on above-five-population basis and that for Gujarat and India on above-seven-population basis. Insofar as the literacy rate among children five to seven years in age is likely to be lower than that for the above-seven population, if calculated on above-seven-population basis, the starting-year literacy rate of Kerala (and Maharashtra) would be higher than that shown in Figure 5.7. This would make the gains in Kerala by year 30 even less impressive. We suspect, however, that since the population between five and seven years is a small proportion of the total above-five population, any bias on this account is likely to be tiny.

13. The unwillingness of progressive developmental groups to concede Gujarat's success on these social (and sometimes even economic) dimensions is partly attributable to their insistence on looking at everything

related to the state through the lens of the 2002 massacre of Muslims in the wake of the burning of fifty-eight innocent passengers in a train by a Muslim mob. This is like looking at the Congress Party performance through the lens of the similar massacre of many more Sikhs in 1984 following the unfortunate and deplorable assassination of Prime Minister Indira Gandhi by her Sikh guards. All such communal violence is a blot on the Indian secularism, but it is not the exclusive experience of Gujarat, whose great citizen Mahatma Gandhi gave his life in defense of Muslims and secularism. We concentrate in the text, however, on Gujarat's performance along the social dimension.

Chapter 6: Yet Other Myths

1. Bhagwati has appeared on two prominent TV shows in the United States, a documentary partially broadcast on *NewsHour* on PBS and one with Christiane Amanpour on CNN, where Sainath was cited and Vandana Shiva made a cameo appearance with claims about farmer suicides and their causes (such as the use of new BT seeds), which Bhagwati challenged. Interestingly, the PBS documentary, which was produced with great finesse, concentrated on one suicide, attributed to the use of the new BT seeds; later, during a panel discussion of the film at Asia Society in New York where Bhagwati appeared, the producer made a frank admission: they had discovered that this suicide had nothing to do with the farmer's use of the new seeds.

2. Bhagwati raised this issue on the previously cited Christiane Amanpour show when he observed that suicides by indebted farmers had been part of what he had read about in Indian agriculture when he was a student almost half a century ago, and farmer suicides were not a new phenomenon.

3. We may note that Nagaraj calculates suicide rates per 100,000 farmers and finds them substantially higher than the suicide rates in the general population per 100,000 people. But in doing so, he is comparing apples and oranges. To be consistent, farmer suicides per 100,000 farmers should be compared to suicides in the general population per 100,000 working people, rather than to the entire population.

4. None of this is to deny the existence of problems that would accompany any new technology that shows promise. Therefore, there have been problems with fake seeds being sold and farmers lacking proper information on the use of pesticide.

5. See www.newageweekly.com/2011/09/economic-reforms-fountain-head-of.html (accessed October 5, 2011).

6. The following discussion draws on Panagariya (2011e).

7. Recall our discussion in Part I.

8. "2G spectrum" refers to electromagnetic frequencies used to transmit calls via second-generation wireless phone technology. The scam involved the allocation of the 2G spectrum to certain companies at exceptionally low prices, with numerous politicians and bureaucrats from the latter or their agents allegedly receiving bribes.

9. This reform has been most associated with the Peruvian intellectual Hernando de Soto. Whereas the micro-credit program, which Elaben Bhatt pioneered and promoted through the Self-Employed Women's Association two years earlier than Muhammad Yunus, and the priority-sector lending program of the Reserve Bank of India, initiated even earlier, provide loans to very small, poor borrowers without collateral, de Soto intriguingly argued that the poor did in fact have assets but that the lack of clear titles prevented them from turning them into effective collateral.

10. He also has edited with Narcis Serra a book of essays, with a contribution by Deepak Nayyar at Jawaharlal Nehru University who clearly shares Stiglitz's views, titled *The Washington Consensus Reconsidered* (New York: Oxford University Press, 2009).

11. The revolution in postwar theory of commercial policy has been described, and its main findings summarized by Bhagwati (who led this revolution starting in 1963), in his Stockholm Lectures, published as *Free Trade Today* (Princeton, NJ: Princeton University Press, 2001). The contributions by the late V. K. Ramaswami and by T. N. Srinivasan also played a major role.

12. Panagariya was a member of the Bank mission for the Trade and Investment Liberalization Loan during its first visit to Delhi in late March 1993. Senior officials at the Bank had held the view that the loan

would not proceed unless India agreed to abolish import licensing on consumer goods. When the mission was told, however, that this was not in the cards, the Bank leadership quickly changed its mind and proceeded with the loan anyway. As a postscript, India liberalized consumer goods imports almost a decade later on April 1, 2001. But the World Bank kept lending to India in the meantime without so much as a hiccup.

13. See Ahmad (1995).

Chapter 7: Track I and Track II Reforms

1. In using the adjective "redistributive," we do not necessarily imply that the enhanced revenues come from the rich and the expenditures go to the poor. In fact, one of the main worries that we address in Part III devoted to such redistributive programs is that unless they are handled with care to ensure proper targeting and prevent massive leakage into political predation, they may fail to reach the poor.

2. Gary Fields (1980), one of the leading experts of his time on poverty, had expressed the gloom on India's poverty problem in these words: "India is a miserably poor country. Per-capita yearly income is under $100. Of the Indian people, 45 percent receive incomes below $50 per year and 90 percent below $150. Of the total number of absolutely poor in the world . . . more than half are Indian. During the 1960s, per capita private consumer expenditure grew by less than 1/2 percent per annum. India's poverty problem is so acute and her resources so limited that it is debatable whether any internal policy change . . . might be expected to improve things substantially" (p. 204). Fields did not seriously consider the possibility, however, that the reform of India's counterproductive economic-policy framework could accelerate growth sharply and produce a noticeable impact on poverty.

3. These two tracks are, of course, not entirely independent. Growth directly impacts the volume of revenues and therefore determines the possible scale of the redistributive programs. Symmetrically, education and health will generally create a more skilled and healthier workforce, which should help growth. Sometimes a conflict between the two tracks

may arise as well, though this is likely to be rare. Thus, for example, a macroeconomic crisis such as the one India faced in 1991 may necessitate large cuts in the fiscal deficit so that the economy is stabilized and returned to a rapid-growth trajectory. In turn, this may require cutting some of the social programs in the short run. Symmetrically, a redistributive program such as the National Rural Employment Guarantee Scheme, which progressively pulls the workforce out of the private economy for employment in public projects of unproven quality, can have an adverse effect on growth.

4. We concentrate on Track I reforms in Part II, leaving issues relating to Track II policies for Part III. We alert the reader that we do not try to be exhaustive but, instead, consider issues that are most critical in each area and require the government's urgent attention. For more detailed and leisurely treatment of a wider array of issues, the reader is invited to consult the recent book by Panagariya (2008a).

5. See Government of India (2007).

6. See Dehejia and Panagariya (2012b) for further details.

7. See Hasan and Jandoc (2012) for further details.

8. Recall our discussion in Chapters 4 and 5.

Chapter 8: A Multitude of Labor Laws and Their Reform

1. See Economic Survey 2010–2011, Appendix Table 3.1, p. A52.

2. In India, the term "organized sector," which principally relates to manufacturing activity, refers to the collection of manufacturing firms registered under the 1948 Factories Act. Firms with ten or more workers using electricity and those with twenty or more workers even if not using electricity are required to register under this act. Because services firms are not required to register under the 1948 Factories Act, even large services firms such as WIPRO, Infosys, and TCS are technically in the unorganized sector. This is the reason we used the term "formal sector" previously to include both manufacturing and services firms with ten or more workers.

3. Clothing accessories refer to Category 84 in the UN SITC classification.

4. In fact, the evidence in favor of a declining trend in the labor–capital ratio in Indian manufacturing generally is overwhelming. Thus, Rani and Unni (2004) find a sharply rising trend in the capital–labor ratios in both the organized and unorganized manufacturing sectors. Chaudhuri (2002) computes the labor–capital ratio in three-digit organized manufacturing sectors from 1990–1991 to 1997–1998 and also finds it to decline progressively. Again, Das, Wadhwa, and Kalita (2009) find a sharply declining trend in the labor–capital ratio in thirty-one labor-intensive organized manufacturing industries between 1990–1991 and 2003–2004.

5. Earlier work on firm-size distribution in India includes Mazumdar (2003) and Mazumdar and Sarkar (2008). These authors have drawn attention to the fact that employment in India is heavily concentrated in small enterprises. While large enterprises have some presence, medium-size enterprises are entirely missing.

6. Although a handful of the products remain subject to the reservation, a March 2000 executive order allows firms willing to export at least 50 percent of their output to manufacture large-scale firms to produce even these products. Therefore, for all practical purposes, the reservation no longer binds.

7. See http://labour.nic.in/act/welcome.html (accessed October 29, 2011). A report of the working group of the Planning Commission on "Labor Laws and Other Labor Regulations" lists forty-three labor laws. See http://planningcommission.nic.in/aboutus/committee/wrkgrp11/wg11_rplabr.pdf (accessed October 29, 2011).

8. Mamata Benrjee replaced the long-standing communist government in the latest State Assembly elections.

9. Amit Mitra made this statement on the NDTV show *Big Fight* at www.ndtv.com/convergence/ndtv/new/Ndtv-Show-Special.aspx?ID=289#VPlay (accessed October 29, 2011).

10. Manish Sabharwal, CEO of TeamLease, made the remark on the NDTV *Big Fight* episode on labor laws mentioned earlier (www.ndtv.com/convergence/ndtv/new/Ndtv-Show-Special.aspx?ID=289#Vplay) (accessed October 29, 2011).

11. More precisely, the act says that seven or more workers in an establishment can form a trade union as long as they represent at least 10 percent of the labor force. Alternatively, one hundred workers in an establishment can form a trade union even if they are less 10 percent of the workforce.

12. All employees earning 6,500 rupees per month or more have to join the provident fund scheme.

13. Shah told this story at a conference in New Delhi several years ago and recently confirmed it in e-mail correspondence with Panagariya.

14. Economist Yasheng Huang of the Sloan School at MIT made this argument to Panagariya some years ago.

15. A bill amending the 1948 Factories Act to allow women to work night shifts has been before the parliament since at least 2008.

16. Debroy (2001) quotes a Supreme Court judge from the *Excel Wear v. Union of India* case of 1978 who wrote, "Gradually, the net was cast too wide and the freedom of the employer tightened to such an extent by introduction of the impugned provisions that it has come to a breaking point from the point of view of the employers. . . . It is not quite correct to say that because compensation is not a substitute for the remedy of prevention of unemployment, the latter remedy must be the only one. If it were so, then in no case closure can be or should be allowed. . . . But, so long as the private ownership of an industry is recognized and governed on an overwhelmingly large proportion of our economic structure, is it possible to say that principles of socialism and social justice can be pushed to such an extreme so as to ignore completely, or to a very large extent, the interest of another section of the public, viz. the private owners of the undertakings?"

17. See www.nlcindia.com/news/news_awardficci.pdf (accessed November 4, 2011).

Chapter 9: Land Acquisition

1. A wrinkle in this episode was the firing by the police on the demonstrators which inflamed the latter. Such tactics have long been

given up in India and their use by the West Bengal government was perhaps attributable to the fact that the communists were in charge of the government and they do not accept dissent without tough counter-measures. In fact, the West Bengal government had until then been the only state government that had not been turned out by the electorate once they got in, unlike most other states that have experienced turnover. A reason often cited is that they simply exterminated opposition in the countryside.

2. See Sukumaran and Bisoi (2011).

3. If the farmer has no knowledge of how to do this, owing to illiteracy or unfamiliarity, there is a role for the government to ensure that these farmers are given the necessary guidance. NGOs can also play this role. This is surely better than denying these farmers the ability to profit from the sale of their land at better prices.

4. The area under forest is 22.8 percent. The remaining 23 percent is barren, fallow, or uncultivated.

Chapter 10: Infrastructure

1. It is common, therefore, to see trucks carrying produce overturned on the congested roads, making road travel hazardous. Once Bhagwati was in the Lufthansa lounge in New Delhi and a German couple entered. The man had a collar around his neck and the woman's arm was in a sling. It turned out that they had run into a truck on the road from Agra to Delhi.

2. A more comprehensive treatment of the issues can be found in Panagariya (2008a, Chapters 17 and 18).

3. This airline ran up losses for several reasons, such as the issuance of automatic upgrades to politicians (a practice that has since been curtailed) as distinct from customers who show loyalty and offer more business later; and the award of free lifetime travel to people chosen by the government. The ministers making such awards act like Evita Peron and have no accountability because the losses they entail go to Air India, where they get absorbed in the yawning deficit that plagues the airline

anyway. Perhaps the way to get at this type of depredation on Air India is to insist on transparency so that the airline has to make public who has benefited, and how often, of such expensive largesse so that opprobrium attaches to them.

4. See Panagariya (2009b).

5. See "Kamal Nath, Ahluwalia Spar over Roadblocks," *Economic Times,* July 5, 2010, at http://articles.economictimes.indiatimes.com/2010–07 –05/news/27569574_1_kamal-nath-planning-commission-plan-panel (accessed November 7, 2011).

6. According to a newspaper report, road construction recently has accelerated to eleven kilometers per day, but it remains to be seen whether even this pace will be sustained. See "11 km Added Per Day, Highways Back on Track," *Economic Times,* October 17, 2011.

7. The floor-space index is usually fixed by the urban authorities. In the central business district of Mumbai, this index has been fixed at 1.3 since the early 1990s. This means that only 1,300 square meters of floor space can be built on a plot of 1,000 square meters. The restriction has resulted in buildings with one or two floors in areas where land is extremely scarce and therefore expensive.

Chapter 11: Higher Education

1. For more extensive analysis of the Browne report, see Panagariya (2010b).

2. See Panagariya (2010c) for details.

Chapter 12: Other Track I Reforms

1. Panagariya (2008a) addresses Track I reforms in yet other areas, such as Indian bankruptcy law, civil service, subsidies, privatization, land titles, and financial sector policies. In fact, the full agenda of reforms that we could usefully implement is so large, because of the counterproductive nature of our policy framework prior to 1991, that the task before our reformers is akin to cleaning up after a tsunami.

2. See, in particular, the comprehensive analysis in Kohli and Bhagwati (2012) and a more abbreviated discussion in Bhagwati and Kohli (2011).

Chapter 13: Track II Reforms

1. These issues and policy proposals to address them were discussed at length twenty-five years ago by Bhagwati (1988), drawing on much economic research, in the Vikram Sarabhai Lecture in 1987 in Ahmedabad on "Poverty and Public Policy."

2. The wages paid in such public works has important implications, as discussed below.

3. Note here that whether the payment is provided in cash or in kind is a separate issue that we consider below. In principle, both the transfer and wage can be provided in cash or in kind.

4. For example, the food security bill that is under consideration proposes to encourage increased consumption of rice and wheat by offering these grains at highly subsidized prices through the public distribution system.

5. The only way the government can eliminate the possibility of turning in-kind transfer into cash is by offering subsidy on unlimited quantity. In this case, the market price will drop down to the subsidized price, making it impossible to turn in-kind subsidy into cash. In this case, the lower effective price of rice will also lead to increased consumption.

Chapter 14: Attacking Poverty by Guaranteeing Employment

1. NREGA has recently been renamed as the Mahatma Gandhi National Rural Employment Guarantee Act scheme. But we shall continue to refer to it by its original acronym in this volume.

2. Consequently, the specified wage rose from 17 percent in Meghalaya to 79 percent in Haryana beginning January 1, 2011.

3. The dollar conversion is done using the average dollar–rupee exchange rate for the fiscal year reported in the RBI *Handbook of Statistics on Indian Economy*, 2011.

4. See Government of India (2009b).

5. One might argue that setting wages at piece rates, as provided by the law, would solve this problem. But this is unlikely since the piece rate must be sufficiently high to give the worker the minimum daily wage that the legislation sets. Moreover, enforcement of work as per the piece rate is likely to be lax in public works programs, especially since the primary purpose of such programs is to create employment.

6. Panagariya has found this to be the case in his informal conversations with businessmen from Bhilwara district in Rajasthan, who told him that workers refuse to work at wages similar to NREGA wages, arguing that the latter are available to them for limited effort while employment in the private sector requires a lot more effort.

Chapter 15: Adult Nutrition and Food Security

1. See National Sample Survey Organization (1996).

2. See National Sample Survey Organization (2001a and 2007a).

3. Data on the first three surveys are from the National Sample Survey Organization (2001b) and for the last one from National Sample Survey Organization (2007b)

4. To quote the authors (Deaton and Drèze 2009), "As has been suggested by several authors, including Palmer-Jones and Sen (2001) and Ray and Lancaster (2005), we could take the calorie intakes associated with the original lines as fixed poverty norms and compute the fraction of the population living in households whose per capita calorie consumption falls beneath 2,400 calories in the rural sector and beneath 2,100 calories in the urban sector. Such calculations are shown in Table 5. Because the distribution of per capita calories is moving to the left over time, these numbers show *rising* poverty rates, from two-thirds of the rural population in 1983 to four-fifths in 2004–05, and from 65% to more than 75% in India as a whole" (p. 45).

5. In principle, there is one qualification. Earlier work by Bhagwati and Balbir Sihag (1980) showed that the lower the offtake of the rations at lower prices in the public distribution system, the lower the differential between these prices and the higher free-market prices. The reason,

they argued, was that an opportunity cost is attached to lining up to get the ration. But the difference between the current market prices and the subsidized prices in the proposed bill is too large to be offset by such opportunity costs for most poor households.

6. See Panagariya (2011f) for additional details.

7. For example, a recent article even by the leading agricultural economist Ashok Gulati in a *Wall Street Journal* blog (http://blogs.wsj.com/indiarealtime/2011/03/17/india-journal-how-to-achieve-food-security), which discussed at length possible measures to engineer a second Green Revolution to improve food security, made no mention whatsoever of the role imports can play in enhancing food supply.

8. See blog http://blogs.wsj.com/indiarealtime/2011/03/17/india-journal-how-to-achieve-food-security (accessed December 5, 2011).

Chapter 16: Reforming Health Care

1. Economists distinguish between private and public goods. Public goods have two properties, non-rivalry in consumption and non-exclusion. Non-rivalry means that consumption of the good by one individual does not reduce its availability to others. Non-exclusion means that once a good is made available, individuals cannot be excluded from its consumption even if they did not pay for its provision. Defense is the commonest example of a public good. Its availability to one citizen does not reduce the availability to others, and once it is provided, no citizen can be excluded from benefiting from it. Private goods exhibit rivalry and exclusion. If an individual drinks a bottle of Coca-Cola, it is no longer available to another individual (rivalry in consumption). Moreover, once the individual buys the bottle, she can exclude others from drinking it (exclusion). Usually, the market would adequately supply private goods but not public goods. In the latter case, government intervention is required.

2. It is arguable whether India also needs campaigns to emphasize personal hygiene. As the economist Padma Desai has written, middle-class Indians, devoted to personal hygiene and a clean home, will typically collect garbage at home but will then dump it in the street outside.

Nonetheless, many households could use advice on other health-related matters, such as the health effects of traditional cooking stoves and the dangers from wearing rayon and nylon saris close to fire when cooking.

3. In its surveys, the National Sample Survey Organization distinguishes between non-hospitalized and hospitalized treatments. These can be approximately identified with what we call routine health care and major illnesses, respectively, in this chapter but the correspondence is not exact. In particular, the surveys most likely include treatment at home of prolonged illnesses and outpatient surgeries in "non-hospitalized" treatment, whereas we include them in the major-illnesses category.

4. Most, though not all, major illnesses require hospitalization. Therefore, we can get at least some rough idea of the incidence of major illnesses at the aggregate level from the data gathered by the National Sample Survey Organization (2006) mentioned earlier. According to it, during January–June 2004, the average rate of hospitalization was 2.3 per 100 individuals in rural and 3.1 per 100 individuals in urban areas. The associated average expenditure per hospitalization was 5,695 rupees in rural and 8,851 rupees in urban areas in current rupees. In comparison, the average expenditure on non-hospitalized care per ailing person in a fifteen-day period was 257 rupees in rural and 306 rupees in urban areas.

5. See http://sahakara.kar.gov.in/Yashasivini.html (accessed December 10, 2011) for details.

6. See www.rsby.gov.in/overview.aspx and www.rsby.gov.in/about_rsby.aspx (both accessed December 10, 2011) for further details.

7. K. Srinath Reddy, president of the Public Health Foundation of India, chaired the group.

Chapter 17: Elementary Education

1. Whereas courts are empowered to enforce the fundamental rights in the Constitution, similar enforceability does not exist with respect to the directive principles of the state policy.

2. According to *Aser 2010*, enrollment of children age six to fourteen years in private schools rose from 16.3 percent of the total enrollment

in 2005 to 24.3 percent in 2010. In the four southern states, where growth has been more robust and which also happen to be relatively rich, the ratio rose from 29.7 percent to 36.1 percent in just one year, between 2009 and 2010.

3. The findings by Muralidharan and Kremer (2006) and Tooley and Dixon (undated) mirror those documented earlier in the comprehensive report by the PROBE Team (1999) and Kingdon (2005).

4. The provisions of the RTE Act legally bind the local government to seek out and enroll every single child within its jurisdiction in an elementary school. The model rules accompanying the act require the local government to conduct household surveys to identify all children within its jurisdiction and to maintain records on them from birth to fourteen years of age. The record, which is to be in the public domain, must include information on name, sex, date and place of birth, parents' names and occupation, preschool of the child, disability if any, and whether the child belongs to a weaker section or disadvantaged group.

5. Indeed, it is quite unlikely that many public schools will be able to satisfy these norms and standards either.

India: Past and Future

1. Thus, as we have argued in this volume (Myth 3.1), the thesis advanced by Dani Rodrik and Arvind Subramanian—that the dramatic turnaround in Indian performance was a result of "attitudinal" changes prior to 1991 rather than the reforms begun in 1991 like a blitzkrieg and steadily intensified thereafter—flies in the face of these massive changes, none of which was expected to be reversed. Novelty sometimes has virtue, but in this case, it is an unmitigated vice.

2. See James Lamont (2010), Amartya Sen (2011), and critiques by Panagariya (2011a, 2011b).

3. We do not address here the India–China comparison on social indicators, as against growth rates, that Drèze and Sen have written on. We have already demonstrated its errors (Myth 5.1).

4. *Samizdat* refers to clandestine copying and distribution of literature banned by the state, especially in the Union of Soviet Socialist Republics.

Appendix 1: Socialism Under Nehru

1. Nehru (1946, pp. 438–439) records this objective in clear terms when describing the deliberations of the 1938 Planning Committee in *Discovery of India*. He states, "The objective for the country as a whole was the attainment, as far as possible, of national self-sufficiency. International trade was certainly not excluded, but we were anxious to avoid being drawn into the whirlpool of economic imperialism. We wanted neither to be victims of an imperialist power nor to develop such tendencies ourselves."

2. Export pessimism reinforced the self-sufficiency argument from the side of economics. If you could not export more jute to buy machinery, which you needed to raise investment, then you had to produce the machinery yourself. This pessimism came from the early views that exports of traditional primary and agricultural products were under strain because of continued economizing on the use of such products in manufactures and because of substitution by synthetics for them. It also came from the view that Western governments, faced with growing exports from the developing countries, would enact trade barriers.

3. The First Five-Year Plan (p. 422) stated the policy in these terms: "The scope and need for development are so great that it is best for the public sector to develop those industries in which private enterprise is unable or unwilling to put up the resources required and run the risk involved, leaving the rest of the field free for private enterprise."

4. Later, starting with the Third Five-Year Plan, the targets were derived with more economic sophistication, in optimization models. But the optimization was academic; the targeting approach remained an albatross around the neck of Indian planners until the post-1991 reforms.

5. According to the Third Five-Year Plan, 32 percent of the total imports in the First Five-Year Plan (1951–1952 to 1955–1956) and 23 percent in the Second Plan (1956–1957 to 1960–1961) were accounted for by consumer goods. "Established importers" who were licensed to import goods for sale to other buyers were allowed to operate relatively freely.

References

Ahluwalia, Deepak. 1993. Public Distribution of Food in India: Coverage, Targeting and Leakages. *Food Policy* 18(1): 33–54.

Ahmad, Zainon. 1995. "India to Push On with Economic Reforms." *New Straits Times* (Malaysia), August 3, p. 16.

Alfaro, Laura, and Anusha Chari. 2012. Does Liberalization Promote Competition? In Bhagwati, Jagdish, and Arvind Panagariya, eds., *Reforms and Economic Transformation in India*. New York: Oxford University Press, pp. 200–226.

ASER. 2010. *Annual Status Education Report (Rural)*. Mumbai: Pratham Resource Center.

Balachandran, Kamala. 2010. Understanding RTE. *Deccan Herald,* August 10.

Bhagwati, Jagdish. 1958. Immiserizing Growth: A Geometrical Note. *Review of Economic Studies* 25: 201–205.

Bhagwati, Jagdish. 1988. Poverty and Public Policy. *World Development* 16 (5): 539–555. Also reprinted in Bhagwati, J., *A Stream of Windows: Unsettling Reflections on Trade, Immigration and Democracy.* Cambridge, MA: MIT Press, 1999.

———. 1998a. The Capital Myth: The Difference Between Trade in Widgets and Dollars. *Foreign Affairs,* May/June.

———. 1998b. Review of India's Economic Reforms: 1991–2001 by Vijay Joshi and I. M. D. Little and India: Economic Development and Social Opportunity by Jean Drèze and Amartya Sen. *Economic Journal* 108: 196–200.

———. 1999. The "Miracle" That Did Happen. In Thorbecke, Erik, and Henry Wan, eds., *Taiwan's Development Experience: Lessons on Roles of Government and Market.* Boston: Kulwer Academic Publishers, pp. 21–39.

———. 2010. Indian Reforms: Yesterday and Today. The 3rd Professor Hiren Mukherjee Memorial Annual Parliamentary Lecture, December 2. Available at www.columbia.edu/~jb38/papers/pdf/Lok-Sabha -speech-FINAL-EXPANDED-Deceber-14.pdf (accessed April 13, 2012).

———. 2011a. The Misplaced Fear of the East in the West. *Bank Votobel Magazine,* November.

———. 2011b. Designing Institutions for Governance Reforms. 24th Intelligence Bureau Centenary Endowment Lecture, Home Ministry, Government of India. Available at www.equilibri.net/ nuovo/es/node/2011 (accessed April 13, 2012).

Bhagwati, Jagdish, and Padma Desai. 1970. *India: Planning for Industrialization.* London: Oxford University Press.

———. 1975. Socialism and Indian Economic Policy. *World Development* 3(4), pp. 213–221.

Bhagwati, Jagdish, and Rajeev Kohli. 2011. Selling the Wrong Idea. *Times of India,* December 12.

Bhagwati, Jagdish, and Arvind Panagariya. 2004. Great Expectations. *Wall Street Journal,* May 24.

———. 2012. Introduction: Trade, Poverty, Inequality, and Democracy. In Bhagwati, Jagdish, and Arvind Panagariya, eds., *India's Reforms: How They Produced Inclusive Growth.* New York: Oxford University Press, pp. 3–17.

Bhagwati, Jagdish, and Balbir Sihag. 1980, December. "Dual Markets, Rationing and Queues." *Quarterly Journal of Economics* 95(4): 775–779.

Bhagwati, Jagdish, and T. N. Srinivasan. 1975. *Foreign Trade Regimes and Economic Development: India.* New York: National Bureau of Economic Research.

Cain, J., Rana Hasan, and Devashish Mitra. 2012. Trade Liberalization and Poverty Reduction: New Evidence from Indian States. In Bhagwati, J., and Arvind Panagariya, eds., *India's Reforms: How They Produced Inclusive Growth.* New York: Oxford University Press, pp. 91–185.

Chakrabarty, Bidyut. 1992. Jawaharlal Nehru and Planning, 1938–41: India at the Crossroads. *Modern Asian Studies* 26(2): 275–287.

Chakraborty, Pinaki, Sudipto Mundle, Arvind Panagariya, and Govinda Rao. 2011. *Economic Policies and Outcomes in the Largest Fifteen States in India.* New York and New Delhi: Columbia University and National Institute of Public Finance and Policy.

Chaudhuri, Sudip. 2002. Economic Reforms and Industrial Structure in India. *Economic and Political Weekly* 37(2): 155–162.

Das, Deb Kusum, Deepika Wadhwa, and Gunajit Kalita. 2009. The Employment Potential of Labor Intensive Industries in India's Organized Manufacturing. ICRIER Working Paper 236, June.

DasGupta, Monica, Rajendra Shukla, T. V. Somanathan, and K. K. Datta. 2009. How Might India's Public Health Systems Be Strengthened? World Bank Policy Research Working Paper Series, No. 5140.

Das, Jishnu, and Jeffrey Hammer. 2007. Money for Nothing: The Dire Straits of Medical Practice in Delhi, India. *Journal of Development Economics* 83(1): 1–36, May.

Das, Matreyi Bordia, Gillette Hall, Soumya Kapoor, and Dennis Nikitin. 2011. "India's Adivasis." *India: Country Brief 4.* World Bank, http://siteresources.worldbank.org/EXTINDPEOPLE/Resources /407801–1271860301656/India_brief_clean_0110.pdf (accessed November 11, 2012).

Deaton, Angus, and Jean Drèze. 2002, September 7. Poverty and Inequality in India: A Reexamination. *Economic and Political Weekly* 37 (36): 3729–3748.

———. 2008. Food and Nutrition in India: Facts and Interpretations. *Economic and Political Weekly* 44 (7): 42–65.

Debroy, Bibek. 2001. Why We Need Law Reform. *Seminar,* January. Available at www.india-seminar.com/2001/497/497%20bibek%20 debroy.htm (accessed November 4, 2011).

Dehejia, Rajeev, and Arvind Panagariya. 2012a. Entrepreneurship in Services and the Socially Disadvantaged. In Bhagwati, Jagdish, and Arvind Panagariya, eds., *Reforms and Economic Transformation in India.* New York: Oxford University Press, pp. 253–277.

———. 2012b. Services Growth in India: A Look Inside the Black Box. In Bhagwati, Jagdish, and Arvind Panagariya, eds., *Reforms and Economic Transformation in India.* New York: Oxford University Press, pp. 86–118.

DeLong, J. Bradford. 2003. India Since Independence: An Analytic Growth Narrative. In Rodrik, Dani, ed., *In Search of Prosperity: Analytic Narratives of Economic Growth*. Princeton, NJ: Princeton University Press, pp. 183–204.

Deshpande, R. S. 2002. Suicide by Farmers in Karnataka: Agrarian Distress and Possible Alleviatory Steps. *Economic and Political Weekly* 37(25): 2601–2610.

Dev, S. M., and M. H. Suryanarayana. 1991. Is PDS Urban Biased and Pro-Rich: An Evaluation. *Economic and Political Weekly* 26(41): 2357–2366.

Drèze, Jean. 2004. Bangladesh Shows the Way. *The Hindu,* September 17.

Drèze, Jean, and Reetika Khera. 2010. The BPL Census and a Possible Alternative. *Economic and Political Weekly* 45(9): 54–63.

Drèze, J., and A. K. Sen. 1995. *India: Economic Development and Social Opportunity*. Oxford: Clarendon Press.

———. 2011. Putting Growth in Its Place. *Outlook,* November 14.

Dumont, Rene. 1966. *False Start in Africa*. London: Andre Deutsch.

Dutta, B., and B. Ramaswami. 2001. Targeting and Efficiency in the Public Distribution System: Case of Andhra Pradesh and Maharashtra. *Economic and Political Weekly* 36(18): 1524–1532.

Dutta, Puja, Stephen Howes, and Rinku Murgai. 2010. "Small but Effective: India's Targeted Unconditional Cash Transfers." *Economic and Political Weekly* 45 (52): 63–70.

Fields, Gary. 1980. *Poverty, Inequality, and Development*. Cambridge: Cambridge University Press.

Franke, Richard W., and Barbara H. Chasin. 1999. Is the Kerala Model Sustainable? Lessons from the Past, Prospects for the Future. In Oommen, M. A., ed., *Rethinking Development: Kerala's Development Experience, Volume 1*. New Delhi: Institute of Social Sciences, pp. 118–148.

Frankel, Jeffrey, and Andrew Rose. 2002. An Estimate of the Effect of Common Currencies on Trade and Income. *Quarterly Journal of Economics* 117(2): 437–466, May.

Ghate, Chetan, and Stephen Wright. 2008. The "V-factor": Distribution, Timing, and Correlates of the Great Indian Growth Turnaround. Discussion Papers of DIW Berlin 783, DIW Berlin, German Institute for Economic Research. Revised version forthcoming in the *Journal of Development Economics*.

Government of India. 2005. *Report of the National Commission on Macroeconomics and Health.* New Delhi: Ministry of Health and Family Welfare.

———. 2007. *Report on Conditions of Work and Promotion of Livelihoods in the Unorganized Sector.* New Delhi: National Commission for Enterprises in the Unorganized Sector.

———. 2009a. *Nutrition in India: National Family Health Survey (NFHS-3) 2005–06.* Mumbai: International Institute for Population Sciences.

———. 2009b. *Guidelines for Implementation of Works on Individual Land Under NREGA,* January draft. New Delhi: Ministry of Rural Development. Available at http://nrega.nic.in/draft_guidelines.pdf (accessed November 19, 2011).

Gruere, Guillaume P., Purvi Mehta-Bhatt, and Debdatta Sengupta. 2008. Bt cotton and Farmer Suicides in India: Reviewing the Evidence. IFPRI Discussion Paper 00808, October.

Gupta, Poonam, and Arvind Panagariya. 2011a. Rich, Educated, and Criminal? *Times of India,* April 5.

———. 2011b. Crime-Tainted MPs Have Little to Do with Corruption. *Economic Times,* September 21.

———. 2012. Economic Reforms and Election Outcomes. Columbia Program on Indian Economic Policies. In Bhagwati, J., and Arvind Panagariya, eds., *India's Reforms: How They Produced Inclusive Growth.* New York: Oxford University Press, pp. 51–87.

Hasan, Rana, and Karl Robert L. Jandoc. 2012. Labor Regulations and Firm Size Distribution in Indian Manufacturing. In Bhagwati, Jagdish, and Arvind Panagariya, eds., *Reforms and Economic Transformation in India.* New York: Oxford University Press, pp. 15–48.

Hasan, Rana, Devashish Mitra, and Asha Sundaram. 2010. The Determinants of Capital Intensity in Manufacturing: The Role of Factor Endowments and Factor Market Imperfections. Mimeo. New York: Syracuse University.

Hasan, Rana, Devashish Mitra, and Beyza P. Ural. 2006–2007. Trade Liberalization, Labor Market Institutions, and Poverty Reduction: Evidence from Indian States. *India Policy Forum* 3: 70–135.

Haq, Mahbub ul. 1972. Let Us Stand Economic Theory on Its Head: Joining the GNP Rat Race Won't Wipe Out Poverty. *Insight,* January.

Himanshu and Abhijit Sen. 2011. Why Not a Universal Food Security Legislation? *Economic and Political Weekly* 46(12): 38–47.

Hnatkovska, Viktoria, Amartya Lahiri, and Sourabh B. Paul. 2012. Castes and Labor Mobility. *American Economic Journal: Applied Economics* 4(2): 274–305.

Howes, Stephan, and Shikha Jha. 1992. Urban Bias in Indian Public Distribution System. *Economic and Political Weekly* 27(19): 1022–1030.

———. 1994. Public Distribution of Food in India: A Comment. *Food Policy* 19(1): 65–68.

International Institute for Population Sciences (IIPS) and Macro International. 2007. *National Family Health Survey (NFHS-3), 2005–06: India.* Mumbai: IIPS.

Jeffrey, Robin. 1992. *Politics, Women, and Well-Being: How Kerala Became "A Model."* Hampshire: Macmillan Press Ltd.

Jha, Shikha. 1992. Consumer Subsidies in India: Is Targeting Effective? *Development and Change* 23(4): 101–128.

Jha, Shikha, and Bharat Ramaswami. 2011. The Percolation of Public Expenditure: Food Subsidies and the Poor in India and the Philippines. Paper presented at the India Policy Forum Conference, July 12–13, and available at www.ncaer.org/popuppages/EventDetails /IPF_2011/Shikha_Jha&Bharat_Ramaswami.pdf (accessed December 5, 2011).

Kingdon, Geeta Gandhi. 2005. Private and Public Schooling: The Indian Experience. Paper presented at the conference Mobilizing the Private Sector for Public Education, Kennedy School of Government, Harvard University, October 5–6.

Kohli, Atul. 2006. Politics of Economic Growth in India, 1980–2005— I. *Economic and Political Weekly* 41(13): 1251–1259.

Kohli, Rajeev, and Jagdish Bhagwati. 2012. Organized Retailing in India: Issues and Outlook. In Bhagwati, Jagdish, and Arvind Panagariya, eds., *Reforms and Economic Transformation in India.* New York: Oxford University Press, pp. 119–137.

Krishna, Pravin, and Guru Sethupathy. 2012. Trade and Inequality in India. In Bhagwati, J., and Arvind Panagariya, eds., *India's Reform: How They Produced Inclusive Growth.* New York: Oxford University Press, pp. 247–278.

Lamont, James. 2010. Nobel Laureate Attacks India on Growth. *Financial Times,* December 21. Available at www.ft.com/cms/s/0/554 eab3e-0d33–11e0–82ff-00144feabdc0.html#axzz1sDTPdVyV (accessed April 16, 2012).

Marathe, S. S. 1989. *Regulation and Development: India's Policy Experience of Controls over Industry,* 2nd ed. New Delhi: Sage Publications.

Mathew, George. 2001. Amartya Sen and the Kerala "Model." *The Hindu,* January 9.

Mazumdar, D. 2003. Small and Medium Enterprise Development in Equitable Growth and Poverty Alleviation. In Edmonds, Christopher M., ed., *Reducing Poverty in Asia: Emerging Issues in Growth, Targeting, and Measurement.* Chaltenham, UK: Asian Development Bank, Edward Elgar.

Mazumdar, D., and S. Sarkar. 2008. *Globalization, Labor Markets, and Inequality in India.* London and New York: Routledge.

McGregor, Richard. 2010. *The Party: The Secret World of China's Communist Rulers.* New York: Harper, 2010.

Mudaliar, A. Lakshmanaswami. 1961. *Report of the Health Survey and Planning Committee.* Ministry of Health, Government of India.

Mukim, Megha, and Arvind Panagariya. 2012. Growth, Openness, and the Socially Disadvantaged. In Bhagwati, J., and Arvind Panagariya, eds., *India's Reform: How They Produced Inclusive Growth.* New York: Oxford University Press, pp. 186–246.

Mukim, Megha, and Arvind Panagariya. 2013. A Comprehensive Look at Poverty Measures in India. Columbia University, in progress.

Muralidharan, Karthik, and Michael Kremer. 2006. Public and Private Schools in Rural India. Mimeo, Department of Economics, Harvard University.

Nagaraj, K. 2008. Farmers' Suicide in India: Magnitudes, Trends, and Spatial Patterns. Available at www.macroscan.org/anl/mar08/pdf/ farmers_suicides.pdf (accessed December 20, 2011).

National Sample Survey Organization. 1996. *Nutritional Intake in India NSS 50th Round: July 1993–June 1994.* Report No. 405, New Delhi.

———. 2001a. *Nutritional Intake in India 1999–2000: NSS 55th Round (July 1999–June 2000).* Report No. 471 (55/1.0/9), New Delhi.

————. 2001b. *Reported Adequacy of Food Intake in India 1999–2000: NSS 55th Round (July 1999–June 2000)*. Report No. 466 (55/1.0/7), New Delhi.

————. 2006. *Morbidity, Health Care, and the Condition of the Aged: NSS 60th Round (January–June 2004)*. Report No. 507 (60/25.0/1), New Delhi.

————. 2007a. *Nutritional Intake in India 2004–05: NSS 61st Round (July 2004–June 2005)*. Report No. 513 (61/1.0/6), New Delhi.

————. 2007b. *Perceived Adequacy of Food Intake in India 2004–05: NSS 61st Round (July 2004–June 2005)*. Report No. 512 (61/1.0/5), New Delhi.

————. 2007c. *Public Distribution System and Other Sources of Household Consumption 2004–05*. Report No. 510, Ministry of Statistics and Program Implementation, GOI, New Delhi.

Nayyar, Deepak. 2006. Economic Growth in Independent India: Lumbering Elephant or Running Tiger? *Economic and Political Weekly* 41(15): 1451–1458.

Nehru, Jawaharlal. 1946. *Discovery of India*. New Delhi: Penguin Books India, 2004 ed.

Nundy, Madhurima. 2005. Primary Health Care in India: Review of Policy, Plan, and Committee Reports. In Government of India, *Background Papers of the National Commission on Macroeconomics and Health*. New Delhi: Ministry of Health and Family Welfare, pp. 39–42.

Palmer-Jones, Richard, and Kunal Sen. 2001. On Indian Poverty Puzzles and Statistics of Poverty. *Economic and Political Weekly* 36(3): 211–217, January 20.

Panagariya, Arvind. 2004a. Miracles and Debacles: In Defense of Trade Openness. *World Economy* 27(8): 1149–1171, August.

————. 2004b. Growth and Reforms During 1980s and 1990s. *Economic and Political Weekly* 39(25): 2581–2594.

————. 2008a. India: The Emerging Giant. New York: Oxford University Press.

————. 2008b. El Nano: A Perfect Storm. *Economic Times,* September 25.

————. 2009a. Is Anti-incumbency Really Passé? *Economic Times,* May 28.

————. 2009b. The Fall of the Holy Trinity. *Economic Times*, March 26.

————. 2010a. India on the Growth Turnpike: No State Left Behind. In Kochhar, Samir, ed., *India on the Growth Turnpike*. New Delhi: Academic Foundation.

————. 2010b. Raising Investment in Higher Education. *Economic Times*, October 27.

————. 2010c. Pursuing Excellence and Equity. *Times of India*, April 10.

————. 2011a. I Beg to Differ, Professor Amartya Sen. *Economic Times*, February 23.

————. 2011b. Does India Compare Poorly with China on People's Well-Being? *Economic Times*, March 23.

————. (2011c). Trade Openness and Growth Miracles: A Fresh Look at Taiwan. Forthcoming in Heyden, Ken, and Stephen Woolcock, eds., *Ashgate Research Companion to International Trade Policy*. London: Ashgate Publishing Limited.

————. 2011d. Are We Living in a Gilded Age? *Economic Times*, May 19.

————. 2011e. Reforms to the Rescue. *Times of India*, September 8.

————. 2011f. The Problem with the Food Bill. *Economic Times*, December 28.

————. 2011g. The Art of Graft. *Times of India*, May 9.

————. 2012a. Myths About Poverty Lines. *Times of India*, March 30.

————. 2012b. Slew of Reforms: Manmohan Singh Scores a Decisive Victory, Stakes Claim to His Legacy. *Economic Times*, September 19.

————. 2012b. Empowering the Poor: Abandon the Broken Model. *Times of India*, August 25.

Pant, Pitambar. 1962. Perspective of Development, 1961–1976, Implications of Planning for a Minimum Level of Living. Paper originally circulated in August 1962 by the Perspective Planning Division, Planning Commission, and reproduced in Srinivasan, T. N., and P. K. Bardhan, eds., *Poverty and Income Distribution in India*. Calcutta: Statistical Publishing Society.

Parikh, K. S. 1994. Who Get How Much from the PDS—How Effectively Does It Reach the Poor? *Sarvekshana* 17(3): 34.

Planning Commission. 2011. *Report on Universal Coverage for India*. New Delhi: Author.

PROBE Team. 1999. *Public Report on Basic Education in India*. New Delhi: Oxford University Press.

Ranadive, K. R. 1973. Growth and Social Justice: Political Economy of "Garibi Hatao." *Economic and Political Weekly* 8(18): 834–841, May 5.

Rani, Uma, and Jeemol Unni. 2004. Unorganized and Organized Manufacturing in India: Potential for Employment Generating Growth. *Economic and Political Weekly* 39(41): 4568–4580.

Rao, Sujatha. 2012. Long on Aspiration, Short on Detail: Report on Universal Health Coverage. *Economic and Political Weekly* 47(6): 12–16.

Ray, Ranjan, and Geoffrey Lancaster. 2005. On Setting the Poverty Line Based on Estimated Nutrient Prices: Condition of Socially Disadvantaged Groups During the Reform Period. *Economic and Political Weekly* 40(1): 46–56, January 1.

Rodrik, Dani. 1995. Getting Interventions Right: How South Korea and Taiwan Grew Rich. *Economic Policy* 20: 55–107.

———. 2003. Institutions, Integration, and Geography: In Search of the Deep Determinants of Economic Growth. In Rodrik, Dani, ed., *In Search of Prosperity: Analytic Narratives of Economic Growth*. Princeton, NJ: Princeton University Press, pp. 1–19.

Rodrik, Dani, and Arvind Subramanian. 2005. From "Hindu Growth" to Productivity Surge: The Mystery of the Indian Growth Transition. *IMF Staff Papers* 52(2): 193–228.

Sainath, P. 2009. The Largest Wave of Suicides in History. Available at http://85.92.88.218/the-largest-wave-of-suicides-in-history-by -pasainath.pdf (accessed December 20, 2011).

Sanyal, Sanjeev. 2006. Post-liberalization India and the Importance of Legal Reform. www.idfresearch.org/gov_parent/Sanjeev%20 Sanyal%20Indian%20Legal%20Reforms%20Jul06.pdf (accessed December 20, 2011).

Sau, Ranjit. 1972. The "New Economics." *Economic and Political Weekly* 7(31/33): 1571–1573, August (Special Number).

Sen, Amartya. 2011. Growth and Other Concerns. *The Hindu,* February 14.

Sen, Amartya, and James D. Wolfensohn. 1999. Development: A Coin with Two Sides. *The Hindu,* Opinion Section, May 6.

Sharma, Anil. 2009. *Evaluating the Performance of the National Rural Employment Guarantee Scheme.* New Delhi: National Council on Applied Economic Research. Also at www.ncaer.org/downloads/Reports/NCAER-PIFStudyNREGA.pdf (accessed November 19, 2011).

Shiva, Vandana. 2004. The Suicide Economy of Corporate Globalization. Available at www.zcommunications.org/the-suicide-economy-of-corporate-globalisation-by-vandana2-shiva.pdf (accessed December 20, 2011).

Shrivastava, J. B. 1975. *Health Services and Medical Education: A Program for Immediate Action.* Ministry of Health and Family Planning, Government of India.

Singh, Kartar. 1973. *Report of the Committee on Multipurpose Workers Under Health and Family Planning Programs.* Ministry of Health and Family Planning, Government of India.

Sinha, Jayant, and Ashutosh Varshney. 2011. It Is Time for India to Rein In Its Robber Barons. *Financial Times,* Comments and Analysis, January 6.

Srinivasan, T. N. 2005. Comments on "From 'Hindu Growth' to Productivity Surge": The Mystery of the Indian Growth Transition. *IMF Staff Papers* 52(2): 229–233.

Sukumaran, Ajay, and Dilip Bisoi. 2011. Not Too Much of a Stretch. *Financial Express,* July 29.

Svedberg, Peter. 2012. Reforming or Replacing the Public Distribution System with Cash Transfers? Economic and Political Weekly 47(7): 53–62, February 18.

Tanizaki, Junichiro. 1988. *Childhood Years: A Memoir.* Tokyo and USA: Kodansha International. English Translation by Paul McCarthy.

Tarozzi, Alessandro. 2008. Growth Reference Charts and the Status of Indian Children. *Economics and Human Biology* 6(3): 455–468.

Thorat, Sukhdeo, and Amaresh Dubey. 2012. Has Growth Been Socially Inclusive During 1993–94–2009–10? *Economic and Political Weekly* 47(10): 43–53, March 10.

Tooley, James, and Pauline Dixon. Undated. Private Schools Serving the Poor: A Study from Delhi, India. Working Paper, Viewpoint 8, Center for Civil Society, New Delhi.

Topalova, Petia. 2007. Trade Liberalization, Poverty, and Inequality: Evidence from Indian Districts. In Harrison, Ann, ed., *Globalization and Poverty.* Chicago: University of Chicago Press, pp. 291–336.

United Nations. 1975. Poverty, Unemployment, and Development Policy: A Case Study of Selected Issues with Reference to Kerala. New York: UN Publication No. ST/ESA/29.

United Nations Development Program (UNDP). 1990. *Human Development Report.* New York: Oxford University Press.

Wade, Robert. 1990. *Governing the Market: Economic Theory and the Role of the Government in East Asian Industrialization.* Princeton, NJ: Princeton University Press.

Wallack, Jessica. 2003. Structural Breaks in Indian Macroeconomic Data. *Economic and Political Economy* 38(41): 4312–4315.

Weisskopf, Thomas E. 2011, November 19. Why Worry About Inequality in the Booming Indian Economy? *Economic and Political Weekly* 46(47): 41–51.

Wolfensohn, James, and Joseph Stiglitz. 1999. Growth Is Not Enough. *Financial Times,* Comments and Analysis, p. 22, September 22.

World Bank. 1999. Annual Review of Development Effectiveness: Toward a Comprehensive Development Strategy. Operations and Evaluation Department.

World Health Organization (WHO). 2011. World Health Statistics 2011. Available at www.who.int/gho/publications/world_health _statistics/2011/en/index.html (accessed December 19, 2011).

Index

Jagdish Bhagwati is university professor of economics at Columbia, and a longtime fellow at the Council on Foreign Relations in the United States. He has combined scientific scholarship with a substantial public policy presence through writings in leading media worldwide and much-acclaimed books aimed at the general public. He has received many prestigious prizes and several honorary degrees. Widely recognized as the intellectual pioneer of India's reforms, he has also received the Padma Vibhushan.

Arvind Panagariya is professor of economics and Indian political economy at Columbia University, a non-resident senior fellow at the Brookings Institution and a past chief economist of the Asian Development Bank. A leading trade theorist of his generation, Panagariya has written prolifically on global trade policy issues and economic reforms in India. Author of a dozen books, his technical papers have been published in the leading journals, including the *American Economic Review*, *Quarterly Journal of Economics*, and *Review of Economic Studies* while his policy papers have appeared in *Foreign Affairs* and *Foreign Policy*. Panagariya writes an influential monthly column in the *Times of India* and has been honored with the Padma Bhushan.

PublicAffairs is a publishing house founded in 1997. It is a tribute to the standards, values, and flair of three persons who have served as mentors to countless reporters, writers, editors, and book people of all kinds, including me.

I. F. STONE, proprietor of *I. F. Stone's Weekly*, combined a commitment to the First Amendment with entrepreneurial zeal and reporting skill and became one of the great independent journalists in American history. At the age of eighty, Izzy published *The Trial of Socrates*, which was a national bestseller. He wrote the book after he taught himself ancient Greek.

BENJAMIN C. BRADLEE was, for nearly thirty years the charismatic editorial leader of *The Washington Post*. It was Ben who gave the *Post* the range and courage to pursue such historic issues as Watergate. He supported his reporters with a tenacity that made them fearless and it is no accident that so many became authors of influential, best-selling books.

ROBERT L. BERNSTEIN, the chief executive of Random House for more than a quarter century, guided one of the nation's premier publishing houses. Bob was personally responsible for many books of political dissent and argument that challenged tyranny around the globe. He is also the founder and longtime chair of Human Rights Watch, one of the most respected human rights organizations in the world.

·   ·   ·

For fifty years, the banner of Public Affairs Press was carried by its owner Morris B. Schnapper, who published Gandhi, Nasser, Toynbee, Truman, and about 1,500 other authors. In 1983, Schnapper was described by *The Washington Post* as "a redoubtable gadfly." His legacy will endure in the books to come.

Peter Osnos, *Founder and Editor-at-Large*